WHEN IS DISCRIMINATION WRONG?

Deborah Hellman

When Is Discrimination Wrong?

HARVARD UNIVERSITY PRESS

Cambridge, Massachusetts, and London, England

First Harvard University Press paperback edition, 2011

Library of Congress Cataloging-in-Publication Data

Hellman, Deborah, 1963–
  When is discrimination wrong? / Deborah Hellman.
      p.   cm.
  Includes bibliographical references and index.
  ISBN 978-0-674-02797-8 (cloth: alk. paper)
  ISBN 978-0-674-06029-6 (pbk.)
  1. Discrimination.   2. Interpersonal relations.   1. Title.
  HM1106.H42 2008
  305—dc22

                                    2007043734

For my parents, Rusty and Sam Hellman,
who encouraged me at every step,
and talked me through each argument.

For my husband, Derek Brown,
for being so extraordinarily flexible and supportive
and for everything else.

Contents

WHEN IS DISCRIMINATION WRONG?

Introduction:
The Discrimination Puzzle

A law requires black bus passengers to sit in the back of the bus and white passengers to sit in the front.

A school principal asks the students with last names beginning with A–M to sit on the left side of the auditorium and those with last names beginning with N–Z to sit on the right side.

An employer at a casino requires female employees to wear makeup and prohibits male employees from wearing makeup.

A nursing home with a predominantly female clientele refuses to hire a male nurse's aide for a job requiring assisting residents with bathing and toilet needs.

A personal advertisement under "Men Seeking Women" in a local paper reads: "Looking for a single woman, age 30–40, for a long-term relationship or marriage. Seeking a woman who is not afraid to be feminine. Prefer someone slim, who wears makeup and likes to dress fashionably."

A worker who is biologically male but dresses and lives as a female requests that her employer designate some bathrooms as unisex or alternatively allow her to use the women's bathroom. The employer refuses and instructs the employee to use the men's bathroom. The employee refuses and is fired as a result.

The U.S. Food and Drug Administration approves a drug specifically for use by African American heart failure patients.

1

A public school's "gifted and talented program" and a selective private school screen kindergarten admissions according to children's IQ test scores.

A university in Iran uses political affiliation as a criterion for selecting students and faculty.

A business prefers to hire job applicants from the local community.

An airline refuses to continue to employ pilots older than 62.

A state refuses to license drivers under age 16.

A company prefers not to hire women between the ages of 20 and 40.

Each example above draws a distinction between people on the basis of a certain trait: race, the first letter of the person's last name, sex, appearance, ability, age, or another attribute. Our intuition suggests that while some of these laws, policies, or practices are morally wrong, some are benign, and the nature of still others is unclear. The aim of this book is to examine why it is sometimes permissible and sometimes impermissible to draw such distinctions among people. In other words, the aim here is to present a general theory of discrimination.

The term *discrimination* has come to have a negative connotation. To call something "discrimination" is to criticize it, to assert that it is wrong. But of course the term has positive associations as well. One can be complimented for discriminating taste (in art, wine, literature, etc.). Someone who is astute and has a subtle mastery of his subject is often described as "discriminating," as in "the manager of the mutual fund is very discriminating in his investments." This positive use of the term is more marginal, however, overwhelmed by its negative associations with wrongful discrimination. By resurrecting it here, I do not mean to downplay the harms of wrongful discrimination. Rather, I want to emphasize the positive as well as the negative aspects of discrimination in order to unsettle our certainty about *which* instances of discrimination are wrong and especially about whether we know *why* they are wrong.

Discrimination—used in this way that captures both its negative and its positive connotations—is both ubiquitous and necessary. We routinely

draw distinctions among people in public policy and law as well as in business, school settings, and private life. Laws require that drivers must be a
certain age (16 is common) and must pass a test to be licensed to drive in
all states. These laws distinguish (i.e., discriminate) between people on the
basis of age and their ability to pass a test; they treat those 16 and over
who have passed the driving test more favorably (they are allowed to
drive) than the group of people who are either under 16 or have failed the
driving test. Employers and school admissions officials draw distinctions
among applicants on the basis of grades, test scores, and myriad other,
sometimes quite controversial, traits. Some firms are in the very business
of discrimination: Insurers draw distinctions among people on the basis of
traits that reflect the likelihood that the insured will file a claim during the
policy period. For example, health and life insurers distinguish among
people on the basis of health status—people with high blood pressure,
who are overweight, and who smoke will pay more for health and life insurance (if they can get insurance at all) than non-smokers with low
blood pressure and average weight. Private and family life calls for discrimination as well. A mother who puts her 2-year-old daughter in her
crib for an afternoon nap but allows her 4-year-old to continue playing is
drawing a distinction between her children on the basis of age—and is
limiting the freedom of the 2-year-old in a way that she is not limiting
that of the 4-year-old.

Much of this distinction drawing is important or even unavoidable. While
we could treat everyone the same in some of the instances described above,
there would be a significant cost in doing so. To take the last and perhaps
most mundane example first, if the mother were to treat both her children
the same, she would have to either put both down for naps or allow both to
play all afternoon. Any parent of a 2-year-old could tell you that this latter
suggestion is folly. Come about four or five o'clock, the 2-year-old would be
miserable, as would anyone within earshot of the child. If the mother were
to put both children down for a nap, there are a number of not very appealing scenarios that might ensue. One cannot make a child sleep, so
merely putting a child to bed doesn't mean she will sleep. She may simply
yell, cry, and require continuous parental intervention to stay in the bed-
room. Alternatively, she may fall asleep. The problem with this outcome is
that she would then be unable to fall asleep at a reasonable bedtime that
night, which would leave her tired the next day and her parents with no
time for themselves at night. While a well-behaved child might simply play

quietly in bed, it seems unreasonable—at least I think so—to insist that she do so *merely* because her sibling needs a nap.

In the case of laws and public policies that distinguish among people, the stakes are much higher. I doubt that we would be willing to either license all drivers regardless of age or to bar everyone from driving—the two options that would treat everyone the same. Nor would we be willing, I imagine, to license anyone who wanted to practice law or medicine regardless of whether the person had passed the tests demonstrating the requisite knowledge and skill.

Finally, where there are limited openings, for jobs or places at school, for example, it is simply not possible to treat one and all the same. Not everyone can be hired or admitted. Thus, we must draw distinctions among the applicants on some basis. The question then becomes, when is such distinction-drawing morally problematic and when is it not?

This book will address the moral question posed by the fact that it is often desirable and sometimes necessary to treat people differently. Laws govern when it is *legally* permissible to do so, either in the form of local, state-wide, or national statutory prohibitions on discrimination of various types or, in the United States, in the form of judicial interpretation of the constitutional guarantee of Equal Protection. While in some ways one could view this statutory and constitutional law as itself providing an answer to the question of when it is morally permissible to draw distinctions among people, there are other important issues that play a role in determining when something ought to be legally prohibited. Some things that are morally wrong are not legally prohibited, and for good reason (being mean to others, for example). And some things are legally prohibited that are not morally wrong, except to the extent that it is wrong to break the law (driving without a license, for example). And yet, perhaps because the U.S. constitutional guarantee of equal protection is itself vague and open to interpretation, much of the legal debate—in this country and elsewhere—has a moral cast. For that reason, the legal literature provides an important starting point for wrestling with what I call the *discrimination puzzle*.

The fact that we often need to distinguish among people forces us to ask when discrimination is morally permissible and when it is not. This puzzle has no easy answer. While people may have a fairly settled sense that certain instances of drawing distinctions among people on the basis of particular traits in particular contexts are wrong, it is harder than one might expect to explain what makes these cases wrong in a way that also works to explain other cases of wrongful and permissible discrimination.

One might think that drawing distinctions on the basis of certain traits is always forbidden—race and sex, in particular. But if so, does that mean that the U.S. Food and Drug Administration (FDA) necessarily acts wrongly in approving a particular drug for use by African American patients? And does it mean that single-sex bathrooms are clearly impermissible? While there may be problems with each of these practices, which we will discuss in later chapters, I don't think either one could be easily written off as impermissible based solely on the fact that it discriminates on the basis of race or sex respectively.

Another facet of the discrimination puzzle that makes it difficult to untangle is that wrongful discrimination sometimes occurs in contexts where the difference in treatment seems unimportant. Nelson Mandela reports in his autobiography that the apartheid regime in South Africa required black prisoners to wear shorts while white and colored prisoners were required to wear pants. In the heat of southern Africa, shorts might be the more comfortable option. Nonetheless, the symbolism of being required to wear shorts, which were commonly seen as infantilizing in this postcolonial regime, was a means of demeaning black prisoners. On the other hand, distinguishing among and treating people differently may deny some an important benefit or opportunity, and yet seem perfectly permissible. An employer might choose the person who types the fastest with the fewest errors for a word-processing job, for example. This policy distinguishes among job applicants on the basis of typing speed and skill and as a result treats one group (the slower typists) far less favorably (they lose out on a well-paid job) than the other (faster typists). So the fact that someone or some group is denied something important, like a good job, doesn't provide a clue as to whether the discrimination is wrongful or permissible.

One might think that one could easily explain why the first of these two cases is impermissible and the second permissible (conclusions I share) by looking at some obvious differences between them. First, in the case of the South African prison garb, the policy was likely imposed to stigmatize black prisoners, while the typing requirements were set for the benign purpose of increasing the productivity of the employer's business. Second, skin color is irrelevant to what uniform prisoners ought to wear, while typing speed and accuracy are relevant to the job of a typist.[1]

Do these differences matter morally? Sometimes morally troubling policies are enacted with the same intention as that of the employer who selects the best typist—that is, to enhance business productivity. Suppose an employer refuses to hire women between the ages of 20 and 40 on the grounds that they are likely to take time off to have children, which would disrupt work schedules and raise the business's medical costs. The employer might adopt this policy merely to enhance business productivity, but does this benign intention insulate the policy from moral criticism?

The fact that a trait is "relevant" or "irrelevant" also fails to distinguish permissible from impermissible discrimination. In the previous example, sex is a relevant job qualification if by "relevant" we simply mean that it is positively correlated with something important. Here sex is likely correlated with work schedules and the costs of childbearing, as the employer supposes. If relevance is merely a matter of the fit between a distinguishing trait and a target, like efficiency, and such relevance is what matters morally, then many practices that our intuitions suggest are morally problematic would be deemed legitimate—like employers refusing to hire women of child-bearing age.

Perhaps the concept of relevance can be refined. The prison-garb case and the typist case differ in that the typist *merits* the job whereas the white prisoners do not *merit* long pants. Doesn't the idea of merit then provide an answer to at least some discrimination puzzles? I think not. Consider the employer who gives a preference to local job candidates in order to support the local community in which she is based. Do the locals thereby merit the jobs? The concept of merit is itself contested such that it will be unlikely to resolve questions regarding what is wrongful discrimination.

In attempting to answer the question posed by the discrimination puzzle, I begin with what I consider a bedrock moral principle—the equal moral worth of all persons. I take it that this bedrock principle is comprised of two sub-principles: First, there is a worth or inherent dignity of persons that requires that we treat each other with respect. What violates this principle may be contested (and is something that the argument of this book will address), but I will assume that the inherent worth of a person sets moral limits on how others may treat her. Second, this inherent dignity and worth of all persons does not vary according to their other traits. While some people are smarter, faster, and more talented at tasks that benefit others, or even kinder and more gentle, these and other differences do not affect how important each of us is from a moral perspective. The inherent worth of persons is not something that comes in degrees. Rather, all people are equally important from the moral point of view and so are equally worthy of concern and respect.[2]

I begin with this bedrock principle because I suspect the moral concern that fuels our worries about drawing distinctions among people is that in doing so we may act in ways that fail to treat others as equally worthy. The discrimination puzzle asks when it is morally permissible to draw distinctions among people on the basis of some trait that they have or lack. We can further refine that question, in recognition of the fact that our concern springs from our commitment to the principle of equal moral worth, and ask, when does drawing distinctions among people fail to treat those affected as persons of equal moral worth? It is this question that this book will address.

It is important to emphasize here the conventional and social nature of wrongful discrimination. We all have many traits: race, age, sex, appearance, abilities, height, weight, voice tone, our names, religion, and so on. As simply traits, they are inert. What matters about them is their social significance in particular contexts. Drawing distinctions on the basis of certain traits in certain contexts has meaning that distinguishing on the basis of other traits would not. Separating students by last name feels quite different than separating students by race, for example—though each can be done for good or bad reasons and each may be related or unrelated to some legitimate purpose. In addition, drawing distinctions among people on the basis of the same trait in different contexts feels different as well. As Justice Marshall once observed: "A sign that says "men only" looks very different on a bathroom door than on a courthouse door."[3] It "looks very different" not because women can practice law as well as men. After all, women can also use men's bathrooms as well as men, too. Nor does the fault lie in the fact that the law prohibiting women from practicing law was enacted in order to keep women out or was grounded in stereotypes about men and women. The prohibition of women from the men's bathroom was also enacted to keep women out and is based on stereotypes about men and women (and privacy norms concerning certain bodily functions). Rather, the problem with the courthouse prohibition is that it distinguishes between men and women in a way that *demeans* women whereas the bathroom prohibition does not.

Part I builds the argument that it is morally wrong to distinguish among people on the basis of a given attribute when doing so demeans any of the people affected. Chapter 1 lays out the argument for this account of wrongful discrimination. Whether a particular distinction does demean is determined by the meaning of drawing such a distinction in that context, in our culture, at this time. In focusing on whether a distinction demeans, this account does not rest on the consequences or the effects of a classification. Rather, some classifications demean—whether or not the person affected *feels* demeaned, stigmatized, or harmed. As such, this account of wrongful discrimination grounds moral impermissibility in the wrong rather than the harm of discrimination.

Chapter 2 develops the argument by exploring in more detail what "demeaning" is and why it is important. It begins by explaining why actions that distinguish among people in a way that demeans are thereby wrongful. The chapter argues that because to demean is to treat another in a way that denies her equal moral worth, it picks out a wrong that is intimately tied to the value that underlies our moral concern with differentiation in the first place. The chapter then provides a more detailed account of "demeaning": to demean is both to express denigration and to do so in a way that has the power or capacity to put the other down.

Chapter 3 explores the important questions of *how* we determine whether drawing a particular distinction in a particular context does demean and whether the fact that people will likely disagree about whether particular distinctions demean is problematic for the theory I advance.

Part II explores some common answers to the discrimination puzzle and argues that each is ultimately unsatisfactory. Chapter 4 considers the concept of merit and argues that it cannot separate permissible from impermissible discrimination. The concept of merit is unable to help because any discussion about whether drawing a particular distinction in a particular context is permissible can simply be recast as a debate about what constitutes merit in that context. For example, universities in Iran use political affiliation as a criterion in selecting students and professors. One might think that this practice constitutes wrongful discrimination because these students and professors don't merit their positions. But why not? The university administrators surely believe that the best students and teachers are those with the best moral values—as they define them. In other words, critics and supporters of this policy can best be understood as arguing about what *constitutes* merit in a university context. If so, the concept of merit itself will not be useful in sorting out permissible from impermissible discrimination.

Chapter 5 argues against the moral relevance of the accuracy of classification. One might think that if one distinguishes among people on the basis of, say, age, in determining who is able to apply for a driving license, that it should matter morally whether age is indeed a good predictor of driving ability. If it is not, then perhaps there is something problematic about using it. There is surely *something* problematic about using age if it is unrelated to driving ability, but the relevant question is whether that something is a moral concern or merely a pragmatic one. Chapter 5 contends that the use of inaccurate classification is inefficient and stupid but not a moral wrong.

Finally, Chapter 6 argues against the view that it is the intention of the person who draws a distinction that is important. This chapter considers two arguments for the relevance of intentions: First, one might think that the actor's intention determines whether an actor in fact distinguishes on the basis of a particular trait or not. Second, one might think that distinguishing among people for a bad purpose renders the action morally suspect. In this chapter I argue against each of these claims, concluding that as far as discrimination goes, it's not the thought that counts.

The book concludes by exploring the ways in which the conception of wrongful discrimination I advance has affinities with the recent emphasis of moral philosophers on the importance of equality of respect when considering what the equal moral worth of persons requires.

PART I

When Is Discrimination Wrong?

CHAPTER 1

The Basic Idea

We routinely draw distinctions among people on the basis of characteristics they possess or lack. This practice is ubiquitous and commonplace. Moreover, much of it—perhaps most—is morally permissible or benign. Some of it however is morally troubling, even deeply so. What explains this difference?

"Discrimination"

I put the term *discrimination* in scare quotes because there is an important ambiguity in the term. *Discrimination* can be used in a *descriptive* or *moralized* way. Descriptively, to "discriminate" is merely to draw distinctions among people on the basis of the presence or absence of some trait. For example, the requirement that one must be at least 16 to drive discriminates between people under 16 and people 16 and over. The requirement that one must pass the bar exam to practice law discriminates between those who pass the bar and those who do not. When the term *discrimination* is used in a moralized way, it means to *wrongfully* draw such distinctions. For example, state laws that required separate seating for black and white passengers on buses and trains wrongfully discriminated between passengers on the basis of race. To avoid confusion about which sense of discrimination I am discussing, I will try to avoid using the words *discriminate* and *discrimination* standing alone. Instead, perhaps forfeiting elegance for clarity at times, when I have in mind the descriptive sense of discrimination, I will say that the law, policy, or action "classifies," or "draws a distinction" or "distinguishes" on the basis of X trait, or something similar. When I have in mind the moralized sense of discrimination, I will say that the law, policy, or action "wrongfully discriminates" so that the moral judgment is explicit.

Motivating the Idea

I want to begin with an artificial and unlikely example. Suppose an employer or a school admissions official were to decide to refuse to hire or admit any candidate whose last name begins with the letter A. On this basis, Adams is rejected. Is this wrongful discrimination? The claim I want to advance in this chapter is that there is nothing wrong with this decision—at least nothing wrong that violates the principle of the equal moral worth of persons. Rejecting Adams because his name begins with A is therefore not wrongful discrimination.

Contrast that example with another. Suppose an employer or school admissions official refuses to hire or admit women. What makes this case different? One salient difference between drawing distinctions on the basis of sex as compared to the first letter of a person's last name is that our society as well as others has a long history of treating women poorly. There are extreme examples of this mistreatment such as disenfranchisement, laws prohibiting women from owning property, laws that defined rape in ways that excluded a husband's rape of his wife from the prohibited conduct, etc. One can obviously go on. There is clearly no comparable history of mistreating people whose last names begin with the letter A. In addition, women currently have a lower socioeconomic status than men in most areas of the world whereas people whose names begin with A are, as far as I know, no more or less well off than those whose names begin with the other twenty-five letters of the alphabet. Women today continue to earn less than men, to be dramatically overrepresented among the poor, and to be vulnerable to violence in the home. My goal is not to establish these facts, which have been more than amply demonstrated by others, and are, I hope, not controversial. Rather, I want to sketch an argument for why these facts matter.

The view that a history of mistreatment and the current social status of people with a particular characteristic are relevant to whether instances of differentiation are wrong is itself not terribly controversial. Courts, commentators, and scholars have made this point before. The interesting question to untangle is why and how history and current social status matters.

Here are some possible answers to that question:

1. The ideal of equality prohibits a certain state of affairs—one in which caste-like distinctions among people exist. According to this view,

refusing to hire or admit someone on the basis of sex is wrong because it risks reinforcing or exacerbating the male hierarchy of our society.

2. The systemic disadvantaging of women matters when evaluating a policy that distinguishes among people on the basis of sex because, as a group, women are likely to have been either entirely excluded from the processes through which the policy was adopted or to have had their interests discounted in that process.

3. The history of mistreatment and the current status of women in society both matter because they determine the nature of an action refusing to hire or admit a woman because of her sex. Being denied a job on the basis of being female demeans women in a way that being denied a job because one's last name begins with A does not.

There are surely other theories about why or how the history and current social status of a particular group matters. I concentrate on these because theory 1 roughly articulates Owen Fiss's anti-caste understanding of the Equal Protection Clause and theory 2 reconstructs John Hart Ely's account of when courts ought to scrutinize enactments under the Equal Protection Clause.[1] Given the prominence—even many years later—of Ely's and Fiss's accounts and the role that legal and jurisprudential understandings of that clause play in both popular and academic debates about when drawing distinctions among people is morally permissible and when it is not, their accounts seem worthy of note. The third proposition, by contrast, is the view I intend to argue for in this chapter.

Wrongful and Discrimination but Not Wrongful Discrimination

So far I imagine most readers would agree that there is a difference between refusing to hire or admit Adams because her last name begins with A and refusing to hire or admit a woman because of her sex. However, though one might agree that history does make a difference—perhaps making one differentiation worse than the other—one might object to the perhaps counterintuitive suggestion that Adams suffers no wrongful discrimination. In order to make that view more plausible, let me make clear that there may well be *something* wrong with the fact that the employer or school admissions official refuses to take Adams because her name begins with A. But while it may be wrong to deny someone a place for this reason, it is not a wrong that offends against the norm of equality and thus is not wrongful discrimination.

Denying someone a job or place at school because her name begins with the letter A could be wrong for an entirely different reason. For example, a law school admissions official may have certain criteria that she is supposed to apply, as provided to her explicitly by the faculty committee charged with determining admissions criteria. If the official uses the first letter of the candidate's last name, in addition to or in lieu of these established criteria, she acts wrongly. This action is wrong because she has acted outside of her delegated authority, has failed to do what she promised to do, or something of this nature. We can criticize her action for these reasons without thereby concluding that Adams has been wrongly discriminated against. So part of what seems troubling about denying someone a job or place at school because of the first letter of her last name may be that there are constraints on the criteria that the official is supposed to use, constraints that derive from her obligation to fulfill her role in the organization.

Consider another example: Zora, a university student, signs up for a poetry class which has limited enrollment. She is rejected. She suspects that the teacher denied her admission because her father (a professor at the university) had previously had an affair with the poetry teacher.[2] Has Zora been wrongly discriminated against? The poetry teacher, call her Professor Malcolm, draws a distinction between students who are related to people with whom she has been sexually involved and students who are not. Malcolm then treats the first group less favorably (denying them entry into class) than the second. Is this distinction-drawing wrong? If so, on what grounds?

One reason Malcolm's denying Zora entry might be wrong is that it goes against the internal rules or codes of the university—either those that are explicitly stated or those that are implicit in its values and mission. University professors are no doubt supposed to exercise their discretion to admit or deny students entry into their classes in a way that is consistent with the university's goals and values. If this is a class in poetry, the teacher should choose the most promising poetry students, perhaps. Even if the university's rules and values do not mandate that criterion, they no doubt forbid the criterion Malcolm used. In this regard, her action is wrongful. But what kind of wrong is this? Malcolm has acted in a way that her job requirements or role as a university professor forbids. She has violated the rules and obligations that the university lays down for its faculty. If we understand this wrong as one that offends the rules of conduct that the university has enacted, then it is a wrong analogous to using her office phone to make lengthy personal calls. If we understand the wrong as one that offends the values internal to the role of "university professor," then it is a wrong analogous to plagiarism. Perhaps it is a bit of both. Either way, though wrongful and discrimination, it is not wrongful discrimination. This is because the source of the wrongfulness does not have anything to do with failing to treat each person as a person of equal moral worth. Rather, the source of the wrong is the violation of the university's internal rules or values—ones that could be otherwise if it were a different sort of institution.

And what if it were a different sort of institution? What if the university officially sanctioned the use of such criteria in selecting students for entry into classes? Would that be wrong? And if so, on what basis?

Consider another example. In *Reading Lolita in Tehran*, Azar Nafisi reports that after the Iranian revolution, universities began accepting students on the basis of political affiliation rather than academic performance or scholarly promise.[3] Is this wrongful discrimination? This case differs from Zora's in that here the admissions officials are not violating official university policy. In that sense, they are (we assume) neither acting outside of their roles nor violating the standards laid down by those with authority within the university. Rather, the university officials have changed the admissions standards to include political affiliation as one of the criteria that admissions officials must consider. So the admissions officials do not commit the wrong of violating the obligations of their role (as admissions officials) or of ignoring the admissions criteria adopted by the university. That is not the wrong they commit—as was the case with Professor Malcolm. Have they done anything else wrong? Nafisi seems to think so. She thinks there is something terribly wrong in using political affiliation as an admissions criterion at a university. But what exactly?

As I will argue in more detail in Chapter 4, which discusses merit and its relationship to wrongful discrimination, Nafisi's objection can best be understood as resting on an argument about what a university is. She sees a university as committed to the values of teaching and scholarship and thus sees the new criterion as a violation of these values. Is then the university's decision to change its admissions criteria wrongful discrimination? The first thing to note is that Nafisi and the university officials are debating precisely whether the criterion is acceptable or not. Is a political affiliation admissions criterion compatible with the mission of a university rightly understood? Second, if Nafisi is right and the criterion is incompatible, this makes the rejection of the better-qualified candidates wrong but does not thereby make it wrongful discrimination. As with Zora, the source of the wrong is not an offense to the norms of equality. Rather, the source of the wrong is the incompatibility of the political-affiliation criterion with the best understanding of the aims of a university.[4]

Consider one final example: genetic discrimination. People with certain known genetic mutations are more likely to develop particular diseases than people without them. Should insurance companies be allowed to either deny coverage or charge higher rates to people with genetic mutations that predispose them to disease? A person might hold the view that justice demands that everyone have health insurance. If so, drawing distinctions between insurance applicants on the basis of their genetic traits is wrong for reasons unrelated to equality. For such a person, genetic discrimination is no more or less wrong than other ways in which health insurance providers distinguish among customers. If so, then the wrongfulness of denying someone insurance because of a genetic mutation would lie not in a violation of the norm of equality but rather in a violation of the demands of justice. This is not wrongful discrimination. It is wrongful and it is discrimination (in the nonpejorative sense of drawing distinctions) but the wrong does not arise from the differentiation, rather it arises from the denial of what justice demands.[5]

When we differentiate among people and treat them differently as a result, it is thus possible for this act to be (a) permissible or (b) impermissible for reasons unrelated to the moral concerns underlying our worries about classification, or (c) impermissible because it offends the principle of the equal moral worth of persons. By giving readers a sense of how a classification could be wrongful, yet not wrongful discrimination, I hope to begin to answer doubts about my claim that refusing to hire Adams because her last name begins with A is *not* wrongful discrimination. There may well be something wrong with such an act—that depends on the criteria adopted by the institutions involved and the internal values that ought to guide their choice of criteria—but it is not the wrong of wrongful discrimination.[6]

Let me tie this point back to the moral principle with which I began—the equal moral worth of persons. If each person has an inherent worth, there are things one could do to her that would violate or deny that worth that have nothing to do with a concern for equality. If X kills Y, he fails to respect her inherent worth—but there is not an equality issue here. If X kills some people and not others, he fails to respect their inherent worth *and* perhaps does so in a way that offends against the norm of equality, in that he selectively kills. However, in such a context we are unlikely to focus on the equality issue, as the killing itself is such a heinous violation of rights (inherent worth). But what of contexts where there is no right at issue other than the right to be treated as an equal? Here it is the value of equality that is most salient. Suppose there are many apartment seekers who want the same apartment and only one can get it. The inherent worth of a person is not violated by not getting the apartment. However, the equal worth of a person may be offended by the selection criteria used—whites only, for example. Where the problem lies in the selection criteria themselves, rather than in the failure to provide a good or a service, there is a potential equality problem.

But not all selection criteria do raise equality issues. Sometimes the failure to use particular selection criteria conflicts with norms or standards that derive from sources specific to the institution itself. In Zora's case, for example, the university has norms and values that guide its operations and the conduct of its faculty. What underlies these norms and values is a conception of the university itself and the sorts of standards appropriate to it. When selection criteria used to distinguish among people conflict with the internal standards of an institution, then the wrongness of distinguishing on such grounds resides in its conflict with the institution's goals and values—rather than with the commitment to people's equal moral worth.

Distinctions that conflict with an institution's (or an individual's) own goals and values can constitute serious wrongs. I carve these off not to suggest they are unimportant. However, where a classification conflicts with internal values or goals, the institution or individual can choose to modify those values or goals to obviate the conflict. This consistency requirement is not an empty check, but its availability means that institutions or individuals can determine for themselves which selection criteria to use—unless there are limits that come from elsewhere. If people are of equal moral worth, then a commitment to this principle requires that we not draw distinctions among people in a manner that fails to treat them as moral equals.

Before moving on, I want to consider one more reason one might be concerned about distinguishing among people. Suppose a college admissions officer was to deny admission to applicants whom he or she did not find likable. Here I am not asking whether in fact the school has permitted or prohibited likability as a factor to be considered in the admissions process. If the school has prohibited it, and the official uses that factor in decision-making anyway, then she clearly violates the obligations of her role or employment contract. Rather, we are looking at the more fundamental question of whether likability is the sort of quality that, when officially authorized, nonetheless constitutes wrongful discrimination.

On what basis might one object to this criterion? One possibility is the one considered above—that likability is not the sort of quality a university ought to be concerned about. This objection, as I argued above, is best conceived as resting on what a university is and is thus focused on determining what sorts of values it can adopt while still remaining a university. What does being a university require? But are there other grounds to object? I imagine that someone might object that the criterion of likability is too subjective. But what does that mean exactly? It might mean that it is too dependent on the individual tastes of the person applying the criterion. If multiple people must apply the criterion, the sorts of people identified as likable could vary dramatically. This is a problem if one values uniformity. But is it a deep problem if one does not? If different officials, using the likability criterion, select applicants with different sorts of attributes, the worst one can say about this is that the selection criteria are arbitrary or irrational. This is an important concern, as many people believe that arbitrariness itself is morally significant. Indeed, the Supreme Court's Equal Protection doctrine requires—at least in theory—that classifications be rational, and thus seemingly endorses the moral relevance of rationality.[7] In my view, the irrationality of classifications is not a wrong that has its roots in the norm of equality—the concern with the equal moral worth of persons—because we are all equally at risk of suffering from arbitrary treatment. It is a reason to get rid of the idiots (to vote them out or whatever) who adopt irrational criteria, but no more. But this is an argument that must be developed in detail. Chapter 5 takes up this task.

In claiming that a likability test is too subjective, one might have an entirely different worry. One might worry that people who are deemed unlikable will not form an arbitrary assemblage but rather will fall into some socially salient group—perhaps even a group that historically has been mistreated or that currently occupies a lower socioeconomic status. For example, Jews might be excluded on the grounds that they are not likable, if we imagine that establishmentarian WASPs are making the judgments.[8] If this example seems outdated, one could easily imagine another, more current scenario. In such a case, the worry is not that likability itself ought not to be the basis for excluding people, but rather that, under the guise of considering likability, we are really excluding people based on religion or ethnicity. In other words, to gin up a criterion that offends against the norm of equality, we need to imagine not just that someone is excluded for a reason that seems unrelated to the institution's goals but instead that the exclusion is really based on a trait that defines a group with either a history of mistreatment or a lower social status currently.

Perhaps likability still seems a troubling admissions criterion to some readers. I use it as an example because it is one that many people are likely to find troubling. And it *is* troubling. But what makes it troubling is something different than one might think. First, it may be troubling if it is not the officially sanctioned policy—in other words if an official acts outside of his authority in using likability as an admissions criterion. Second, it may be troubling because its vagueness allows officials surreptitiously to use other traits as admissions criteria—religion or ethnicity, for example. If so, the problem is not that likability is an admissions criterion. Rather the problem is that under the guise of considering likability, admissions officials are really admitting or rejecting people based on race or ethnicity. Likability itself may feel like an odd criterion, but one can easily reword what one is after in a more appealing way. Suppose that a policy directs admissions officials to admit students who can work cooperatively with others, for example. An ability to cooperate is useful in many employment settings and is, generally, a useful trait. A school's decision to promote that value hardly seems objectionable. What troubles us, if anything, is the concern that because it is hard to identify people who can work cooperatively with others (there is no test one could take), the discretion necessary for implementing this selection criterion would allow officials to use other traits in its stead—intentionally or unintentionally.

History and Current Social Status: How It Matters

We have established that drawing distinctions on the basis of attributes that define a group that has been mistreated in the past or is currently of lower status *feels* morally different than drawing distinctions on the basis of other traits. I say "feels" because we are still exploring why this is so and if this feeling is justified. For ease of exposition, let us call traits that define such a group "HSD" traits—for history of mistreatment or current social disadvantage. What makes differentiation on the basis of HSD traits morally different in a way that violates the norm that we should treat people with equal concern and respect? If HSD traits really do make a difference in evaluating whether a distinction is permissible or not, *what* difference do they make and *why?*

The fact that HSD traits seem to make a difference has led some commentators to contend that it is the equal treatment of *groups* rather than the equal treatment of *individuals* that matters.[9] Thus, one influential answer to the question of why distinguishing on the basis of HSD traits is different is that the requirement that we treat one another as moral equals forbids establishing or strengthening social castes. Another familiar answer to the question of why we ought to be troubled by policies that draw distinctions among people on the basis of HSD traits is that such groups may lack the ability to affect the political process in a regular and fair way. For example, if blacks are regularly excluded from the political process, it is more likely that laws and policies that distinguish among people will do so in a way that disadvantages blacks. This reconstruction of John Hart Ely's famous account of when and why courts should closely scrutinize laws that affect "discrete and insular minorities" can be extended beyond the context of law. What I term the *disproportionate burden* argument, considered below, was inspired by Ely's concerns.

Anti-Caste and Disproportionate Burden

Distinguishing on the basis of HSD traits may be morally different than doing so on the basis of non-HSD traits because the former reinforces or entrenches the caste-like aspects of our society. Laws that disadvantage groups without a social identity—people whose last names begin with A, for example—cannot reinforce a caste as there is no such social group whose status can be harmed or reinforced. In order to ask whether a law, policy, or practice reinforces caste, we must first determine whether the group identified is one to which the concept of caste is relevant. The history of how a group has been treated or its current social status is what largely determines whether we are dealing with such a social group.[10] One caveat before proceeding: The initial comparison between not hiring someone on the basis of the first letter of her last name and not hiring someone on the basis of her sex led to the hypothesis that the history or current social status of a group defined by a trait makes a moral difference. How and why history and social status matter has yet to be determined. I do not mean to say they are determinative; a distinction on the basis of a non-HSD trait can also be wrongful. Rather, the contrast between the cases *suggests* that history and social status matter. We are mining that insight—not a novel one, but one that has been inadequately explored—to determine why and how. To do so, we are considering two prominent accounts (one being a reconstruction) of when distinction-drawing runs legally afoul of the Equal Protection Clause to see if they shed any light. While both accounts of why and how HSD traits matter are flawed, understanding where they go wrong will guide our inquiry to an alternative.

According to anti-caste approaches, history or current social status matter because they determine, to a large degree, which are the groups whose relative status we must safeguard. This view is appealing in many ways, yet ultimately unsatisfactory. It taps a powerful intuition that laws that disadvantage individual African Americans, for example, are morally troubling because of the social status of African Americans as a group. However, this view does so at the cost of relinquishing the individual nature of a violation. A black man denied an opportunity is wronged because this action contributes to the relative disadvantage of blacks as a group. Though the status of the group may be relevant, as I argue below, it ought to be relevant in a way that allows us to maintain that a wrong is done to the individual and not just to the group.[11]

What about the second explanation, which I term the *disproportionate burden* account? If drawing distinctions among us is necessary to affect many valuable goals, we would hope that the interests of each of us in not being disadvantaged by such distinction drawing are weighed equally in the political and private processes through which such distinctions are drawn. If some groups find it difficult to have their interests considered in these processes, then we may worry about the fairness of the classifications or differentiations brought to bear.[12]

This Ely-inspired account of why the history of mistreatment of particular groups matters fails to capture something important about *how* drawing distinctions on the basis of these traits is morally problematic. On this view, any one instance of line drawing that does not adequately consider the interests of a particular group is not problematic. Rather, it is the *cumulative* disadvantage that is problematic.[13] After all, there will always be winners and losers with individual policies, particularly in a political process. A problem arises when a "discrete and insular minority" (to use those famous words) is unable to break in so as to insure it is not repeatedly a loser.

It is the fact that the wrongfulness of any individual policy depends on prior policies that is problematic. Consider the case of a privileged white woman who is denied some job or opportunity because she is a woman. If, up until now, she has not been subject to much line drawing on the basis of sex—and the interests of women have been considered in drawing the distinctions that have affected her—what would this account say about this particular instance? Is it wrong? If so, why? One might say that here she is entitled not to be disadvantaged on the basis of her sex *but only* because in general the interests of women are not adequately considered in the drawing of distinctions in most policies and laws. If so, the sex discrimination that affects her is wrong only derivatively. Something is thereby lost.

The fact that these sorts of accounts relinquish the individual nature of the wrong of wrongful discrimination is sometimes directly embraced. For example, Glenn Loury argues that the commitment to "race-egalitarianism" that he defends "focuses explicitly on the status of groups." This focus entails, in his view, a rejection of "the precepts of liberal individualism," by which he means "the tendency of thought that seeks to critically assess the justice of a society's distribution of resources solely in terms of the welfare of individuals, while giving no independent weight to the economic or social position of identity-based groups."[14] While I am quite sympathetic with much of Loury's excellent book, I find his approach sets up a false dichotomy. It is possible to claim that the historical treatment and current social status of the *group* matter in assessing current policy and still maintain that they also matter in determining whether the policy treats *individuals* unfairly. To mediate the pull of the claim that group status matters with the intuition that an individual has been wronged, we need to find a way that the group status matters to the determination of how the individual has been treated.

An alternative way to make sense of the intuition that the history of mistreatment of a group matters in the assessment of wrongful discrimination is to notice that the history or current status of the group actually affects what one does in drawing such a distinction. What one *does* in drawing a distinction on the basis of some characteristic is not just separate people into two or more groups and allocate different treatment on the basis of that distinction. Sometimes one also demeans some of the people one classifies. But not always. The employer who does not hire job applicants whose last names begin with the letter A does not demean this group of people. She may intend to. Perhaps she believes people whose last names begin with A are idiots because she has known quite a few over the years. Still, de-meaning is partly a conventional act as will be explained below, so her ac-tion does not demean people with names beginning with A because there is nothing for her intentions to grab onto.

Discrimination as a Social Fact

The history or current social status of a group affects what one does in *clas-sifying* on the basis of a particular trait. When a person or institution sepa-rates people on the basis of certain characteristics in certain contexts, the actor not only distinguishes but may also demean some of those affected. If so, distinguishing in this way is wrong.

How might that be so? Meaning can come from three sources: the intent of the speaker, the perception or understanding of the listener, and the con-text in which the "utterance"[15] is made. Philosophers of language debate the relative importance of each of these. Moreover, there is an additional debate that focuses on the relative importance of semantics (the conven-tionally understood meanings of individual words and sentence structures) versus what are called "pragmatics" (context, use). One philosopher on the pragmatics side uses the following example to illustrate the importance of context. You ask him, "Can you cook?" and he replies, "I am French." While "I am French" normally means that the speaker is of French nationality, in this context it means that the speaker—François Recanati—is a good cook.[16] Here, what the sentence says is seemingly unconnected to the meaning of the individual words or indeed of the sentence, taken on its own. Whether one thinks, like Recanati, that use, context, and pragmatics are the central determinant of meaning or instead that this sort of case is an exception to the way language generally works—a debate I do not wish to enter here— one thing is clear: Sometimes, at the least, words have a meaning that is un-related to or goes beyond the ordinary meaning of the words and the sen-tence structure in which they are used. Recanati is surely right about this case: In that context "I am French" means Recanati is a good cook.

When laws or policies group people on the basis of traits, sometimes the context and culture invest these distinctions with a meaning that other dis-tinctions do not have—but not always. If so, then this meaning—the more complex one that depends in part on culture and context—matters to how we ought to assess the moral significance of the action as a whole. Consider the following example: A school principal issues the order: "Black students shall sit on the left side of the auditorium and white students shall sit on the right side of the auditorium." In this example, as first suggested by Paul Brest and later discussed by John Hart Ely,[17] the principal orders this seating arrangement because he likes the aesthetic effect thereby created. The reason for this contrived example was to elucidate some problems of intent-based understandings of the wrong of wrongful discrimination. When we recognize that the meaning of the principal's order depends not only on his intentions and the meanings of his individual words, but also on their context and the culture in which they are spoken, we see that the problematic nature of this classic example dissipates and our instincts about it are fairly easily accounted for. How should we understand the principal's order? Well, first, it is important to note that it *is* an order. In addition, it has an effect on the students and other teachers, getting them to do something. This much is uncontroversial.

In addition, and perhaps most salient, the principal demeans the black students. To see how this is so, consider a more loaded example. Suppose the principle had said: "Black students shall sit in the back of the bus and white students shall sit in the front." Separation by race in seating on buses, trains, and so on in our culture is conventionally understood to connote inferiority so that the treatment meted out by this classification is more symbolically loaded than is that of the left versus the right side of the room. This order—blacks in the back—has an effect as well. The principal's order is likely to produce a feeling of being stigmatized in the students. But it is the fact that the order demeans that I want to emphasize. In ordering the blacks to the back of the bus, the principal thereby demeans the black students.[18] This distinction bears emphasis.

The claim that a classification demeans the black students is easily confused with the claim that they are stigmatized. While the notion of stigma is important, I avoid it because I think it is often used in a way that is ambiguous. Sometimes claims about stigma refer to the effect produced by a classification and other times they refer to what one does in classifying—demean. The effect of classification refers to the harm suffered by those affected, either psychologically or socially. *Brown v. Board of Education*'s famous assertion that segregating African American public school children "generates a feeling of inferiority as to their status in the community that may affect their hearts and minds in a way unlikely ever to be undone"[19] is a classic example of the notion of stigma as a psychological harm. In addition, scholars have emphasized the ways in which groups can be stigmatized socially. For example, Glenn Loury builds on the work of Erving

Goffman in claiming that blacks are a socially stigmatized racial group, by which he means that "the meanings connoted by race-symbols undermine an observing agent's ability to see their bearers as a person possessing a common humanity with the observer—as 'someone not unlike the rest of us.'"[20] Both the conception of stigma as psychological harm and as a social harm emphasize the effect produced by a classification.[21]

What I want to call attention to is different. Rather than emphasize the effect (psychological or social) produced by classification, I claim that sometimes it is wrong to classify because of what one expresses—regardless of whether the person or people affected feel demeaned, stigmatized, or degraded. The term *stigma* can also be used in this way; one may stigmatize, meaning to demean or degrade. But because the term *stigma* is more commonly used to call attention to the effects of actions, I find it more confusing than helpful to use here.

Another way of capturing the distinction I am drawing is as follows: an approach that looks at the effect of classification focuses on the *harm* thereby caused, whereas an approach that looks at what one does in classifying focuses on whether that action is *wrong*. In my view, classification is sometimes wrong because of what one does in classifying and this wrongness is not reducible to the harm that one may inflict.

Context and Culture Make Drawing Certain Distinctions Demeaning

Whether distinguishing among people demeans any of those affected is determined by the social context in which the action occurs. In our culture, ordering African Americans to the back of the bus is conventionally understood as denigrating. This is not because there is something worse about the back of the bus, however. Teenagers covet that spot. Ordering blacks to the back of the bus is dramatically different because it is *blacks* that are ordered to the *back* and because of the history of racial segregation in public transport and much else in this country. In addition, the fact that one *orders* blacks to the back makes a difference in what one does—ordering (rather than requesting, for example) has a greater potential to demean.

Other countries—with their own histories—render various sorts of treatment meaningful in much the same way that the back versus the front of the bus is for us. When Nelson Mandela was imprisoned on Robin Island, the black prisoners were required to wear shorts while the white and colored prisoners could wear long pants.[22] This policy demeaned the black prisoners because wearing shorts in postcolonial South Africa was conventionally understood as infantilizing. Notice also that this classification occurs in the context of an order—an exercise of power in which the possibility of demeaning is more likely.

While the left side of the auditorium is not generally understood to be inferior to the right,[23] merely classifying on the basis of race without there being anything about the context that dilutes or saps the order of racial separation of its demeaning potential, risks, at the least, demeaning. This is because separation on the basis of race has a socially or conventionally understood meaning in our culture—particularly an *order* of racial separation. It can be neutralized by other aspects of the situation. But if it is not neutralized, it remains charged. For example, were a high school teacher teaching about the Jim Crow era to ask his racially mixed class to separate by race in order to illustrate how this separation felt, the fact that this racial separation takes place in the context of educating the students about racial discrimination changes the meaning of this order. And perhaps it is only a request, as the teacher may be open to allowing students who feel too uncomfortable to opt out—which would further modify the meaning of the teacher's action.

Notice that the way in which social context and culture determine whether an act separating people demeans and thereby wrongfully discriminates operates at two levels. First, and most important, is the following aspect: Whether the characteristic one uses to classify has the potential to demean is determined largely by how that characteristic has been used to separate people in the past and the relative social status of the group defined by the characteristic today. Race is different from the letter that begins one's last name. Second, when we distinguish between people on the basis of some characteristic, we then accord different treatment to each group. Sometimes that different treatment is better or worse in a way that would be true across cultures—loss of a job, health care, education, and so on. Other times, the difference in treatment resides in the cultural significance of that treatment—the back of the bus, wearing shorts, and so on. In these cases, the conventionalism of discrimination occurs at a second level as well.

One caveat before we proceed. Drawing distinctions on the basis of HSD traits has more *potential* to demean because of the social significance of such distinctions. But as I explained above, not all distinction-drawing on the basis of HSD traits is demeaning, as other aspects of the situation also affect whether one demeans. Moreover, categorizing on the basis of non-HSD traits can also demean; however, more contextual factors are required for this to be the case.

Let me recap the argument thus far. To classify (or to draw distinctions among people on the basis of some attribute) is to do several things at once. First, to classify is to distinguish, to separate, to divide. Second, classifying generally produces an effect—different treatment is accorded to different persons and, at times, some of those affected feel stigmatized. Third, in classifying sometimes we demean. It is this third aspect of classification that is crucial and determines whether the action constitutes wrongful discrimination.

Whether classification demeans depends on the social or conventional meaning of drawing a particular distinction in a particular context. Context and culture play a significant role in determining the meaning of actions. Sometimes to classify is to demean—and when it is, this denigration is relevant to its moral permissibility.

Why Demeaning?

The discrimination puzzle is of moral concern because treating people differently risks running afoul of the idea that people have equal moral worth. We cannot treat all people the same; laws, policies, and practices must draw distinctions among people on various bases. This fact of necessary differentiation gives rise to the moral question of when different treatment is morally permissible and when it is not. When does differentiation fail to treat people as moral equals?

To demean is to treat someone in a way that denies her equal moral worth and thus picks out a wrong that is intimately tied to the value that underlies our worries about differentiation in the first place. To demean is not merely to insult but also to put down, to diminish and denigrate. It is to treat another as lesser. Interestingly, some have argued that demeaning is the core moral wrong, not only relating to differentiation but more generally. Jean Hampton, for example, offers the following as a definition of a moral wrong (as distinguished from mere harm): "A person wrongs another if and only if (while acting as a responsible agent) she treats him in a way that is objectively demeaning."[24] This conception of moral wrong springs from the same intuition that I have offered to explain when and whether differentiation is wrong. After all, people harm one another in many ways.

If one is trying to distinguish harms that are wrongs from those that are not, one could propose a theory of rights (like bodily integrity, control of property, etc.). Alternatively, one could say that harms that demean are wrongful and harms that do not are benign. Here, the idea of demeaning helps one to identify which harms treat the other in a way that conflicts with the bedrock principle of the equal moral worth of persons.

While I am sympathetic to Hampton's account of moral wrong, I do not want to argue for or against it here. Rather, I point it out to show the reader the general appeal of *demeaning* as a moral concept. Moreover, I think the more modest claim that demeaning is the core moral concept separating permissible from impermissible differentiation is especially plausible. First, this is because our worries about differentiation spring from the particular concern that in treating people differently we may fail to treat them as moral equals. And second, differentiation occurs in many contexts in which there is no way to define the "right" that someone may otherwise be entitled to (like bodily integrity or use of property). Rather, the employer or school admissions official is free to use whatever criteria he or she wants to decide whom to hire or admit—within limits. These limits are what we are trying to sketch.

Demeaning is not equivalent to subordination. It may lead to subordination, but that is the effect—one that is likely from repeated demeaning actions, but an effect that may not occur. So, in any particular instance, if a person is demeaned by a policy (that distinguishes among people), she need not *feel* demeaned to have a moral claim. Demeaning is wrong because the fact that people are of equal moral worth requires that we treat them as such. We must not treat each other as lesser beings even when doing so causes no harm. Hampton draws a similar distinction between demeaning and degradation. When one person wrongs another (defined as acting in a way that is "objectively demeaning"), the person wronged may feel that her status has been lowered or she may not. If she does not, "she perceives herself to have suffered *no literal degradation* as a result of the wrongdoing. Her high value is, she believes, unchanged despite the action. But she is nonetheless *demeaned* in the sense that she has been forced to endure treatment that is too low for her. So there is a difference between being demeaned and being literally lowered in value."[25]

In saying that it is wrong to demean I do not mean to claim that one can never demean. Rather, like other claims of moral right or wrong, it is possible that in a particular instance, one could demean to avoid a worse wrong or perhaps a very great harm. Rather, the goal here is to analyze when differentiation is wrong—not to say when the wrongfulness of this action may be overridden by other concerns.

Is Demeaning Enough?

I have argued that demeaning especially offends against the requirement of treating others as having equal moral worth. To demean is to treat someone as less worthy and to do so in a way that is reasonably powerful. What it takes for an action to demean will be discussed in more detail in Chapter 2. But, one might wonder, are not there other ways besides demeaning that offend the equal moral worth of others? After all, killing someone surely does (though perhaps it would be more natural to say that killing offends the inherent worth of a person rather than the *equal* worth of the person). If so, then perhaps demeaning is only one sort of wrongful discrimination and perhaps there are others. The question that is the focus of this book is this: When does drawing distinctions among people fail to respect their equal moral worth? The answer I have argued for in this chapter is that when distinctions demean, they wrongfully fail to treat people as moral equals. This answer leaves open the possibility that some distinctions that do not demean may also fail to treat people as moral equals, but for other reasons. While I cannot conclusively reject this possibility, Chapters 4, 5, and 6 attempt to convince the reader that several promising arguments for thinking that non-demeaning distinctions can also fail to treat those affected as moral equals fail. In Chapter 4, I argue that treating people as equals does not require that distinctions be drawn on the basis of merit. In Chapter 5, I argue that treating people as equals does not require that distinctions be rational. Taking these two arguments together *suggests* that treating people as moral equals does *not* require that one have a good reason for distinguishing among people. (I say "suggests" because clearly these two arguments do not cover all possible alternatives, but the fact that they fail is suggestive.) Rather, to classify people in a way that treats them as moral equals, we must simply refrain from doing so in a way that demeans. This is a less demanding requirement— differentiation need not be justified, it only needs to refrain from demeaning. Respect for the diversity among people, among aims, and among institutions argues for this more modest approach. There is unlikely to be a defined list of permissible reasons to distinguish among people. Rather, there is one clear reason not to. When differentiation demeans it is wrongful.

When it does not, we ought to let the complexity and diversity of our goals and values flourish.

An Individual Wrong

This account of wrongful discrimination provides an explanation of why the history and current social status of groups are relevant. At the start of this chapter, I ventured the contrast between not hiring someone because her last name begins with A and not hiring someone because he is black or she is a woman suggests that distinguishing among people on the basis of HSD traits matters. I then asked why it matters and endeavored to develop a theory to explain the relevance of these HSD traits without losing track of our intuition that wrongful discrimination is an individual wrong. The account provided here satisfies both of these requirements. History and current social status are relevant because they are part of what determines the meaning of a law, policy, or practice that draws distinctions on the basis of a particular trait.

Let us return to our original comparison: discriminating on the basis of the first letter of one's last name versus discriminating on the basis of race or sex. If the school principal were to ask students whose last names begin with the letters A–M to sit on the left side of the auditorium and those whose last names begin with N–Z to sit on the right, what does he do in issuing this request or command? He requests or commands but he does not demean. Segregating people on the basis of the first letter of one's name has no social significance in our culture, so that what he does is request or command, but not demean. He does not demean because his request or order does not have a loaded meaning in our culture. This is an interpretive claim about our culture. Of course at that school it is possible that there has been a history of treating people whose last names begin with the letters A–M poorly so that the social significance of his command would then demean. But this possibility only emphasizes what it takes to make it the case that in classifying he demeans.

The account presented here avoids another important pitfall in debates about equality. Some influential scholars have claimed that equality is an empty idea—that equality requires simply that persons be treated in accord with how they ought to be treated.[26] For example, if each of us is entitled to be judged by academic merit when applying to a college or university, then what is wrong with deviations from this norm in some cases is not an offense against equality but instead an offense against the requirement that academic merit is the right criterion to apply. On this view, the concept of equality is doing no real work. The account of wrongful discrimination provided here avoids this pitfall, giving real teeth to the concept of equality without simultaneously putting forward a controversial conception of positive human rights.

Discrimination is wrong when it demeans. To demean is to treat another as less worthy. In this sense, demeaning is an inherently comparative concept. What will be demeaning will surely vary from context to context and from culture to culture, and thus it is unlikely that a norm of non-demeaning will require that people have access to some particular conception of rights or minimum level of goods. What it does require is that laws, policies, and practices not draw distinctions among people in a way that treats some as less worthy than others, however that is interpreted in that culture. This account thus neither reduces equality to an entitlement to a specific good or right nor leaves it empty of bite or content.

I have presented the view that it is morally wrong to draw distinctions among people and treat them differently as a result when doing so demeans any of those affected. For this account to be convincing, there are important questions that must be addressed. The next two chapters will elaborate the basic idea presented here. First, Chapter 2 will further explore what is demeaning. Next, Chapter 3 will address how one determines whether a particular classification demeans, and what we should say about the fact that people are likely to disagree about whether particular classifications demean. Part II will consider alternative answers to the question of when discrimination is wrong. Chapter 4 argues against the claim that the concept of merit helps determine when a classification fails to treat people as equals. Chapter 5 considers the more modest claim that distinctions must at least be rational. Lastly, Chapter 6 explores and rejects the view that it is the intention of the person who draws a distinction that is important.

CHAPTER 2

Demeaning and Wrongful Discrimination

In 2000, Harrah's (a company operating casinos, including one in Reno, Nevada) instituted a Personal Best program that required female employees to wear makeup, but prohibited male employees from doing so. Specifically, the policy required that "[m]ake up (face powder, blush and mascara) must be worn and applied neatly in complimentary colors," and that "[l]ip color must be worn at all times" by female beverage servers. For males the policy stated: "Eye and facial makeup is not permitted."[1]

In *Fesel v. Masonic Home of Delaware, Inc.*, the court allowed a nursing home serving a largely female population to continue its policy of only hiring women as aides. Aides were responsible for the personal care of the residents, including "dressing, bathing, toilet assistance, geriatric pad changes and catheter care." Many of the clients would not consent to being attended by male aides.[2]

A personal advertisement under "Men Seeking Women" in a local paper reads: "Looking for a single woman, age 30–40, for a long-term relationship or marriage. Seeking a woman who is not afraid to be feminine. Prefer someone slim, who wears makeup and likes to dress fashionably."

This chapter and the next will address two questions central to the view that drawing distinctions among people in a way that demeans is wrongful. This chapter will explore exactly what demeaning is. Chapter 3 will address how one determines whether a classification demeans and what disagreement about whether a classification demeans portends for the theory I advance.

What Is Demeaning?

To demean is to treat another as not fully human or not of equal moral worth. To demean therefore is partly an expressive act. One's action expresses that the other is less worthy of concern or respect. In addition, to *treat* another in such a way also requires that one's action have a certain efficacy. Generally speaking, one needs a degree of power or status to demean another. We must be careful, however, not to confuse this power/status requirement with the actual effect of the action. An employer might demean women by requiring that they be twice as good as men to get the job in question, nonetheless a particular woman may not feel demeaned or stigmatized.[3] The actual effect of the action does not determine what sort of action it is. For example, a person who presents himself as a minister may perform a marriage ceremony and thereby induce the bride and groom to believe they are married, but he has not actually married the couple unless he has the status or power required by law to do so.

To demean is to put down—to debase or degrade. To demean thus requires not only that one express disrespect for the equal humanity of the other but also that one be in a position such that this expression can subordinate the other. For example, if I spit at a colleague or my boss, I act disrespectfully, given conventions in our culture about the meaning of spitting. But it is unlikely that I demean my colleague or boss. I do not *put her down*. I do not demean her because my actions (except in unusual circumstances) lack the power to put her down. I do not mean that she does not feel degraded or debased—though she probably does not, she is probably just insulted and angry. Rather, I mean that in spitting I do not demean her because my action, given our relative status, likely lacks the power to demean. Contrast this scenario with one in which I spit on a homeless man lying in the street. Here I demean him. In spitting, I put him down. This act of spitting constitutes demeaning because (a) spitting is a conventional way of showing disrespect *and* (b) the relative disparity in status between a homeless person and myself allows my expression of disrespect to put him down.[4]

Demeaning thus has a conventional and a non-conventional aspect, or a social dimension and a power dimension. It is our common history and culture and its conventions and social understandings that determine which actions express a rejection of the equal humanity of others. And it is the power or status of the speaker that allows the expression of this sentiment to demean.

Consider another example: suppose a mother says to her child, "you stupid kid, you're not good at anything." She both expresses disrespect for her child and demeans him. Compare this to the case where the child's classmate says the same thing to him. In such a case the classmate insults the child and expresses disrespect but does not demean—that is, unless we tell a story of unequal status or hierarchy in the classroom. Now of course neither of these situations are examples of drawing distinctions among people—of *discrimination* as I have been using the term. Nonetheless, they are helpful in illustrating an important feature about demeaning. Because drawing distinctions among people on the basis of some trait they have or lack is wrong when doing so demeans, according to the view I am advancing here, it is crucial to establish what demeaning is. So, while neither a pedestrian spitting on a homeless man nor a mother berating her child are instances of distinction drawing, they help to clarify what it takes for an action to demean.

Demeaning is related to being disrespectful and to that extent depends on convention. There are conventional methods of expressing respect—taking off one's hat when entering a room, writing a thank you note to one's dinner host, looking someone in the eye when speaking. In fact, one way of understanding manners is as respect-conventions.[5] In a similar way, albeit less formalized and defined, there are conventions for disrespect as well— giving someone the finger, spitting on someone, looking over someone's shoulder when she is speaking to one, and so on. Demeaning is, in part, expressing disrespect (in an especially strong way as it is an expression of a lack of respect for the equal humanity of the other) and as such depends on conventions regarding how disrespect is expressed in a particular culture.

But, as the above examples illustrate, not all disrespectful action is demeaning. First, demeaning requires an especially strong expression of disrespect—that of a lack of respect for another's equal moral worth. Second, in most instances, demeaning also requires that the speaker hold a higher status than the person demeaned. To demean, rather than merely to insult, requires a certain degree of power. If this is correct, then a theory that defines wrongful discrimination as differentiating among people in a manner that demeans will have interesting implications.

For example, suppose I am considering renting my house while I am away for a year. I plan to rent the house furnished, leaving not only my furniture, rugs, and dishes but also books, vases, paintings, and other personal possessions. To safeguard my property, I decide to try to rent the house to another family and to avoid renting it to groups of single, young people, in particular. Under no conditions will I rent to a group of twenty-something men just out of college. My renting policy distinguishes among prospective tenants on the basis of sex, age, and family status. Does it wrongfully discriminate? I think it does not. It does not, in my view, in part because of the lack of a power differential between prospective tenants and myself. Though the implication of my refusal to rent can surely be read as insulting ("they're going to trash the place") and would-be tenants surely are denied the possibility of renting a house they may like, my action does not demean them for several reasons. First, there are plenty of other apartments and houses the prospective tenants could rent. Second, my choice not to entrust my personal belongings to certain others expresses something different than would a professional landlord's refusal to rent a vacant apartment. Third, the implication that young men just out of college like to party and do not take good care of possessions does not implicate their equal moral worth—in part because they do not form a group that has been subordinated in our culture. Finally, given my status as a one-time landlord, I lack power in this context.

That said, my view that a refusal to rent to a group of young, single men is not wrongful discrimination does not entail that a law forbidding discrimination in housing on the basis of age, sex, or family-status is unjustified. On the contrary. Laws must generalize. Because many instances (perhaps most) of housing discrimination based on age, sex, and family status are likely to involve rent refusals that do demean, general laws prohibiting housing discrimination on these bases are morally defensible.

Amnon Reichman notes that at common law, professionals were forbidden from drawing distinctions among prospective clients on the basis of traits like race and sex because the profession required one to offer one's services to all comers.[6] If so, this norm was internal to the profession itself. However, one could also understand the ban as an instantiation of the more general claim that drawing distinctions is wrongful when it demeans. When a blacksmith refuses to shoe a horse for a prospective customer, this action is likely to demean his client because the significance of such a professional's refusal of service is different from that of a non-professional's, because a professional generally serves all who can pay and because a professional occupies a position of power or status in our culture.

Context and Convention

Demeaning action thus requires (1) an expression of the unequal humanity of the other and (2) that the speaker occupy a position of status such that this expression is one that can put the other down. Whether or not any particular action expresses this deep disrespect depends crucially on context and convention. In this way, the unique history and traditions of a particular society play a central role.

Context and culture play a significant role in determining meaning. For example, conventions often allow words to perform actions.[7] To say "double" in bridge *is* to double; the officiant's statement, "I now pronounce you husband and wife," *marries* the couple; the umpire's call, "out!" at the baseball game *calls* an out. What accounts for the force these words have, for their ability to do the things they do, are the *conventions* that govern the games of bridge and baseball and the legal institution of marriage. It is not simply the meanings of the words that are significant here, rather it is primarily the broader social conventions about how the games of bridge and baseball are played and what it takes to marry two people in our culture. It is easy to see how social conventions enable the actions at issue in these examples because these examples depend upon highly stylized, formal social practices that define and create them.

Consider next a more complicated but fairly uncontroversial example: promising.[8] If I say, "I promise to do X," I have not only asserted something, I have done something. I have committed myself to do X (so long as nothing occurs that excuses me from this obligation). Promising is an important example because it demonstrates how one is able to change the moral landscape by saying something. The promiser has an obligation that he or she did not have prior to making the promise.[9] This example is also important because how promising is accomplished is conventional but not highly formalized or stylized like a game or a marriage ceremony. There are many ways to so commit oneself. One might use straightforward language like "I promise to do X," but one need not. Suppose my friend is about to have a dangerous medical procedure from which she may not recover. She asks me in a serious tone whether I will care for her children if she dies. I reply, "you bet," and squeeze her hand. I do not think there is any question here that I have promised. Of course there are likely many cases in which it is difficult to determine whether someone has promised and about which people might disagree about whether a person has promised. Nonetheless, promising is possible because there are conventions (though loose and difficult to specify) about how one commits oneself.

As promising illustrates, the conventions that enable promising and other verbal acts must be clear enough to be recognizable but need not be highly stylized or formal. Moreover, they may be in flux. As a result, words uttered at time T1 may have a meaning that the same words uttered at time T2 fail to have. Consider the case of accepting responsibility. It used to be the case—at least I *think* so—that one could accept responsibility by saying so either directly ("I accept responsibility") or through conventionally understood locutions (like "The buck stops here"). When these words were generally understood as ways of accepting responsibility, uttering them *was* to accept responsibility. Such an acceptance of responsibility meant that the speaker then had moral obligations that she had not had prior to the acceptance of responsibility. What those obligations were exactly would depend on what the speaker was accepting responsibility for, of course, but *some* obligations attached from accepting responsibility.

The verbal acceptance of responsibility has been undermined as a way of accepting responsibility (perhaps not completely but substantially) by the fact that it has been too often used insincerely. Because the explicit acceptance of responsibility has often not been accompanied by the required follow-through, two consequences have occurred: First, to say, "I accept responsibility for X" may no longer be a way of accepting responsibility. This power, if you will, is nullified. One cannot accept responsibility just by saying one does. One can accept responsibility in other ways though—perhaps by resigning from one's post. Second, saying, "I accept responsibility," no longer has the moral consequences it once did. Now, when people say, "the buck stops here," they no longer perform a morally significant action. What each of us can accomplish through our words is thus limited and the moral obligations that entail from explicit acceptances of responsibility are deflated. These consequences are really two sides of the same coin, but it is worth emphasizing each.

The example of promising illustrates how social conventions can determine the actions that words constitute even when those social conventions are informal. The example of accepting responsibility shows how these conventions can change—they can disintegrate, thereby eroding the force of the words, and they can also develop. Both of these processes are fairly slow. When a convention is growing or changing (and perhaps conventions are always doing so), it may be unclear whether an utterance has a particular force or not. Perhaps this explains the current state of affairs with regard to stating that one accepts responsibility. Though it is not a significant moral act, neither is it insignificant.

But what of social conventions regarding classification? Classification sometimes demeans the people classified. This is so because of the ways these traits have been used in the past. Cultural meanings have become attached to certain traits—race and sex paradigmatically, but there are others. If so, a law, policy, or practice that classifies on the basis of these traits risks demeaning. To distinguish among people on racial grounds is therefore not merely to distinguish among them on racial grounds (which might be rational or irrational in the particular context or motivated by good or bad intentions). To distinguish among people on racial grounds is to use a category that does not merely refer to certain differences in appearance (skin color, hair texture, etc.). Rather, classification on the basis of these traits carries with it baggage of social signification, or association with other traits that are deeply derogatory. As Glenn Loury explains, "the social meanings imputed to race-symbols have had profound, enduring, and all-too-real consequences—consequences due not to any race-dependent biological processes but rather to a system of race-dependent meanings, habitual social significations, that can be more difficult to 'move' than the proverbial, all-too-material mountain."[10]

What these social understandings are, regarding the use of race and sex-based classifications as well as many others, is not easily specified. Neither is it easy to articulate the myriad ways in which one can promise in our culture. With promising, at least one can do so explicitly by stating, "I promise." So, too, with demeaning. While one cannot say, "I demean you," and thereby demean someone, there are equally clear ways of demeaning in our culture, nevertheless. Ordering blacks to sit in the back of the bus is probably equally fixed by social convention as an instance of demeaning blacks (so long as it does not occur in a play or documentary, but so too of promising) as saying "I promise" is an instance of promising. And if laws requiring African Americans to sit in the back of the bus—especially laws embedded in a web of other legal restrictions such as where they can go to school, drink water, and so on—are a quintessential example of demeaning, then we can use this example to guide our inquiry into whether other practices demean. Thus the inquiry into whether a particular differentiation demeans is guided by three questions: Does the differentiation express that the person or people affected is or are of unequal moral worth? Is the person or institution drawing the distinction one with power or status in the situation? How similar is the differentiation at issue to a paradigmatic demeaning that "stamps the colored race (or whomever) with a badge of inferiority"?[11] If to demean, in our culture, is to stamp a person or group "with a badge of inferiority," then the example of segregative laws can guide our inquiry.

Are the practices and social understandings I am referring to really conventions? They are surely far less formalized and stylized than the rules for bridge or baseball, but I have been referring to them as conventions nonetheless. In my view, the ways of promising, accepting responsibility, and demeaning (to use the examples so far discussed) are largely conventionally determined. Sometimes conventions are highly formal—as in games—but they need not be. Where the meaning of an utterance is fairly clearly determined by its context, it is conventional in the sense that is important here.

This discussion is not meant to imply that the meanings of classifications in particular contexts are always easy to determine. Rather, judging whether a particular classification in a particular context does demean calls for a complex interpretive judgment. Many factors about the context may be relevant. Moreover, the cultural context at issue may at times be fairly local. Sometimes use of a particular trait to distinguish among people has meaning in a local community that it does not in the country as a whole. A point made in the last chapter bears emphasis here, in light of this complexity. While drawing distinctions on the basis of HSD traits has more demeaning potential than drawing distinctions on the basis of other traits, this is only a rule of thumb. It is surely possible to distinguish among people in a way that demeans without doing so on the basis of an HSD trait, and it is surely possible to draw a distinction on the basis of an HSD trait that does not demean. A state law forbidding people with freckles from voting would likely be an instance of the former; a teacher's direction that white students sit the front of the classroom and blacks in the back in the context of a lesson about racial segregation, accompanied by appropriate framing discussion, would likely be an example of the latter.

Some Examples Considered

To make this discussion both more real and more concrete, it will be helpful to consider some examples that are more than stripped-down hypotheticals.

I have chosen the three examples that head this chapter because their similarities and differences highlight the two dimensions of demeaning acts: the expressive dimension and the power dimension.

In the first example (based on the legal challenge the employer's policy spawned), the owners of a chain of casinos instituted a policy requiring female employees to wear makeup and forbidding male employees from doing so. The policy, which the employer termed a Personal Best policy, distinguishes between female and male employees and treats each differently, in this case requiring sex-specific grooming standards. In the second example, again drawn from a legal challenge to the employer policy at issue, a nursing home serving an elderly, largely female, population refused to hire men as aides. The responsibilities of an aide were to attend to the intimate and personal needs of the residents, including toilet assistance, dressing, and bathing. Here again, the policy distinguishes between men and women and treats each differently. In this case, however, the difference in treatment is more dramatic, as men are considered ineligible for the job in question. Finally, the third example is a hypothetical. A personal advertisement is placed by a man seeking a woman within a specific age range who is "feminine"—which the ad defines as wearing makeup and enjoying fashion. Here again there is a distinction drawn between men and women (the ad seeks women only), as well as between women who dress in a "feminine" way and those that do not. This third example is thus similar to the first two (by excluding men and by identifying sex-specific grooming standards) but also different in that it is a prospective dater who draws the distinctions rather than an employer. Do any of these policies demean? If so, why?

An action that distinguishes among people on the basis of their attributes is demeaning if the distinction-drawing and differential treatment express the unequal moral worth of the persons in question and if the person or entity adopting the policy or practice has sufficient power or status such that its actions can put others down. Let us apply that definition to the cases under discussion. First the casino case.

The first question to address is whether sex-specific grooming standards requiring only women to wear makeup denigrate women or express extreme disrespect for women. A good case can be made that they do. Requiring women to wear makeup—which should be distinguished from a policy permitting only women to wear makeup—conveys the idea that a woman's body is for adornment and the enjoyment by others. The stereotypical aspect of this grooming requirement—makeup for women—is one in a whole set of stereotypes about gender-specific roles. In addition, the fact that the employer *requires* women to comport with this stereotype reinforces its meaning and strengthens its expressive force. Not all grooming requirements are objectionable, though all may limit the employee's liberty in some way. The makeup requirement is significantly different from a requirement that all employees wear, say, blue pants and a white shirt. That policy is also a requirement, but it does not incorporate any particular concept of gender role. The makeup requirement is also significantly different in degree, even as compared to other sex-specific appearance requirements—short hair for men, long or short hair for women, for example. In our culture, the makeup requirement is associated with a certain understanding of women's bodies as objects in a way that distinguishes it from the less-derogatory hair-length requirement.[12]

Moreover, the fact that it is an employer who adopts this sex-based grooming policy is significant. An employer's actions are more likely to demean her employees than the reverse because the employer's status vis-à-vis her employees makes her actions powerful. As a result, this policy likely[13] demeans women and is therefore wrong.

Contrast that policy with both the refusal to hire men as nursing home aides and the dating policy, which combines a refusal to date men and a preference for women who wear makeup. The nursing home policy seems at first blush to be more problematic than the casino's makeup requirement in that the nursing home's policy forbids hiring men at all (versus merely instituting different grooming requirements for men and women). Yet the nursing home's refusal to hire men does not express that men are of unequal moral worth. There is surely an important cultural meaning to the home's deferral to its residents' preference to be attended to in personal matters by someone of the same sex, but it is not a cultural meaning that denigrates men or women.

Perhaps an argument could be made that it does demean. It would look something like this: Male nursing home residents are unlikely to have a similar complaint (at least not with the same intensity) to being attended by female aides. If so, there is perhaps a conflation of two important cultural understandings of the female-aides-only policy. On the one hand, it may simply reflect the cultural practice that intimate bodily functions be carried out only in the company of people of the same sex. On the other hand, it may also incorporate an understanding that these caring roles are women's roles so that women aides attending men is not likely to be perceived as a significant problem (despite the preference for same-sex privacy), while male aides attending women *is* (as it cuts against both cultural preferences). Which interpretation of the policy is best requires an interpretive judgment—as will be discussed in the next chapter—but suffice it to say that the cultural meaning of this policy is, at the least, more ambiguous than the makeup requirement.

Now compare these two policies with the personal advertisement. Here the prospective dater refuses to date men and expresses a preference for "feminine" women who wear makeup. Like the preference for women as nurse's aides attending female nursing home residents, the simple preference for women as romantic partners is probably best understood as not denigrating men or women. In the case of the personal ad, the prospective dater's preference for "feminine," makeup-wearing women likely also expresses something significant about women's bodies as objects. But the different context makes all the difference. In the case of a personal ad, the man simply states his dating preferences. As such, the ad is more like a request than an order or demand. Second, we are dealing with the dating context rather than the employment context. These two factors crucially affect whether the man's distinction drawing demeans women. I think it does not demean women because his preference lacks the power to put women down. It lacks that power because of the man's status (as a seeker of dates) and because it is a request rather than a command. In addition, the fact that this preference for makeup-wearing women occurs in the dating context (rather than the employment context) modifies how one would interpret its expressive meaning.

The discussion of these three examples helps elucidate the factors that affect whether distinction drawing in a particular context demeans. Demeaning is determined by a conventional and a non-conventional aspect. The use of a classification demeans in a particular context if it expresses the unequal moral worth of some person or group of people and does so in a manner that puts that person or people down. To demean thus requires both an action with a particular expressive content and that the speaker occupy a position such that his or her actions have some power.

The discussion of these examples is offered to clarify the factors at issue and not to assert that my reading of these practices is correct. I argue that classifications that demean are wrongful and that demeaning actions are those that express that the other is of unequal moral worth in a manner that puts the other down. I do not, however, claim any interpretive expertise about whether particular classifications do demean. Controversial policies are likely to spawn disagreement as to whether they do indeed demean. What such disagreement means for my theory of wrongful discrimination will be addressed in Chapter 3. The examples discussed here are offered to show the reader the sort of analysis that the theory I offer would entail.

Conventional Meaning versus Conventional Practice

It is important to emphasize the role convention plays, according to the theory I present here. In arguing that conventions determine whether a classification practice demeans, my theory is not *conventional* in the sense of acquiescing to or validating conventional practices. The fact that things have always been done a certain way surely cannot make them right. Because meaning is inherently conventional, however, social understandings about the meaning of certain distinctions in certain contexts affect whether they demean and are thereby wrongful.

Consider again the two examples dealing with sex-based discrimination in employment. In one, female employees were required to wear makeup while male employees were prohibited from doing so. In the second, the employer hired only women as nursing aides. In both instances, let us suppose the employer adopts the policy to satisfy customer preferences. And, in both instances these customer preferences reflect conventional practices regarding makeup use and bathroom privacy. In each case, thus, there is a conventional practice: sex-linked grooming habits and sex-segregation for intimate bodily functions. The theory I propose does not simply focus on whether the policy reflects current practice, however; it also requires that we examine the conventionally determined meaning of that practice. How should we best understand the social meaning of wearing makeup by women but not men? How should we best understand the fact that people sex-segregate for intimate bodily functions (toilet use and bathing)? A plausible answer would be that a policy requiring women, but not men, to wear makeup demeans women as it implies that women need adornment to be presentable and it emphasizes sexual attractiveness as a primary value of women. By contrast, the practice of preferring that only people of the same sex see one's body and help with private functions does not demean either men or women. It has a social meaning, indeed, one that is complex and multifaceted, but not one that demeans men or women.[14]

The approach I take here helps to explain why sometimes it makes sense to respect current practices and sometimes it does not. Robert Post has puzzled over this seeming inconsistency in the way that courts sometimes defer to conventional practice and sometimes do not.[15] For example, Post asserts that the courts' approach to precisely these cases fails to explain why, "if the nursing home residents in *Fesel* had claimed a privacy right not to be touched by nurse's aides who were African American, their expectations would no doubt properly and ruthlessly be overridden by Title VII."[16] This seems puzzling if one were to think that the *fact* of customary practice (say of preferring only to be touched by someone of the same race) is what is morally significant.[17] If we look to the *meaning* of each practice—sex-linked versus race-linked privacy concerns—we see that the latter is denigrating in a way that the former is not. In our culture, a customer preference for not being touched by someone of another race conveys a fear of racial contamination—and only in one direction. Indeed, one can understand the racial segregation of schools, drinking fountains, and especially swimming pools in exactly this way. No similar cultural understanding is associated with sex-linked privacy practices. These practices clearly also carry social meaning. Indeed, the sex segregation of private functions is permissible to the extent that it is, because this practice does not denigrate men or women.

Kimberly Yuracko offers a different interpretation of this line of cases[18]—in which courts generally (and probably rightly in my view) allow employers to differentiate between male and female job candidates in order to defer to the privacy preferences of their customers, but courts generally do not permit employers to treat men and women differently in ways that sexualize certain jobs (like the makeup requirement in the casino case). In Yuracko's view, the case law cannot be explained without reference to *perfectionist* concerns. For example, according to Yuracko, the interest in bodily privacy is protected because courts believe that "human dignity and flourishing is tied to one's ability to shield one's body and sexuality from unwanted and forced exposure."[19] Yuracko may be right as a descriptive matter—courts may indeed be moved by perfectionist concerns about what is good or valuable in life. But this perfectionist rationale is surely troubling. Are courts then justified in protecting customer preferences for privacy but not in protecting their preferences to be served drinks by attractive young women on airlines *because* a good life entails bodily privacy but not sexual titillation in the provision of goods and services?

The approach I endorse in this book provides a way to analyze the claims made in these cases without positing a conception of the good life. Rather than asking if bodily privacy is part of a valuable way of life, I ask whether the employer's deferral to customer preferences for bodily privacy expresses denigration of men or women. Similarly, in deciding whether to defer to customer preferences to be served drinks by an attractive female flight attendant (one of the cases discussed by Yuracko), one would ask not whether a largely sex-free workplace is important to human flourishing but rather whether deferring to such customer preferences demeans men or women. A good case can be made that it does. This approach avoids resting governmental restrictions on particular conceptions of the good life and of human flourishing. Instead, employer and customer freedom is curtailed in order to respect the rights of others to be treated in a non-demeaning fashion.

Is Demeaning Really an Equality Concern?

I have argued that treating people in a demeaning way is wrong because people are moral equals and such treatment denies this aspect of their humanity. But why consider this a concern grounded in *equality*? Perhaps we ought to say instead that all people have an inherent right to be treated with respect. Demeaning treatment fails to treat people with respect and thus violates this right. This account bypasses equality altogether. Is equality then "an empty idea" as Peter Westen argues,[20] or a principle that "has no moral force" as Harry Frankfurt claims?[21]

Let us scrutinize this argument—focusing on how it is presented by Harry Frankfurt. In Frankfurt's view, respect and equality are distinct. Each person is entitled to respect but the respect that each is due has "nothing essentially to do with the respect and consideration and concern that other people are shown or with the rights that other people happen to enjoy."[22] The respect that each is due is defined by virtue of who he or she is rather than by any comparison with how others are treated.

Frankfurt appears to assert that, in general, respect ought to be accorded in light of people's individual qualities: "Treating people with respect precludes assigning them special advantages or disadvantages except on the basis of considerations that differentiate relevantly among them."[23] Nonetheless, I imagine Frankfurt would agree that each person is entitled to some level of respect—call it "minimum respect"—merely by virtue of their common humanity. He would likely, however, insist that this entitlement has nothing to do with *equality*. Rather, each person is entitled to minimum respect, as each person is a person. We are equally entitled to it, not because equality is an important value, but because each person is entitled to it.[24]

But this approach—saying that each person is entitled to the respect that being a person entails—is itself empty. How would one ascertain what treating someone with the respect appropriate to personhood requires? Rather, the fact that we all share a common humanity requires that we be treated *as worthy as* others. We give flesh to the injunction to treat others with the respect that our common humanity demands by saying that no one may be treated as a *second-class* person. In other words, there is something inherently comparative here. Though each person may be entitled to a minimum level of goods or welfare or something else (I express no opinion about these claims), there is not some quantum of respect that each is entitled to, except that each is entitled to be treated as equally worthy of concern as others. Equality is therefore the foundational value.

Is Demeaning Really Enough?

Given that differentiation among people is unavoidable—by public and private actors—we need a theory about when differentiation is permissible and when not. The answer I proposed in Chapter 1 and elaborate in this chapter is that what marks wrongful from permissible discrimination is a feature of the action itself. Because differentiation is a moral problem stemming from a concern with equality, it makes sense to look to that value in formulating a conception of wrongful differentiation. Wrongful differentiation is that which offends against the norm of the equal moral worth of persons. I propose that distinction drawing is morally wrong when it demeans. But is demeaning really enough?

One might argue that though demeaning differentiation is problematic and harmful, not all demeaning differentiation constitutes wrongful discrimination. Perhaps the differentiation must demean *and* hinder an important interest to constitute wrongful discrimination.[25] Suppose distinguishing among people in a particular way in a particular context demeans some of those affected. The claim that this is not enough to be wrongful rests on the view that being demeaned *by itself* does not impede an important interest of the person. I think there is good reason to believe that view is not right. Indeed, avoiding demeaning treatment may instead be a *central* interest of people. Avishai Margalit makes such a claim: "the attitude of others is built into the very concept of the value of humans which the bearer of self-respect is supposed to adopt with regard to herself."[26] In other words, self-respect, surely a central interest, is inextricably tied to avoiding demeaning treatment. There is empirical evidence for this claim. People care immensely about whether they are treated with respect and especially whether they are treated as being *as worthy as* others.[27] The economist Robert Frank has extensively documented how individual spending habits are driven by a desire for *relative* status.[28] If relative status is an important interest,[29] this suggests that demeaning conduct obstructs a person's interest in being treated as equally worthy.

Is there reason to think that some demeaning is morally de minimis? There is good reason to think that not all demeaning action (in general) or all wrongful discrimination (distinction drawing that demeans) is harmful enough to warrant *legal* regulation. But this fact does not distinguish wrongful discrimination from other wrongful actions—some of which are legally regulated and some not. Promise-breaking is generally wrong, yet not all promise-breaking warrants legal regulation. Only certain promises are legally enforceable.[30] It is wrong to hurt another's feelings for no good reason, yet most such hurting of feelings is not legally proscribed. So, while demeaning distinction drawing may be sufficient for wrongful discrimination, there is good reason to suspect it is not sufficient to establish which wrongful discrimination ought to be legally prohibited—either by statute or via an interpretation of the constitutional guarantee of equal protection. Such a legal claim would require consideration of practical concerns like the costs and benefits of restricting certain forms of demeaning discrimination. The aim of this book is to lay the moral foundation on which an inquiry into when wrongful discrimination should be legally proscribed could proceed. Having established that certain distinction drawing is morally wrong, we can then ask which wrongful discrimination ought to be legally prohibited and which, though wrongful, is best left alone.

Is All Demeaning Wrong?

The most likely threat to this account of wrongful discrimination as differentiation that demeans comes from its implications for punishment. Is not punishment demeaning? And if so, does this not suggest that punishment is morally wrong or at least suspect? Given that punishment is not morally wrong (at least not when it is meted out in a proportional way, after an appropriate legal determination of guilt, and in response to a just criminal law, etc.), does the legitimacy of punishment suggest there is something wrong with this definition of wrongful discrimination?

Answering this challenge is difficult without wading into controversial and complex debates about when and for what reasons punishment *is* justified. Some claim that punishment is justified when it is deserved, others when it deters, and still others when it serves to rehabilitate or morally educate the criminal. Though punishment surely harms the criminal (by depriving him of liberty and in other ways) and our current penal system could be faulted for demeaning those convicted of crimes (for example, by tolerating violence, rape especially, within prisons), some theories view punishment in and of itself as not demeaning to the criminal. For example, Jean Hampton adopts a moral-education theory of punishment that sees punishment as a way to communicate the wrongful nature of an action to its perpetrator in a way that respects his autonomy: "it [her theory] attempts to justify punishment as a way to benefit the person who will experience it, a way of helping him to gain moral knowledge if he choose to listen."[31]

Punishment would also be unlikely to demean as it is conceived under a retributivist theory. According to this theory, the criminal deserves his punishment.[32] Michael Moore is especially clear that *failing* to punish the criminal may in fact deny his common humanity. According to Moore, if one would judge oneself guilty and deserving of punishment for doing a certain bad act, then one must so judge the criminal who does the same act. As he explains: "To grant that you would be guilty and deserving of punishment, but that others who do the exact same wrong with the exact same culpability would not be, is to arrogate to yourself a godlike position . . . [and] is an elitist arrogance that denies one's common humanity with those who do wrong."[33] Punishment of those who deserve it, in this view, is not demeaning but instead expresses respect for the moral agency of the person punished.

But even theories that explain and justify punishment as respectful to the person punished suggest limits. Not all punishment is respectful, nor all practices associated with it. Disproportionate punishment may be not only unjust but also demeaning. Many of the recent interrogation tactics used to elicit information from suspected terrorists and others may be demeaning—though that is hardly their worst offense. Lastly, some argue that the treatment of ex-felons is wrong precisely because it is demeaning. For example, George Fletcher has this to say about the practice of disenfranchising convicted felons:

> Despite our efforts to overcome discrimination in the areas of race, gender, illegitimacy, and alienage (at least by state governments), we still yield to the need to stigmatize felons and to treat them as "untouchables." They are the undercaste of American society. And among the untouchables, the worst are clearly the sex offenders, who are treated as inherently suspect for the rest of their lives.[34]

In sum, punishment need not be demeaning, according to some theories. However, many of our current practices may well be. Alternatively, one could argue that all punishment demeans[35] and is thereby at least prima facie wrong. However, the need to safeguard the community overrides this wrong in the case of punishing (most) criminals.

Dignity as Identified by Canadian Law

Interestingly, the *Canadian Charter of Rights and Freedoms* establishes a legal right to dignity that bears a strong similarity to the ban on demeaning differentiation that I argue for here. Section 15 of the Charter (its equality provision) states: "Every individual is equal before the law and has the right to the equal protection and equal benefit of the law without discrimination and, in particular, without discrimination based on race, national or ethnic origin, colour, religion, sex, age or mental or physical disability."[36] This Charter is fairly recent—having been adopted in 1982—thus the case law offers a compressed look at how Canada's Supreme Court interprets its demand for equal protection and prohibition of (wrongful) discrimination. What has emerged is the idea that Section 15 protects the "dignity" of each person.[37] In the 1995 case *Egan v. A-G. Canada*,[38] Justice L'Heureux-Dubé (writing alone but with the majority in finding provisions of the Canadian Pension Act in violation of section 15 for limiting such rights to opposite sex couples) gave this gloss to the section's force:

> Equality . . . means nothing if it does not represent a commitment to recognizing each person's equal worth as a human being, regardless of individual differences. Equality means that our society cannot tolerate legislative distinctions that treat certain people as second-class citizens, that demean

them, that treat them as less capable for no good reason, or that otherwise offend fundamental human dignity.[39]

More recently, the Court solidified its adoption of this conception of Section 15 in *Law v. Canada (Minister of Employment and Immigration).*[40] There Justice Iacobucci, writing for the majority in rejecting a challenge to the government's use of age in determining survivor benefits, describes the purpose of Section 15 as follows:

> to prevent the violation of essential human dignity and freedom through the imposition of disadvantage, stereotyping, or political or social prejudice, and to promote a society in which all persons enjoy equal recognition at law as human beings or as members of Canadian society, equally capable and equally deserving of concern, respect and consideration.[41]

The actual interpretation—in case law and scholarly commentary—of this protection of human dignity has varied. In particular, stereotyping and animus (the intent of the enacting body) has been overemphasized in my view. Nonetheless, one important strand of this jurisprudence emphasizes that what matters is whether a law or policy in question demeans or denigrates those whom it affects. While neither courts nor commentators have analyzed this in quite the same way I have here, the similarities are clear and worth noting. Most clearly, Denise G. Réaume argues:

> In order, then, to find violations of s. 15, we should look for distributive criteria which, in distributing the concrete benefit with which they are concerned in a particular way, thereby fail to accord equal respect to all persons as bearers of dignity, as persons of equal moral status. Legislation that conveys the implication that the members of a particular group are of less worth, not full members of society, violates dignity.[42]

One last point, which the discussion regarding the conception of dignity under the Canadian constitution brings into relief: In *Gosselin v. Québec,*[43] the Supreme Court of Canada upheld the welfare system of the province of Québec despite the fact that it provided a different level of benefits to those over 30 than to those under 30. Those under 30 could increase their level of benefits by enrolling in job training or educational programs—though there was some question about the availability of each. Because the welfare benefits awarded to the under-30 group were so low, the case raised the question whether the conception of dignity included a *substantive* component—requiring that each person is entitled to some minimum level of benefits or some fair share of society's wealth.

The discussion surrounding this case raises the question of the relationship between equality-based and justice-based concerns. My focus in this book is on equality—on the question of when drawing distinctions among people, and then treating them differently, fails to treat those affected as people of equal moral worth. However when a government fails to accord justice to some of its citizens, this may demean them even when distinguishing among people on the basis of the trait used does not itself have much demeaning potential.

Let me explain this point abstractly and then concretely, with a few examples. Suppose the government distinguishes among people on the basis of trait X and awards those with trait X the benefit A, and those without X the smaller benefit B. If distinguishing among persons on the basis of having or lacking X in this context does not demean, then this policy is not wrongful discrimination. In determining whether the policy demeans, we must look at the trait (X) and the context. Part of that context includes being attentive to what justice demands. So, if the government has an obligation based on justice to provide at least A to everyone, then providing B (which is less than A) to those without X demeans them. It does so by virtue of the fact that denying those without X what justice demands is itself demeaning.

To elucidate, consider some examples—one hypothetical and one real. Suppose the government were to decide to deny freckled people the right to vote. Treating people with freckles differently than those without freckles does not carry any baggage, if you will, so that this distinction—though arbitrary and stupid—would likely not demean, except that something vital is at stake. If justice requires that all adults have the right to vote, then restricting the franchise to those without freckles is unjust—and derivatively may also be demeaning. This instance of treating freckled people differently, as it violates justice, may express contempt for the equal humanity of the freckled. As this is an action of government, a good case can be made that this differentiation demeans freckled people.[44]

A similar argument can be made regarding the Canadian case *Gosselin*—though its application is far more controversial. Suppose one believes that justice requires that welfare benefits be greater than provided to the under-30 recipients of Québec's welfare program. If so, this program violates justice. But it may violate the demands of equality as well. The welfare program distinguishes among recipients on the basis of age. It may well be that such differentiation is not itself demeaning. But if only the younger recipients are denied what justice demands, then this selective denial may well demean younger welfare recipients.[45] Of course, the strength of this analysis depends on the claim that Québec's welfare program fell below the level required by justice.

Situating This View

Before closing this chapter, it may be helpful to situate my view in relation to others that it shares affinities with and that it builds upon. The inspiration for my view comes from the famous 1960 article by Charles Black, "The Lawfulness of the Segregation Decisions."[46] In that article, Black defends the *Brown v. Board of Education* decision against the challenge that segregation equally directs each race to a separate sphere and thus does not violate the constitutional guarantee of equal protection. For Black, the unlawfulness of segregation resides in the intent of actors adopting segregation laws and policies and in the effects of such laws. But it is noteworthy that he also stresses what he terms the "social meaning" of segregation. In a forceful passage, Black argues that "it would be the most unneutral of principles, improvised *ad hoc*, to require that a court faced with the present problem refuse to note a plain fact about the society of the United States—the fact that the social meaning of segregation is the putting of the Negro in a position of walled-off inferiority—or the other equally plain fact that such treatment is hurtful to human beings."[47] Thus for Black, the social meaning of segregation is one key to why it is wrong.

Black's emphasis on the fact that the question of when laws and policies violate equality cannot be answered in the abstract is also noteworthy. Other scholars are misled, according to Black, by mistakenly focusing on the question, "Must Segregation Amount to Discrimination?" Black answers that it is "an interesting question" and that "someday our methods of sociology may be adequate to answering it." Black's suggestion that this is a question for sociologists implies that he suspects that in all societies where segregation according to some trait is practiced, the segregation carries a hierarchical meaning. That may well be right. The abstract question gets some traction, however, precisely because we *can* imagine isolated instances of "segregation" on the basis of other traits that do not seem problematic—as in the alphabetic segregation of students in class that I discussed in Chapter 1. Black's key point here is that these cases are different. As he explains: "Our question is whether discrimination [I would say wrongful discrimination] inheres in that segregation that is imposed by law in the twentieth century in certain specific states in the American Union."[48] The right question must focus on the specific, contextually rich instance of separation or classification at issue.[49]

The view I propose here also has affinities to those adopted by legal scholars Charles Lawrence (regarding race discrimination) and Catherine MacKinnon (regarding the subordination of women) in the 1980s—both build on the insights of Charles Black. Lawrence believes, as do I, that the cultural meaning of laws and policies that draw distinctions among people is significant.[50] His insightful emphasis on the fact that racially influenced decision making is often unconscious makes an important contribution to our understanding of the wrong of wrongful discrimination, and offers a convincing argument for the rejection of the doctrinal focus in equal protection law on a finding of bad intentions by the actor in question. However, his work continues to locate the wrong of wrongful discrimination in a process defect—drawing on John Hart Ely's work—in the adoption of the law or policy in question. He believes that the cultural meaning of laws and policies is important for *evidentiary* reasons rather than being important in itself.[51] A racial cultural meaning is important evidence for Lawrence that an unconscious racial bias influenced the decision making that led to the adoption of the policy or practice in question.[52]

Catharine MacKinnon's important "dominance" strand of feminism is perhaps closer to the view I present here. She rejects the idea that the problem of wrongful discrimination is one of inapt or irrational classification (as do I in Chapter 5) and instead sees sexism as better conceived as a problem of power and subordination. MacKinnon also emphasizes the contribution that culture and history make to determining the social meaning of gender.[53] MacKinnon's view locates the wrong of wrongful discrimination in the subordination of women, which is analogous to my view that classifications are wrongful when they demean (women or others). But there is an important ambiguity in MacKinnon's work. MacKinnon is unclear as to whether she locates the moral wrong in the wrong of the action or in its effect.

Moreover, MacKinnon's work is motivated by a rejection of what she calls "difference feminism," or the debate about whether and how women are the same as or different from men. This starting point leads her, mistakenly in my view, to reject the focus on classification. But though the focus on classification has been misleading (in that sense I agree with MacKinnon), the moral issue it presents remains. Sometimes drawing distinctions among people on the basis of traits they have or lack is morally troubling and sometimes it is not. The question of when it is or is not permissible—what I call the discrimination puzzle—lingers even if we reject the difference strand of feminism.[54]

But these are to name only a few, salient scholars whose work I build upon in this book. There are clearly others, only a few of whom I will briefly mention here. Kenneth Karst's conception of "equal citizenship" is importantly similar. According to Karst, this principle requires that "[e]ach individual is presumptively entitled to be treated by the organized society as a respected, responsible, and participating member" or "[s]tated negatively, the principle forbids the organized society to treat an individual as a member of an inferior or dependent caste or as a nonparticipant."[55] Thus for Karst, as for me, the core principle of the equal moral worth of persons (I am downplaying the citizenship aspect of his view) is central to understanding the constitutional command of equal protection and the moral prohibition against wrongful discrimination. These passages make the resonance strong. Yet Karst's conception of equal citizenship grounds the wrong of wrongful discrimination in the harm of exclusion rather than in demeaning treatment. While he powerfully describes Jim Crow as an "officially organized degradation ceremony," he focuses on the "harm of exclusion," "[t]he most heartrending deprivation of all."[56]

Drawing on work from another part of the globe, I found the work of Israeli philosopher Avishai Margalit instructive. Motivated by the Israeli/Palestinian conflict, Margalit attempts to sketch the contours of a decent society—which he sees as less demanding than a just society. A key component of a decent society, according to Margalit, is that it refrains from humiliation. His conception of humiliation is very close to the concept of demeaning that I have been exploring here. According to Margalit: "Humiliation is any sort of behavior or condition that constitutes a sound reason for a person to consider his or her self-respect injured."[57] He too emphasizes that the person's subjective judgment is not determinative, rather it is the objective reasonable judgment that matters: "This is a normative rather than a psychological sense of humiliation."[58] He sees humiliation as a form a cruelty, a "mental cruelty,"[59] and thus argues that it must be eradicated. The requirement of eradicating humiliation needs no further justification, according to Margalit, "since the paradigm example of moral behavior is be-havior that prevents cruelty. This is where justification comes to an end."[60]

Finally, at the broadest level, I see the view I propose here as in line with both Jean Hampton's view of immoral action as that which demeans and with egalitarian moral theories that focus on respect (which will be dis-cussed in the Conclusion). At the level of doctrinal implementation in law, my view agrees with the developing equality jurisprudence of the Canadian Supreme Court, which is working its way toward establishing human dig-nity as the foundation of a constitutional guarantee of equality.

Conclusion

The puzzle of discrimination resides in the fact that we do and we must dis-tinguish among people on the basis of their characteristics on a fairly reg-ular and constant basis. Whereas good decision-making principles may counsel that distinctions be rationally supported, and the ideals of particular institutions may limit the sorts of criteria appropriate in those contexts, these concerns are not based on a concern for equality. How do we know when the criteria mandated by an institution's goals are impermissible? The commitment to the equal moral worth of persons limits the sorts of selec-tion criteria that may be applied in particular contexts. When drawing dis-tinctions among people in a particular context demeans any of those affected, it is wrongful discrimination.

Demeaning actions are those that put the other down. To demean is to express that the other is less worthy of concern and respect and to do so in a manner that has power. Because demeaning is a conjunction of expres-sive action and power, there are circumstances in which demeaning is more likely. For example, private actions are less likely to demean than govern-mental actions. Individual actions are less likely to demean than actions by institutions. This is because governments and institutions generally have more status and power than private individuals. But this statement is simply a rule of thumb. A demeaning action is one that has power, but power can take many forms. In addition, differentiating on the basis of features that define a historically mistreated group or a group that currently occupies a low social position is more likely to demean than doing so on the basis of other features. This is because the history and current status of the group concerned affects the meaning of the distinction drawing. So, treating people differently on the basis of race or sex (especially minority race or female sex) is more likely to demean than is treating people differently according to the first letter of their last names or their eye colors. But again, this is a rule of thumb, not an absolute requirement. It is possible that grouping people according to a novel trait (i.e., one that has not been used to disadvantage people in the past) can be done in such a way that even that first instance of negative treatment itself demeans. If our government were to suddenly declare that all people with last names beginning with A would be ineligible to vote or would be forbidden from working, for example, this instance of distinction drawing would demean those whose last names begin with A.

The discussion of this example and others in this chapter raises the question of what one ought to say about disagreement. Surely there will be disagreement about whether particular classifications demean. What does this disagreement mean for the theory of wrongful discrimination presented here? It is to this question that we now turn.

CHAPTER 3

Interpretation and Disagreement

A worker who is a biological male but dresses and lives as a woman requests that her employer designate some bathrooms as unisex or alternatively allow her to use the female bathroom. The employer refuses and instructs the employee to use the men's bathroom. The employee refuses and is fired as a result.[1]

In 2005 the U.S. Food and Drug Administration (FDA) approved the first drug specifically targeted to a particular racial group. BiDil won approval for use in the treatment of African Americans for heart failure. Shortly after its approval, NitroMed (which holds the patent for and markets the drug) announced that it would sell BiDil for a significantly higher price than analysts had predicted. At the same time, the company announced a complimentary charitable program intended to provide the drug to the 75,000 or so patients the company estimates could benefit from the drug but who have no prescription drug coverage. " 'We believe it's a mandate,' said B. J. Jones, the marketing director for NitroMed, 'that BiDil should be available for every black heart-failure patient.' "[2]

This chapter will address two related questions. First, how do we determine whether drawing distinctions among people in a particular context does demean? Second, given that people are likely to disagree about whether particular policies or practices that distinguish among people demean, what is the significance of this disagreement to the theory of wrongful discrimination I advance?

How Does One Determine Whether a Particular Practice Demeans?

Critics of the FDA's approval of BiDil argue that designating a drug specifically for African Americans sends a message that blacks are genetically or biologically different from whites. For example, Gregg Bloche, a professor of health law and policy at Georgetown University, complained that "It invites people to think there are significant biological distinctions between racial groups when in fact the evidence shows nothing of the sort."[3] To Jonathan Kahn, a professor of law at Hamline University, the problem is that "you have the federal government giving its imprimatur, its stamp of approval, to using race as a biological category."[4] Judy Ann Bigby, director of the Office for Women, Family, and Community Programs at The Brigham and Women's Hospital, worries that "if people get one little inkling that there's a biological basis to race, we could potentially lose ground into understanding racial differences in disease. . . . Biology could be an excuse for not looking at the social basis of disease."[5]

These critiques are largely formulated in terms of the bad consequences likely to flow from the confusion between a social and a biological category. Black or African American is a social category—it refers to those people who self-identify or whom others identify as black. It does not pick out a group of people who share a common genetic or biological trait. The BiDil critics worry that the FDA approval of the drug specifically for treating African American heart failure patients will cause people to confuse these two ways of conceiving of race, which in turn will have negative consequences—failing to investigate the social dimensions of the disease, for example. And they may well be right.

Another way to capture the heart (no pun intended) of their complaint, however, is to say that race-specific drugs demean blacks because the concept of a biologically distinct race is bound up in our culture with notions of racial inferiority. If so, the FDA's action is not just a misguided policy recommendation but possibly worse, possibly wrongful discrimination.

Defenders of the racially targeted drug could reply that while the use of a racial classification in health care runs the risk of demeaning, this one is not. Given the context—where a population long underserved by the health care industry stands to benefit from a targeted treatment—the potential for denigration to the population is neutralized by a clear benefit. In addition, the decision by the drug's maker to price the drug as they did—a mechanism for using insurance companies to subsidize the care of sick African Americans who lack drug coverage by spreading the cost of their care among people of all races—further neutralizes the potential for denigration. How should one determine who is right?

The Nature of the Question

To determine whether the racial classification used in the FDA approval of BiDil demeans requires *interpretation*. To put the point more generally: The determination of whether the use of a classification in a particular context demeans requires an interpretive judgment similar in nature to the determination of whether an utterance is an order or merely advice. The identity of the speaker, the context in which the utterance occurs, and the words of the utterance itself are all important factors affecting this interpretive judgment. For example, when a boss says to his employee, "Get me some milk," this is an order. But when the coworker says the same thing to her colleague who is heading to the cafeteria, this is best characterized as a request rather than an order. Like ordering, demeaning usually occurs in the context of a power imbalance. It is easier for a boss to order or to demean than it is for an employee to do so. The identity of the speaker is thus centrally important to the interpretive judgment about whether distinguishing between people on the basis of a particular trait in a particular context demeans.

An utterance is an order (or is not) whether or not it is obeyed.[6] For example, when a 4-year-old says to his parent at the breakfast table, "Get me some milk," the parent is likely to reply, "I will be happy to when you can ask me politely." In other words, though the parent does not obey the child's order, it is still an order. If the worker above does not heed the boss's order and comes back from the cafeteria without the milk for her boss, it is still the case that the boss ordered the employee. The employee just has not obeyed. To assess whether an utterance is an order, we need only know who is the speaker, what has been said, and in what context. What happens afterwards is not relevant.

Let us return to the example of a 4-year-old. Does this example belie the claim that the identity of the speaker is crucial? One might think that a parent can order a child but that the child cannot order the parent just as the boss can much more easily order the employee than the other way around. The example of the 4-year-old's impolite behavior is useful for clarifying how these interpretive judgments work. First, while the identity of the speaker often matters, it does not always matter. Here I use the term "speaker" loosely to refer to whoever issues the utterance whether orally or in a written form. Second, it is not the case that a coworker can never order another coworker or that an employee can never order her boss. Rather, the fact that an utterance is made by a coworker or employee affects the best interpretation of what has transpired. The difference in status between the speaker and those to whom he speaks affects the interpretation of what has taken place.

So why can the child order the parent? Some might say that she cannot, that the best interpretation of the seeming order is that it is not an order but something else, an awkward request. And perhaps in some households in some cultures that would be the best interpretation of the son's statement. Even in our culture perhaps there would be disagreement about whether the child has ordered the parent or not. The fact of disagreement and its implications for the theory of discrimination I advance will be discussed later in this chapter. For now, let me explain why I think the child has in fact ordered the parent to get him some milk. (Doing so will highlight other factors that affect this kind of interpretive judgment.) First, the relationship between parent and child is one in which the child has some power over the parent as well. In fact, perhaps it is because current parenting styles increasingly minimize the hierarchical aspects of the parent/child relationship that it is possible for the child to order the parent. Second, the child's tone of voice may be relevant. The way in which he says, "Get me some milk" has a different stress or emphasis than the way in which the coworker is likely to speak to a colleague. Third, the speech of children is interpreted differently than the speech of adults because we know that children are just learning the cultural rules that govern polite interactions. We interpret the coworker's speech as a request because we know that coworkers do not generally order each other around. Children, having not learned politeness conventions, are more likely to do so. In other words, the presence of customs about how people generally relate to one another affects the way we interpret individuals' actions. But children are different. In fact, it is in order to teach him precisely these customs that the parent might say: "I'll be happy to get you the milk if you can ask me politely." The parent would be a better teacher yet if he helped the child learn what constitutes asking politely by saying: "I'll be happy to get you the milk if you can ask me by saying 'please.'"

This discussion has taken us pretty far a field from the subject of discrimination, but for a reason. I argue in Chapter 1 that it is wrong to draw distinctions among people when doing so demeans some of them. Next, I explain that assessing whether differential treatment does demean is the same kind of assessment as that involved in judging whether an utterance is an order or advice. This determination depends on the identity of the speaker, on the context, and on the content of the utterance itself. In particular, when the speaker has some power or authority over the person to whom that utterance is directed, this makes it more likely that the utterance is an order. The same can be said regarding demeaning. But context is also key. The example of the child highlights how we interpret utterances through understandings about how people generally use such words.

To flesh out how these three dimensions—speaker, context, and the words used—affect interpretive judgments of speech and action, I started with less controversial and easily accessible examples like the distinction between an order and a request. The next step is to examine an example of discrimination to see how attention to the person, the context, and the content helps one determine whether a particular classification demeans.

In the BiDil example, the FDA approved a drug specifically for use by African Americans. This action is simultaneously a license (allowing the drug to be marketed) and a recommendation. Once the FDA approves a drug, the drug may be used for purposes and in patients other than those stipulated in the approval. This so-called off-label use of drugs is common. In that sense the FDA action that approved BiDil, thereby allowing it to be marketed and sold here in the United States, did not limit BiDil to African American patients, nor even to patients in heart failure. What it did was to recommend that BiDil be used for (and only for) these patients. This recommendation distinguishes between patients on two different grounds—race and health condition. Does this action (classifying on the basis of race and health status) by the FDA demean any of the groups affected: African Americans, non–African Americans; heart failure patients, non–heart failure patients?

The data on which the FDA based its approval are themselves somewhat controversial.[7] For the purposes of this discussion, we will put aside that aspect of the controversy. Assume that the data supporting the approval of BiDil for use in African Americans are solid data that adequately support the recommendation to use the drug in this population.

Does the recommendation demean African Americans? (While one could ask whether the FDA's action demeans non–African Americans, heart-failure patients, or other sick people as well, the claim that it demeans African Americans has the most potential and reflects the actual criticism of the FDA's action so it is this claim I will explore.)

The fact that it is the FDA that issues the regulations matters to the determination of what sort of action the FDA performs. The FDA is an actor with authority (in terms of determining which new drugs are available to patients and doctors) and with status (as an expert in matters of health). In addition, the FDA is an organ of the state and therefore when it acts, acts for the state. I am not here making a legal point about what actions constitute "state action" under constitutional law. Rather, I am making a claim about what sort of action the FDA approval of a new drug is.

To know whether the FDA action demeans African Americans, we need to look at the actor, the content of the regulation, and the context. The authority and status of the actor increase the possibility of demeaning. To demean is to subordinate, to put down, to degrade. An actor with low status may try to subordinate or degrade but his actions are simply less powerful than are those issued by a higher-status speaker—at least in most instances. So the fact that it is the FDA that approves the new drug application raises the possibility of a demeaning classification in a way that would be less pressing if this classification occurred in another context—a recommendation by an author of a scientific article for example.

Next, consider the context. Although it may seem as if the drug approval is a form of license or permission, this is so in a far more limited way than may initially appear. The FDA action makes the sale of this drug legal.[8] But the part of its action that concerns us here is the part that involves classification. The FDA approved BiDil for use in African American heart failure patients. Because physicians routinely prescribe drugs for off-label use, this classification is best understood as a recommendation rather than a license or permission. The interpretation of the action as a recommendation derives not from the language of the approval or from the background law. Rather, the classification is best understood as a recommendation because of the background practice (i.e., the context) in which it is issued.[9]

The context plays a similarly important role in determining whether the agency's action demeans African Americans. Here one must look at the local context (i.e., understanding what FDA approval means, practices of off-label use, etc.) and at the broader society and culture in which the agency action occurs. This latter includes the ways in which race-based classifications, particularly in the context of health and biology, have been made and used in the past. The FDA approval treats patients of one "race" differently from patients of another "race." I put the term *race* in scare quotes because there is an important ambiguity in the FDA recommendation regarding whether the category should be understood as biological or social—and therein lies much of the problem. The term *African American* could refer to a class of people who are biologically distinct from non–African Americans. Alternatively, it could identify the group of people socially understood as black or African American. The use of the distinction (between African American and non–African American) in a health context relating to the approval of a new drug suggests that it is the biological conception of race that the FDA is using and, more importantly, thereby providing its imprimatur to. In fact, the data on which the FDA approval rests does not provide evidence for a biological versus a social basis for the observed difference in treatment outcomes. Here race may be operating as a proxy for any number of factors more germane to why blacks fare better with BiDil than do whites—diet, lifestyle, or any number of unknown environmental factors.[10]

The fact that a government agency responsible for making decisions based on science issues a recommendation using a racial classification is important because it gives the impression that the FDA supports the view that races (understood as social categories) are biologically distinct. This position is troubling if endorsed by an authoritative body like the FDA because claims about the biological differences between races have a troubling history. Biological difference has been used to support the view that blacks are less intellectually capable and morally regulated, more prone to violence and sexual promiscuity. As this background identification of blacks is insulting, one can see how the FDA's racially specific recommendation could demean African Americans. Whether that is indeed the best interpretation of the FDA's racial classification, I am unsure. What I want to suggest here is that it is plausible and, more important, that it is precisely such a concern that troubles some people about the recommendation. In other words, one reason why the FDA's use of the racial classification may be morally problematic is that it risks demeaning African Americans.[11]

But wait, you may be thinking, don't throw the baby out with the bathwater. Maybe the social category "black" significantly overlaps with a relevant genetic difference (i.e., "blacks" may be significantly more likely than "non-blacks" to have a particular genetic trait that would also make them more likely to benefit from a particular therapy). Is there no way to be attentive to these differences without thereby endorsing the falsehoods historically associated with claims of biological difference? In other words, the social category "black" may be one that is useful to employ in recommending drugs or other health care approaches—useful in the sense that it is the best available surrogate for an as yet unknown genetic difference between the group of people who would benefit from a particular therapy and those who would not. If blacks stand to benefit from racially distinctive recommendations, does not one hurt the very people one is allegedly trying to help in prohibiting such racial categorizations?

Given the power of social stereotypes—the ways in which the social category of race has been encoded in our consciousness—this baggage is heavy indeed. Glenn Loury argues that blacks are tainted by what he terms "racial dishonor," which he defines as "an entrenched if inchoate presumption of inferiority, or moral inadequacy, of unfitness for intimacy, or intellectual incapacity, harbored by observing agents when they regard race-marked subjects."[12] If he is right, then any use of racial classifications in the health care context—where racial categories may be read as biological categories—risks "dishonoring" (Loury's term) or demeaning blacks. But risking and doing are not the same. Any use of racial categories in the health care context risks demeaning blacks. Whether it will depends on a more detailed account of the particular context and the content of the policy or practice employing the racial classification.

This risk, however, has moral implications. At the least, it makes sense (moral as well as scientific) to work hard to determine if the racial classification is a proxy for another trait that itself is causally related to the different treatment responses of the two groups. Of course scientists should always strive to disentangle correlation from causation but the moral concern with racial classification in the health care context provides an especially strong reason to do so. As such, it may warrant spending more resources than one would otherwise in trying to untangle these two. Second, to the extent possible, the FDA should act in ways, including speaking, that attempt to mute the degree to which its use of racial classifications endorses the view that race is a biological, as distinct from a social, category.

NitroMed (the company marketing BiDil) did try to take action to mitigate criticism of its decision to market a racially targeted drug. But the action it took was of a very different kind, aimed at a very different conception of what might be morally troubling about its action. NitroMed adopted an unusual pricing policy: pairing a higher than normal price for the drug with a commitment to provide the medication free to African American heart failure patients who lack prescription drug coverage. If the wrong of wrongful discrimination were a matter of whether a policy or practice reinforces the caste-like hierarchies of our society, then this policy would be morally responsive. In other words, one could think that the marketing by NitroMed of a drug for African Americans may harm African Americans as a group (by stigmatizing them or in some other way). If so, a policy designed to benefit the group (providing needed medication to African Americans who lack prescription drug coverage) may well succeed in offsetting the group harm with a group benefit.

The twin policies (high drug pricing combined with free drugs to those in need) may well benefit blacks as a group and may be laudable in *that* respect, but it does not affect whether the racially specific medical recommendation wrongfully discriminates. If instead one conceives of the morally troubling aspect of the racially specific drug recommendation as related to whether the policy demeans African Americans, one gets a very different idea of what actions one could take to avoid this moral wrong. If the wrong lies not in whether the group is harmed (which might be offset with a group benefit) but in what the FDA or the drug company does in issuing its recommendations, then ameliorative actions should be geared to ways in which the actor can change the character of her action. Jonathan Kahn offers a recommendation that is attentive to this conception of the moral wrong. He recommends that "any federal agency or institution conducting research with federal funds that reviews, approves, or itself uses race as a biological category or as a surrogate for a biological category be required to offer a clarification of their terms of analysis and a justification for using them in such a manner."[13] This recommendation would help to change what the FDA or other agency expresses in recommending a drug specifically for African American patients.

If the social category "African American" is helpful in predicting who will likely benefit from the drug and no other substitute can be found (like diet or environment), perhaps the use of this classification does not—after all—demean blacks. Part of the context in which we analyze whether the FDA action demeans blacks includes the fact that the health needs of African Americans have historically been neglected. It is for this reason that ethical guidelines governing clinical medical research require the inclusion of minorities as research subjects.[14] In other words, the context in which we analyze whether the classification demeans is itself multifaceted.

On the one hand, the use of race as a biological category has historically been associated with the dishonoring of blacks. On the other hand, the medical establishment has historically been less sensitive to the health needs of blacks. Both elements—as well as the strength of the data supporting a strong correlation between the social category "black" and the group of people most likely to benefit from the therapy (an issue we set aside because of its controversial nature)—affect how we ought to interpret whether approval of a drug specifically recommended for African Americans demeans them.

Disagreement

People are likely to disagree about whether any particular practice that distinguishes among them demeans any of those affected. BiDil is one example. The issue of whether single-sex bathrooms demean transsexuals and ambiguously gendered people is another. Transsexuals who have not yet completed sex change operations claim that policies requiring them to use the bathroom designated for their birth sex rather than their identified gender demean them. Ambiguously gendered persons (people who do not feel themselves to be clearly one gender or another) find that bathroom segregation practices demean people who do not consider themselves to be either one or the other. Do sex-segregated bathroom practices demean transsexuals or ambiguously gendered people? Earlier I presented single-sex bathrooms as an example of a policy that distinguishes between people on the basis of sex but does not demean. Though single-sex bathrooms do not, in my view, demean either men qua men or women qua women, the claim that they demean trans- or ambiguously gendered men and women has more traction. Others may disagree. Separating bathrooms by sex in deference to the privacy concerns of most men and most women as well as the safety concerns of women does not express disrespect or denigration for trans- or ambiguously gendered persons, one might argue. While it is surely true that trans- and ambiguously gendered people have suffered ill treatment in many spheres of life, this mistreatment is not sufficiently connected to sex-segregated bathroom use to render that practice demeaning. Moreover, the legitimate reasons for sex-segregated bathrooms neutralize any denigrating associations. The best interpretation of the practice is that it is a reasonable accommodation to the privacy concerns of men and the privacy and safety concerns of women.

Who is right? Perhaps more pressing still, is anyone right? Is there *a right* answer to the question whether sex-segregated bathrooms demean trans- sexuals and ambiguously gendered people? Would such an answer be *objec- tive?* How would we go about determining who is right when people dis- agree? And finally, what does disagreement itself mean for the theory of wrongful discrimination that I put forward here? It is to this constellation of questions that we now turn.

Concern about objectivity seems particularly pressing because there is likely to be significant disagreement as to whether particular acts of differ- entiation demean. Perhaps only a subjective sense of whether a practice de- means is possible, and no way to decide among those that differ. If so, per- haps there is no real answer to the question whether a particular practice—single sex bathrooms, for example—demeans.

What Exactly *Is* Objectivity?

A claim to objectivity can have several meanings, of which at least two are relevant to our discussion. Sometimes *objectivity* is used to characterize a judgment or decision in a way that distinguishes it from bias. The umpire's call, the judge's decision, the teacher's grade are objective to the extent that they are made on the basis of the appropriate criteria and not on the basis of inappropriate or distorting criteria. Here objectivity is related to impartiality. Objectivity can also refer to the status, if you will, of the object of the judg- ment. Is there a right call, a correct judicial decision, a proper grade? If so, baseball, law, and scholarship are objective disciplines because there are facts of baseball, law, and scholarship that are capable of being either true or false. Both senses of objectivity seem relevant to our inquiry here. First, one might wonder whether it is possible to specify appropriate versus inappro- priate criteria on which to base a judgment that a particular policy is de- meaning. If the two types of criteria cannot, at least in theory, be distin- guished, then objectivity—in the sense of basing judgment on appropriate criteria—is not possible in this area. Second, one might wonder whether judgments about whether a practice or policy demeans can be true or false. If objectivity requires that there be a right answer to such questions, then disagreement would seem to threaten objectivity.

The claim that a law or social practice demeans is an interpretive judg- ment (i.e., the best understanding of the practice given its cultural context). In this respect, the judgment that a social practice is demeaning is analogous to the claim that a legal decision is correct. Whether A's conduct renders her liable depends on whether there is an answer to the question of what the law requires. To answer such a question requires an interpretive judgment of the relevant legal material. In other words, there must be a way to distinguish appropriate from inappropriate criteria to use in making this decision. And, there must be a fact of the matter such that the claim that *the law requires X* can be either true or false. Similar questions can also be raised about the objectivity of judgments about art ("that painting is beautiful") and literature ("this book is a masterpiece"). Are claims that a painting is beautiful *objective*? In other words, is it possible to specify appropriate versus inappropriate criteria that bear on this question (objectivity as impartiality) and is there a right answer to the question whether a given painting is beautiful (metaphysical objectivity)?

In drawing these analogies to the objectivity of law or aesthetic judgments, I do not mean to suggest that the objectivity of judgments in each of these areas stand or fall together. Of course, it is possible for legal judgments to be objective, while aesthetic and social (as to whether a policy demeans) ones are not, for example. But some of the doubts one might have about the objectivity of judgments regarding whether particular practices demean are the same as those one might have about the objectivity of legal and aesthetic judgments. This is important because the aims of the book should not be understood too broadly. The book attempts to define when and why it is sometimes wrong to draw distinctions among people on the basis of their traits. To summarize the argument so far: It is wrong to draw distinctions among people when doing so demeans any of those affected. Because there are likely to be significant disagreements among people as to whether particular practices demean, the question as to whether objectivity is possible arises. While the concept of objectivity is itself complicated and controversial,[15] two aspects of objectivity, highlighted by the following questions, appear germane: (1) are there appropriate versus inappropriate criteria that bear on such a judgment, and (2) are claims that a practice is demeaning capable of being either true or false? Although I believe that such judgments can be objective, I cannot defend this claim in a way that answers the many philosophical doubts one might have about whether objectivity in law, aesthetics, or morality (which has been subject to similar attacks) is possible. Doing so would make this a very different book.

Instead, what I hope to do here is, first, to briefly describe the sort of objectivity I think is possible for interpretive judgments about laws, policies, and practices in our culture. Second, I hope to address the particular worries one might have about the objectivity of this sort of judgment, over and above any general concerns about the objectivity of law, aesthetics, and morality.

Aside: Type versus Token Objectivity

Gerald Postema draws a helpful distinction between what he calls "type" versus "token" objectivity. Type objectivity refers to whether judgments that fall into a certain *class* or *type* can be objective—regardless of whether any particular judgment is. For example, if one were to ask whether legal judgments are objective in a type-objectivity sense, one is asking whether any legal judgments are objective, whether law is something about which one can be objective, whether legal facts are of the kind that they can be either true or false, and so on. As Postema explains, type objectivity is "an eligibility notion."[16] Token objectivity, by contrast, refers to whether a *particular* judgment is objective—it is taken as given, then, that judgments of that type can be objective. As Postema explains, *"Token objectivity* is a *success* notion and expresses a direct, conclusory assessment of the judgment."[17]

This distinction is important to emphasize because in considering whether interpretive judgments about social practice or policies can be objective, we are discussing *type objectivity*. The relevant question then is whether this *type* of judgment—interpretive judgments about the meaning of social practices—can be objective, not whether any *particular* judgment is objective. A related point worth emphasizing is that in arguing that it is possible to make judgments that a particular practice like single-sex bathrooms does (or does not) demean ambiguously gendered persons, I am not claiming that I am right in any conclusion I might draw. In fact, about this particular issue I am especially uncertain. Rather, in focusing on type-objectivity for judgments about whether particular policies that distinguish among people also demean, I am claiming that these judgments can be true or false, not that any particular judgment is correct or objective.

The Objectivity of Interpretive Judgment

Let us focus more closely on objectivity. Jules Coleman and Brian Leiter describe three conceptions of objectivity, which they call minimal, modest, and strong.[18] A domain—like law, morals, or aesthetics—is minimally objective so long as what is right is fixed by the view of the majority of relevant decision makers.[19] Leiter thinks fashion is like this.[20] What is fashionable is what trendsetters in the fashion industry think fashionable. There are objectively correct answers to the question "what is fashionable" because all we need to do is determine whose opinions count and what they think. Whatever the majority of such people think fashionable *is* fashionable. Leiter himself thinks law is minimally objective in this sense. A legally correct decision is the one that is thought legally correct by the majority of relevant officials.[21]

A minimal conception of objectivity seems inapt—both to law and to interpretive judgments about which policies or practices demean. If what is—objectively—demeaning is (just) what the majority thinks is demeaning, this standard is likely to reproduce the oppression of minorities that a prohibition on wrongful discrimination seems concerned to eradicate. A majoritarian conception of what demeans allows dominant practices and understandings to stand and to be labeled objectively unobjectionable. Surely the majority can be wrong about whether particular practices demean. The most egregious cases of wrongful discrimination are *likely* to be recognized as demeaning by the majority. But there is no guarantee. For example, racial segregation was probably recognized as demeaning by a majority of whites and blacks. Justice Brown's majority opinion in *Plessy v. Ferguson*, if it is sincere, is an important counter-example, though. He famously observed that the plaintiff misinterpreted the meaning of racial segregation: "We consider the underlying fallacy of the plaintiff's argument to consist in the assumption that the enforced separation of the two races stamps the colored race with a badge of inferiority."[22] Whether his opinion reflects the honest assessment of the majority of people at that time is unclear. The first Justice Harlan, dissenting in *Plessy*, interpreted the practice of racial segregation differently—as demeaning. He saw the law as one that "puts the brand of servitude and degradation upon a large class of our fellow citizens."[23] If we agree that Justice Brown has misinterpreted the real meaning of segregation *at that time*, this is because that real meaning is independent of the majority's view about it.

Laws and policies "protecting" women provide another apt example. Although such laws (like those in the past that restricted women's employment[24] or those more recently that restrict women from hazardous employment)[25] may not have been viewed by the most people at the time as demeaning, they *are* (I believe) nonetheless demeaning. Today, the majority of people would likely not find that the practice of sex-segregated bathrooms demeans transgendered or ambiguously gendered people. However, this fact ought not to settle the question about whether such practices demean.

A minimal conception of objectivity has another important flaw. It makes some sense to say that what is objectively fashionable is what the majority of cognoscenti thinks is fashionable because fashion seems to simply *be about* what people think. Some aspects of manners are like this. It is good manners to shake hands when meeting someone just because most people in our culture think that shaking hands is the polite thing to do when meeting someone. But where the judgment is evaluative rather than merely descriptive, a minimal conception of objectivity will be inadequate. What the majority of people think matters to determining what the conventional practice *is*, but the fact that a majority of folks think something is right cannot make it right. Because demeaning carries normative weight—it is, at least prima facie, wrong to demean—a minimal conception of objectivity will be inapt to explain the objectivity of judgments that practice X demeans.

In fact, the minimal conception of objectivity may not work even for fashion or manners. To call something fashionable is sometimes not merely to refer to what others do and think; it can also be a term of approbation, a compliment. If so, it refers to an evaluative judgment as well as a descriptive judgment. The judgment that something is fashionable may be ambiguous as between these two meanings (merely descriptive, or descriptive and evaluative). Sometimes to call something fashionable has no normative connotations, as in "I think nose and lip piercing is creepy, but it is fashionable." But other times, to call something fashionable is more normatively freighted: "she is a very fashionable dresser" generally means not that she follows the fashions but that she culls from the current styles and wears only the best of the current offerings. On this conception, "fashionable" means to be a style that is currently in vogue and a style that is beautiful or artful or whatever the aim of fashion is. To the extent that what is fashionable has this evaluative bite, a minimal conception of objectivity will not suffice. The fact that the majority of relevant decision makers think something is fashionable will not be decisive because the majority *could* be wrong. Nose and lip piercing may only *appear* fashionable, if to be fashionable requires both that the style is one currently in vogue *and* that it is beautiful. If so, a more robust conception of objectivity may be necessary for a style to be objectively fashionable.[26]

The third reason that a minimal conception of objectivity is inadequate to account for the objectivity of judgments that a practice demeans is that it fails to explain rational disagreement about such matters. Connie Rosati makes this point in explaining why a minimal conception of objectivity is inadequate for law:

> First, judicial majoritarianism, like subjectivism, lacks the resources to account for rational disagreement. It is not uncommon to hear apparently legally knowledgeable critics insist that most judges have gotten the law wrong. The majority of judges likely hold, and a majority of justices in their time did hold, that the death penalty is not unconstitutional, yet this fact did not stop Justices William Brennan and Harry Blackmun from arguing otherwise. But if the law just is what the majority of judges say it is, or rather, what they would approve, then how are we to make sense of such a dispute? If we adopt judicial majoritarianism, we must accept the dubious proposition that Brennan and Blackmun were not engaged in genuine disagreement with their fellow justices about what the law is, rather they were either misinformed about what the majority of judges approve or didn't understand what a legal fact is.[27]

People surely disagree about whether a particular practice wrongfully discriminates. If, as I argue, that disagreement can be recast as one about whether a distinguishing practice demeans, then we need a conception of the objectivity of such judgments that captures the nature of such disagreement. In disagreeing about whether single-sex bathrooms demean ambiguously gendered people, we are not disagreeing about whether most people see this practice as demeaning. Rather, the best way to characterize this disagreement about whether practices wrongfully discriminate is to describe it as *genuine*.

Leiter and Coleman contrast minimal objectivity with what they term *strong objectivity*. A fact is strongly objective if it is true or false independently of anyone's reaction to it or perception of it.[28] It would be true or false even if there were no people in the world at all. It is simply the way things are. This conception of objectivity seems inappropriate for interpretive judgments of social practices precisely because they are judgments about social practices and therefore involve us. How could we say that sex-segregated bathrooms objectively demean ambiguously gendered people no matter how anyone, in any context or situation, would interpret the meaning of that practice? While demeaning has normative bite (which is in part what made a minimal conception of objectivity inapt), demeaning also depends on conventional practices and norms. I cannot demean you by folding my hands when speaking to you, even if in my mind that gesture is equivalent to spitting. Because hand folding has no meaning in our culture, my hand folding cannot demean you (unless we tell some complicated story that invests it with meaning). To demean requires a reliance on conventional methods for showing disrespect. As such, the fact that practice X demeans cannot be objectively demeaning in this strong sense because it cannot be true irrespective of how anyone would interpret the action in any context.[29]

A Modest Proposal for Modest Objectivity

Coleman and Leiter articulate and defend a conception of objectivity for law that they term *modest objectivity*. As they define it, "[a]ccording to modest objectivity, what seems right under 'ideal epistemic conditions' determines what is right."[30] What makes it modest is that it stands between minimal and strong objectivity in the following sense. Like minimal objectivity, the truth or true nature of things is not completely independent of human experience and perception. But like strong objectivity, it is possible for everyone to be wrong about the real nature of the thing perceived. As Philip Pettit points out however, this modest objectivity is fairly robust. In defending the objectivity of ethical values, Pettit points out that colors also do not have a true nature independent of how they are normally perceived by people. Yet we think of colors as objective, and statements about color ("the chair is red") as capable of being true or false. As he says with regard to ethical values, "it would be an important win for those who believe in the objectivity of ethics to be able to argue that values and disvalues are on a par, for example, with colors."[31] So too for interpretive judgments about social practice. It would be an important win too for those who believe in the objectivity of these interpretive judgments to be able to argue that they are on a par with the objectivity of colors. Objectivity need not require independence from human experience and perception to be meaningful. If interpretive judgments are objective in a way similar to that of colors, that is pretty good.

Coleman and Leiter's particular idea about what modest objectivity consists of—perception under ideal epistemic conditions—is appealing, but not without problems. It is no easy task to specify what the ideal epistemic conditions are for making ethical judgments, legal judgments, or interpretive judgments about social practices. Coleman and Leiter's list of the ideal epistemic conditions for legal judgment are not, as Connie Rosati points out, as self-evident as they appear to think. For example, Coleman and Leiter specify that the ideal judge should be "maximally empathetic and imaginative," among other criteria.[32] But specifying what it means to be maximally empathetic is not easy—Rosati makes precisely this point.[33] To bring this critique home to the issue at hand, consider how we should specify the ideal epistemic conditions for determining whether single-sex bathrooms do or do not demean ambiguously gendered people. Does maximal empathy require adopting the position of the ambiguously gendered? It cannot simply require the uncritical adoption of their position, else modest objectivity would not be judgment under ideal epistemic conditions but instead the judgment of the aggrieved party, whatever its merits. On this view, any claim of wrongful discrimination would be legitimate. This does not seem objective. Rather, it is simply to adopt one particular perspective.

My rough sense of how to navigate this issue is that one ought to listen closely and well to the perspective of the aggrieved, but then one must, always, make an independent assessment of its value. Is this maximal empathy? Modest empathy? I do not think these labels will help. How much empathy one ought to have and, perhaps more importantly, what one ought to do with this empathic response is not easy to specify.

This difficulty in fully specifying the ideal epistemic conditions that yield objective judgment relates to the first sense of objectivity identified earlier. At the start of this section, I identified two senses of objectivity that are important to the assessment of whether interpretive judgments of social practices can be "objective." First, a person judging is objective if he or she is free from bias, if he or she brings only the relevant criteria to bear in making a decision. This sense of objectivity is related to impartiality. Second, a judgment or assertion is objective if it is capable of being true or false because there is a real truth of the matter against which to test it. So far, we have largely been exploring the ways in which interpretive judgments are objective in this second, metaphysical, sense. Do these judgments assert claims about how things really are that are capable of being true or false? In answering this question, we have explored three senses of what that objectivity may entail (minimal, strong, and modest). We have so far rejected both minimal and strong as unable to provide a good sense of how interpretive judgments could be objective. In settling, tentatively, on the modest conception of objectivity, I am agreeing that we ought to look for a way that such claims can be objective that neither reduces objective truth to mere majoritarianism nor demands complete independence from human experience. One version of modest objectivity defines the objective judgment as that which would be adopted by someone under ideal epistemic conditions. In wrestling with the question of what such conditions might include, I find that we are returning to the first sense of objectivity, as a decision using only appropriate and no inappropriate criteria. Both the methodological and metaphysical conceptions of objectivity thus require that one specify the appropriate criteria for objective judgment.

So where we, tentatively, end up is as follows: For interpretive judgments about social practices to be objective, we must be able to specify relevant from irrelevant criteria for these judgments—so that we can insure that the people interpreting the social practices are being objective (methodological sense) and so that we can tell whether their judgments are objective (metaphysical sense—using a modest conception of objectivity). Can we do that? Yes, but not fully. Coleman and Leiter are surely right that empathy with the perspective of others is important. Also on their list of ideal epistemic conditions is that the ideal judge must be "free of personal bias for or against either party."[34] This is a criterion for the ideal epistemic conditions for judging what the law is, but we can easily translate it to the situation involved in interpreting social practices: The ideal "judge" must be free of personal bias for or against any of the people acted upon by a policy that distinguishes among people. These criteria help us to separate relevant from irrelevant criteria. The subjective experience of those acted upon by a discriminating policy is relevant. The personal like or dislike that the interpreter may feel for the individual people affected by the policy is not relevant. That is a start.

But what should we say about a person who holds the following view? It is wrong, morally, to change genders or it is not healthy to fail to clearly identify with one gender or the other. Do these views count as a personal bias that renders a decision non-objective? What about the following view? I see their point (the position of the ambiguously gendered), but the needs of the majority for privacy and safety should trump the needs of the minority, unless something vital is at stake, which it is not here. Does this view exhibit a lack of adequate empathy? Each of these viewpoints could affect whether one perceives single-sex bathrooms as demeaning. These and other similar questions are not easy to answer. We have some sense of appropriate versus inappropriate criteria, but there are many shades of gray in between.

I am not dismayed by this result or despairing of the possibility of the objectivity of interpretive judgment for several reasons. First, the idea of modest objectivity is promising. Objectivity about interpretive judgment should allow for the possibility that everyone is wrong (about whether a given practice demeans) and make recognizable reasonable disagreement (rather than simply disagreement about what people think). At the same time, objectivity about interpretive judgment cannot require that a practice does or does not demean regardless of how anyone under any conditions would perceive it. So I think the basic idea of modest objectivity sets us on the right track. Second, I am hopeful that as we learn more about what practices demean (through conversations with others, empathetic thought experiments, etc.), we will come to have a clearer sense of what the ideal epistemic conditions are for making such judgments. Though it would be wonderful if we had a firm grasp of these conditions first, and then used them to determine which interpretive judgments are demeaning and which are not, I do not think it will happen this way. I think we will learn about what counts as demeaning through using our best understanding of the ideal conditions for objective judgments about interpretive matters and will, simultaneously, learn about what these ideal epistemic conditions are as we learn more about which practices do or do not demean.[35] The two inquiries will go hand in hand.

Thirdly, the limitations of this account of the objectivity of interpretive judgments about social practices are not unique to this domain. Rather, they are familiar philosophical worries about the objectivity of law and morality. Just as Pettit thought that if values could be seen as objective in the sense that colors are, it would comprise a significant accomplishment, so too I would argue that if interpretive judgments about social practices have no bigger problems with regard to objectivity than do law and morals, that is not too bad. This is a book about discrimination, after all. Its aim is to articulate and defend a conception of what makes discrimination wrong. The view I put forward is that it is wrong to draw distinctions among people when doing so demeans. This position gives rise to the question: Can a judgment that practice X demeans be objective? The answer provided by this section is a tentative yes—modestly objective. But perhaps more important, the worries about its objectivity are the same worries we have about the objectivity of law and morality more generally, at least those worries that have been raised thus far. But are there reasons to be particularly concerned about the objectivity of interpretive judgments about social practices, over and above those that plague claims for the objectivity of law and morality? It is to this question that we now turn.

Special Concerns about Objectivity

Is the claim that the judgment *practice X demeans group Y* particularly problematic in terms of its ability to be objective? In other words, are there reasons to worry about the objectivity of such judgments over and above the more general worries one might have about the objectivity of claims about law or morality? In order to answer this question, we must identify the reasons one might think judgments of this type are particularly problematic in terms of their objectivity. First, one might note that there is likely to be substantial disagreement about whether particular policies or practices that distinguish among people do so in a way that demeans. Second, one might worry that one cannot know whether a social practice that distinguishes among people demeans without being inside the culture and thus that any judgment about the practice may be biased or limited. Third, one might worry that in practice the views about which practices are demeaning that will be *seen as* true will be those of the majority or dominant group so that adoption of this approach will lead to defective and skewed judgments about what practices wrongfully discriminate and which do not. If so the theory I advance could become a tool of legitimation by the powerful.

Disagreement

Let us address each concern in turn, starting with the likelihood of disagreement. It is surely true that there is likely to be significant disagreement about whether many practices that distinguish among people do so in a way that demeans, especially with regard to any practice that is controversial, and even some that are not. Does affirmative action demean black students, who are helped by the preference? Do single-sex colleges demean women or men? Does genetic discrimination in insurance demean people with genetic mutations predisposing them to disease? Do single-sex bathrooms demean ambiguously gendered people? On the other hand, there is likely to be significant *agreement* about the meaning of some practices. Separation by race in the use of public drinking fountains demeans blacks. Barring women from specific professions (like law) demeans women. Laws that prohibit people with disabilities or disfigurement from public spaces demeans such people.

So, while there *is* likely to be significant disagreement about whether certain policies that distinguish among people demean, there is likely to be significant agreement as well. Is the likely amount of disagreement too much? How much is too much? There is also significant disagreement about many other ethical issues: Is abortion morally permissible? What about suicide or assisted suicide for terminally ill patients? In this section, we are asking whether there are *special* reasons to be concerned about the objectivity of judgments that a particular practice demeans. The first reason offered was the likelihood of significant disagreement about such matters. While there is likely to be disagreement, it does not strike me as likely to be more pervasive (or at least not significantly so) than disagreement about moral matters more generally. Thus, the fact of disagreement ought not to pose a special problem for the objectivity of interpretive judgments about social practice.

Moreover, the focus on whether a practice demeans helps to change the discussion in some cases that generate disagreement. Affirmative action provides an apt example. Today discussion about affirmative action (in legal and non-legal contexts) tends to focus on when and whether it is ever permissible to treat people differently on the basis of race. If instead one were to ask whether the practice demeans any of those affected, the claim of wrongful discrimination by white candidates who narrowly miss getting a job, a place at school, or a contract would be substantially undermined. Consider the college or university context as an example. While an affirmative action program may result in a highly qualified white student not being admitted, an affirmative action policy does not express denigration of whites qua whites. While there can surely be disagreement about the best understanding of this social practice, the claim that it demeans whites has little traction. Ronald Dworkin makes precisely this point in a 1985 essay on the Supreme Court's decision in *The Regents of the University of California v. Allan Bakke*. In exploring the nature of the complaint that Bakke could raise against the university, Dworkin asks "He [Bakke] says he was kept out of medical school because of his race. Does he mean that he was kept out because his race is the object of prejudice or contempt?" Dworkin concludes "[t]hat suggestion is absurd."[36] There is no history of whites qua whites being excluded that gives this interpretation traction. More plausible is the claim that the school's decision demeans blacks because the lowering of standards seems to track the stereotype of blacks as intellectually inferior or the claim that the school's decision demeans lower-class whites as it fits with meritocratic understandings that attribute lower economic status to inferior ability.[37] The theory thus helps to identify better and worse arguments regarding controversial policies—the claims of lower-class whites versus the claims of whites qua whites, for example. Thus while the theory of wrongful discrimination as drawing distinctions that demean will not eliminate disagreement about controversial practices, it will channel that disagreement into different (and in my view more fruitful) lines of inquiry.

But will the focus on whether a practice demeans invite people to be extra sensitive to insult or easily affronted by practices that distinguish among them? Will this approach make "grievance the coin of the realm?"[38] If it would, this would be a serious concern as a diverse community such as ours should encourage thick skin as a civic virtue. However, we should note that *if* implementation of this account into law or policy did make grievance the coin of the realm, this failing would not suggest that this account of wrongful discrimination is wrong in theory. Rather, it would provide a reason not to implement it in practice. What is the right theory and what is the best way to implement that theory in practice are two distinct questions. That said, there are reasons to doubt that this account will encourage a culture of complaint,[39] even at the level of practical implementation.

First, this account of wrongful discrimination grounds the moral wrong in whether a practice is *objectively* demeaning, not in whether an individual or group of people feels demeaned or stigmatized. It therefore provides no encouragement for people to be especially sensitive. Rather, it frees them to articulate the complaints they may have about practices they find demeaning while simultaneously developing a strength of character that allows them not to feel lowered by such practices. The fact that a person or group does feel demeaned by a practice is not determinative of whether the practice is best understood as demeaning, though it is surely relevant.

Second, an empathic response to others' suffering can free people to move beyond that suffering and, inversely, a denial of empathy can cause that suffering to grow. If so, a theory that allows people to articulate the ways in which they believe a practice that draws distinctions among people does so in a way that demeans may well liberate people from these feelings of diminishment. Once heard and acknowledged—because the theory provides a way to conceptualize the wrong they feel—they may be able to see the viewpoints of those holding other views. In a diverse society, encouraging such paths to understanding is critical.

Accessible to Insiders Only

Perhaps interpretive judgments about social practices may fail to be objective because one cannot understand or interpret such practices without being *inside* them. If so, these judgments are not accessible to all, and those to whom they are accessible can only provide biased or partial judgments—or so the objection goes. There are two parts to this objection. First, people outside of the culture will be unable to say anything about whether one of its distinguishing practices demeans. For example, one might think that non-Muslims are unable to really understand the practice of veil wearing and its cultural and social significance, so they cannot judge whether veil wearing by observant Muslim women demeans women. Second, the opinion of those on the inside is tainted by their inability to get outside of their individual perspective and view the practice from the outside, to see it how it *really* is. Participants in a culture cannot get outside to see it how it really is because the view from the outside does not include the cultural knowledge required to read and understand the practice. So, one is stuck between a rock and a hard place.

But is this correct? While participants in a culture usually understand the cultural significance of its practices better than outsiders, this is not always so. One can be too close to something to see or understand it well, for example. Also, the fact that one is not a member of a culture or a participant in its practices and rituals does not preclude one from entering it imaginatively. As Joseph Raz points out, such a claim is implausible. He argues that the claim that a culture is inaccessible to outsiders requires one to make the "implausible supposition" that "people have the capacity to acquire the concepts of one culture only."[40] A more plausible claim is that it takes time, investment, and openness to understand the meaning of another culture's practices. This is surely true and an important fact to keep in mind—along with a healthy dose of humility—when interpreting and judging the practice of cultures other than our own.

But what of insiders? The argument against the inaccessibility of culturally laden practices to outsiders also emphasizes how insider judgment can be biased or partial. No more so perhaps than outsider judgment, but both are *views from somewhere.* If, as Thomas Nagel spoke of it, objectivity is the view from nowhere,[41] is not objectivity, in that sense, unattainable?

To the extent that understanding social practices (ours or others') requires drawing on what we know about cultures and practices, it cannot be the kind of knowledge knowable from nowhere. Cultural practices are understood through immersing oneself actually or imaginatively in those cultural practices. Even this imaginative immersion requires drawing on analogies or similarities to concepts or cultural practices one knows or inhabits. Again, I do not think this is necessarily a problem for the objectivity of such judgments. What one must know and understand is the culture, its history, and its way of doing things. This detailed knowledge is what allows one to form judgments about what a cultural practice means.

This does not mean that the moral judgment one makes about a practice—that it is demeaning, for example—is somehow relative to that culture and its traditions. What the practice means is relative to that culture, of course. Taking off one's hat has a different meaning in different cultures but showing respect for others is morally worthy everywhere.

Cultural Hegemony

Finally, one might worry that practices of dominant cultures will be largely unchallenged and practices of subordinate cultures will be more likely to be judged as demeaning. This could happen when members of one culture examine the practices of another or when members of a dominant group within a culture examine the practices of a minority group. Bad intentions need not be the cause of such lopsided judgment. For example, the claim by transgendered people that single-sex bathrooms demean them may be summarily dismissed by non–transgendered people who simply do not see the practice as demeaning anyone—they see it as a reasonable way to accommodate the privacy preferences of most people. The fact that the preferences of some are not accommodated need not condemn the practice, as policies that distinguish between people routinely produce winners and losers. The relevant question is whether the discriminating practice *demeans* the losers or simply denies them something of value. The interpretive judgment of those in power (of the dominant group or culture) may be predictably and routinely flawed such that the claims of minority groups are rejected, notwithstanding their merits, again and again.

This first thing to note about this reservation regarding the objectivity of interpretive judgments is that it raises an objection to the objectivity of *particular* interpretive judgments, rather than to the objectivity of this *type* of interpretive judgment. Remember Postema's distinction between *type* and *token* objectivity. Type objectivity refers to whether judgments of the kind at issue can be objective and is thus, as he terms it, an "eligibility notion." Token objectivity, by contrast, relates to whether any particular judgment— of a type for which objectivity is possible—succeeds in being, in fact, objective and is thus, as he terms it, a "success notion."[42] In claiming that judgments by dominant groups (who may be in control of decision-making in a particular culture) regarding the practices of minority groups are likely to be biased, one is making an assertion about whether these judgments *succeed* in being objective. As such, the objection is more limited and more internal (i.e., one would have to look at particular judgments to determine whether the claim is warranted) than it might initially appear.

That said, let us look at the objection more closely. It raises an important practical worry about how a theory like the one I propose is likely to play out in the real world—the claim being that it is likely to reinforce the dominance of dominant groups. First, is that so? I am skeptical about the degree to which any theory about when or whether discrimination is wrong will either exacerbate or ameliorate the dominance of dominant social groups. For the dominant group to cede power, they must recognize that what they are doing is wrong, when it is wrong. This theory perhaps makes that more explicit, but the ability to *see things differently* is required to change one's mind, whatever theory one is using to evaluate one's actions.

Second, and more important, even if adoption of my view were likely to lead to more wrongful domination by dominant social groups, this fact would not provide a reason to reject the theory at the *theoretical level*. If objectivity is possible but poor judgment likely, we would have reason to substitute other tests for political or judicial decision makers to use when deciding public policy.[43] If another test (of what ought to count as wrongful discrimination) is more likely to reach the right result than asking decision makers to directly examine whether a classification demeans, then this is a reason to adopt another test. But note that to adopt this viewpoint, one must have a prior conception of what counts as the *right* judgment. It cannot be the decision that would be adopted with the substitute test, as that would be circular. It must be the decision that would be right using the right theory of when discrimination is permissible and when not—a theory whose value cannot be assessed in terms of whether people are likely to misapply it.

Finally, I do not believe that telling people to focus on whether a classification demeans will yield more incorrect decisions than would an alternative test with less room for interpretive judgment. Candidly and explicitly focusing on the question of whether a particular practice demeans any of the groups affected may help illuminate the flaws of the dominant position, when it is flawed. It will facilitate critique of the dominant group's outlook—an outlook that would also influence how that group applies any test one might substitute. Use of this approach thus might ultimately lead to more real movement in how a dominant group perceives and understands its differentiation practices.

To recap: When is it morally wrong to distinguish among and then treat people differently? When the differentiation demeans. People are likely to disagree about whether any actual practice demeans. No theory could, nor should, hope to eliminate such disagreement entirely. The theory I propose helps to channel that disagreement to the right question. Of course as a society we need mechanisms for dealing with disagreement, whether disagreement about when discrimination is wrong or anything else. In our society, these methods include democratic and judicial decision making.

Considering Alternatives

Introduction to Part II

In Part II, we examine three alternative approaches to answering this question: When does an act of differentiation constitute wrongful discrimination? Though these competing views may not be offered as comprehensive alternative visions, they suggest that other principles are relevant in assessing whether acts of differentiation wrongfully discriminate. If so, they also offer challenges to the theory presented in Part I.

In Chapter 4, I consider the concept of merit. One might think that distinctions that fail to respect merit are wrongful or, alternatively, that distinctions made in accord with merit are, at least presumptively, valid. Why think this? If we begin with a commitment to the equal moral worth of persons, perhaps this equality requires treating people the same, absent a good reason to do otherwise. If so, then merit provides such a good reason. Or so one might think. In Chapter 4, I argue against this view, arguing instead that merit is an unstable idea. Merit is simply what the person or institution hiring an employee or admitting a student (to take these contexts as examples) seeks, and thus there is no reason to accord a moral pass to such preferences.

But then why does it *seem* that merit-based selections are commendable—the polar opposite of wrongful discrimination? In part, I expect this has a historical explanation. Merit-based hiring, for example, constituted a departure from practices that were wrongful discrimination: refusing to hire blacks or women or religious and ethnic minorities. But this does not mean that being merit-based makes such a practice right, simply that the shift to merit-based hiring provided an avenue away from demeaning wrongful discrimination. Second, there may well be a connection between non-demeaning differentiation and merit-based selection in some instances. Depending on the criteria that make up merit, decisions according to those criteria often will express respect for the people affected by the selection rather than contempt. Thus merit-based selection will, in most instances, not be demeaning. This overlap explains, in part, why merit seems related to assessing when discrimination is wrong. It is important to emphasize, however, that on this account a particular merit-based selection is permissible *because* it not demeaning (which may in part be due to its being merit-based). Moreover, on this view merit-based selection can be demeaning, notwithstanding its being merit-based, and some selections that flout merit may not be demeaning and are therefore not wrongful discrimination.

Chapter 5 considers a related view. One might think that treating people as moral equals requires that one have some reason (and not a patently bad reason) to draw distinctions among them and thus that arbitrary differentiation is morally wrong. In Chapter 5, I argue against this view, contending that arbitrariness itself is not a wrong grounded in a concern with equality. This view leaves open the possibility that certain institutions (most notably the State) are required not to treat those whom they affect or control in an arbitrary manner. But if so, this is a requirement internal to the institution or role, not one that derives from the moral requirement to treat people as moral equals.

But why think otherwise? Why does it *seem* that arbitrary classifications are clear cases of wrongful discrimination? In part, the intuition that arbitrariness matters to equality derives from the very natural outrage we all feel at decisions that lack reasons, particularly decisions with serious consequences for people. For example, if the person selecting which candidate to hire were to say he had decided that morning that Tuesday would be a "T" day and he would thus try to hire a candidate whose name begins with "T," we would be struck by the waste such a decision would wreak and the stupidity it would embody. The outrage at waste and stupidity that occurs in the context of selection among applications thus finds a happy home— or so it would seem—in the claim of wrongful discrimination. Second, arbitrariness seems important, in part, because testing for arbitrariness is often a good way to smoke out the use of other more troubling criteria. The employer who says he hired Tom Smith because his name starts with "T" may have really chosen Tom because he is a man (or using some other more troubling criterion). Third, acting arbitrarily *is* sometimes an important moral wrong for other reasons. For example, a teacher has an obligation to grade students in accord with how well they perform the assignment (or how much progress they have made, or effort they have put in, or some criterion related to the goal of learning). For a teacher to assign grades arbitrarily *is* wrong, but not because it wrongfully discriminates among students. Rather, arbitrary grading is wrong because it violates the norms or values of the educational mission.

Chapter 6 considers a different sort of view—that it is the intention or motivation of the person who adopts a law, policy, or practice that matters, at least to some degree. This view has been influential, particularly in law. In Chapter 6, I argue against this view and contend that the actor's intentions do not determine what the policy or practice at issue is (is it one that distinguishes on the basis of race or not, for example), nor do the actor's intentions determine whether differentiation in a particular context is wrong. But why think otherwise? Why has this view been so influential?

The reasons for the tenacity of the view that intent is important in judging whether differentiation is wrongful or permissible are complex. Though I cannot hope to catalogue and explain them all here, I want to point out two such reasons that are important. First, drawing distinctions among people often occurs in contexts in which the actor has some discretion. For example, the employer deciding whom to hire is not required, morally, to hire one particular candidate (unless one believes in a strong form of the argument for merit discussed in Chapter 4). To know what the criteria are that influenced his decision (i.e., the traits he considered), we need to go inside the head of the actor. This fact makes it *seem* as if it is the actor's intentions or motivation that matter. In part, confusion results from the fact that courts and others often use the term *intention* rather loosely— perhaps they mean only that evaluation of the action depends on knowing the criteria *actually* used to distinguish among people. But what the criteria really are is not the same as what the actor intends the criteria to be or what motivates him to adopt particular criteria.

Second, the judgment that a policy or practice wrongfully discriminates seems to suggest that the actor who enacted the policy or practice is morally blameworthy. Blameworthiness suggests control over one's actions, which in turn suggests that the intentions or the motivation of the actor matters. Though much wrongful discrimination is morally blameworthy as it is adopted intentionally or, most culpably, motivated by a desire to harm those affected, all wrongful discrimination need not be. There is a difference between an employer who decides not to hire African American workers because of animus and an employer who is influenced by racial stereotypes of which she is unaware. But the fact that one of these actors is morally culpable while the other is not (or is less so) need not lead us to conclude that the actions of each (distinguishing among job applicants on the basis of race) are not both wrongful discrimination.

This introduction to Part II aims to explain or diagnose the attraction of the most prominent alternative views of what makes wrongful discrimination wrong. The following chapters argue against each of these views, responding, I hope, to the reader's most pressing reservations to the view presented in Part I. As this book aims to articulate an alternative account and lay out its basic contours, I have no illusions that all questions, objections, or reservations will be answered. Rather, what follows begins that process. Each of these chapters is relatively freestanding and can be read as an argument against the moral significance of each of these factors (merit, rationality, and intention) with regard to the question of when distinguishing among people wrongfully discriminates, and in that sense these chapters could be of interest to readers who remain unmoved by the arguments in Part I.

CHAPTER **4**

Merit, Entitlement, and Desert

In her memoir, *Reading Lolita in Tehran,* Azar Nafisi describes how
university admissions and hiring policies changed after the Iranian
revolution. No longer were students and faculty chosen on the basis of
past academic performance or scholarly promise; instead, revolutionary
zeal became the dominant criterion for admission.[1]

"Since 1992, Business for Social Responsibility (BSR) has helped
companies of all sizes and sectors to achieve success in ways that
demonstrate respect for ethical values, people, communities, and the
environment."[2]

A 3-, 4-, or 5-year-old child applying for admission to a public school's
gifted-and-talented program or to many private schools is required to take
an intelligence test. Admission depends in part on the child's score.[3]

One familiar view about when it is permissible to draw distinctions among
people and when it is not looks to the concept of merit. Roughly, *merit*
refers to an attribute that would contribute to the enterprise that is selecting
applicants. "Careers open to talent"—a classic formulation of the merit
principle—mandates selecting people for positions who will be best able to
do the job. One could endorse a merit-based hiring principle without any
moral implications following. The head of a company has good reason—her
company's profitability, for example—to endorse merit-based hiring. But
this prudent reason to go with merit does not entail that the company president is morally required to employ merit-based hiring or that doing so insulates her from moral complaint.

The merit principle can be cast as one with moral force, in a weak or a strong form. Merit selection is either morally mandated (the strong form of the moral merit principle) or merit selection insulates policies that distinguish among people from moral criticism (the weak form of the moral merit principle).

According to the strong view, when the Iranian universities abandon academic promise in favor of political zeal, they act wrongly in denying admission to the academically best students. Their academic merit *entitles* them to university spots. But perhaps the universities can reply that they *are* using merit as their admissions criterion. They simply have a different conception of merit than does Azar Nafisi—one that makes political affiliation paramount. If that reply seems troubling, consider the above mission statement for the Business for Social Responsibility (BSR). In a business context, a merit-based hiring procedure would seem to dictate that companies choose the employee best able to do the job. But concern for the local community might lead a business to hire local job seekers whenever possible. Is this deviation from merit-based hiring thereby impermissible? A commitment to "values" might warrant keeping on a sick employee who can no longer do a job well rather than replacing her with the best-qualified person. Is this practice—seemingly supported by the BSR principles—impermissible, as the strong form of the merit principle might suggest?

One could make this strong form even stronger, though less plausible, by linking merit to desert. According to this formulation, deviation from the merit principle is morally wrong because people deserve to be treated according to merit. This view seems especially unpersuasive as the traits that form the basis of merit—ability to perform well in work, school, sport, and so on—often result from traits that are unearned like natural intelligence or athleticism.[4]

Even in its weak form, the moral merit principle can be troubling. If students with higher IQs, as measured by standard intelligence testing, generally perform better in school than those with lower IQs, then choosing the students with the highest IQs for entry into a public gifted-and-talented kindergarten or private pre-K or kindergarten would be morally permissible. Yet many people react with hesitation, if not outrage, at the idea of testing kids so young and making school choices on the basis of these tests. Does this suggest that merit selection is not always permissible?

In this chapter, I will use these three examples as well as others to develop the argument that merit selection is not morally mandated (the strong form of the moral merit principle), nor does merit selection insulate policies that distinguish among people from moral criticism (the weak form of the moral merit principle). This argument connects to the concerns left open in Part I. There, I argued that drawing distinctions among people is morally wrong when doing so fails to respect the equal moral worth of persons. In addition, I argued that distinctions that demean are thereby wrongful because they fail to treat people as moral equals. I left open the possibility that some non-demeaning differentiation could also fail to treat people as equals. The strong form of the merit principle identified above (that people are entitled or deserve to be judged according to merit) could provide an account of how or why non-demeaning differentiation fails to treat people as moral equals. If this strong merit principle were defensible, then selection criteria that flout merit would fail to treat people as they are entitled or as they deserve—which could amount to failing to treat them as moral equals.

Alternatively if the weak merit principle is correct—and merit-based selection criteria are immune from criticism—this would challenge the account of wrongful discrimination provided in Part I. According to the weak merit principle, the fact that a selection criterion is based on merit insulates it from moral criticism. Therefore demeaning merit-based hiring would be morally permissible—a view seemingly rejected by the account in Part I.

What Is Merit?

The concept of merit is controversial. Individual responses to the cases with which I began this chapter reveal differing conceptions of merit. In other words, varying views about the moral permissibility of the selection criteria mentioned above may simply reflect adherence to different conceptions of merit. This fact leads some scholars to conclude that merit is not a useful concept. We would do better to argue about the substantive questions that give rise to each of the conceptions of merit than to use the concept of merit itself, as its meaning is so loose as to obfuscate rather than elucidate.[5]

Christopher McCrudden offers the following four inquiries that, in his view, help delineate the various conceptions of merit that are often in play:

1. What are "the differences in the limits and restrictions as to what merit can consist of"?[6] For example, can the fact that a worker is

from the local community be an aspect of merit? In other words, must the traits that make up "merit" be socially useful traits or might they include any characteristic?

2. What are "the differences as to what 'the job' is thought to be"? Though McCrudden's focus is on the concept of merit in the context of employment, this criterion could be expanded to other contexts—differences as to what the position (including jobs or spots at school or on sports teams, etc.) is thought to be. For example, this question would draw attention to what the job of a university professor or the role of a university student consists of. Is this something that the employer or school can define for itself or are there external constraints on its definition? Is the role of business simply to make money or may it moderate that goal with other commitments?

3. What are "the differences on the degree of 'fit' between the job an the merit criterion"? Does the fact that 4-year-olds have cooperative days and uncooperative days that might significantly affect the reliability of an intelligence test for this group (if this is true) matter to whether the IQ test score of a 4-year-old may be considered an aspect of merit? For example, if smart 4-year-olds who slept poorly the night before often perform poorly on IQ tests, then the test score may be a bad predictor of school performance.

4. What are the "differences as to what status should be attached to merit"? Once we have identified what merit is, what does this claim yield? Does the fact that one 4-year-old has a higher IQ test score than another *entitle* her to be admitted to a program or school? Is this because she *deserves* to be admitted? If she is entitled to be admitted, though she does not deserve to be, is this merely because the school or program has announced that IQ test scores will determine admission or is it for some other reason? If entitlement is merely a function of legitimate expectations, could a clear policy statement by the Iranian revolutionary government that university admissions policies will hereinafter favor applicants with demonstrated revolutionary zeal vitiate the claim of the academically talented student denied admission and, similarly, entitle zealous revolutionaries places on the faculty and in the student body?

Common Sense versus Constructed Merit

The conceptions of merit picked out by answers to questions 1 and 2 can be described as either more common sense or more constructed. By *common-sense merit* I mean to suggest the sense of merit that comports with the way the term is ordinarily used. However, the fact that this sense of merit reflects common usage does not mean it is therefore right. Rather, I argue that the commonsense conception of merit is unstable, that its underlying rationale leads ultimately toward a more constructed conception of merit. This is a problem for arguments based on merit as this constructive sense of merit has less intuitive moral appeal and thus cannot justify arguments that merit entails either entitlement or desert.

A conception limiting the traits that constitute merit to those that are socially useful seems to comport best with the common understanding of the word. Skills and abilities are what people generally think of as comprising merit. To say that characteristics that are not socially useful can also comprise merit—where one lives, for example—seems strained because merit is generally understood to be something positive. If person X merits position Y in virtue of *m*, this is because *m* is something good about X. To merit something is, generally, a term of approbation. Robert Fullinwider and Judith Lichtenberg agree; they argue for limiting the term *merit* to skills and talents both because it "conforms more closely to the way we ordinarily talk" and because they believe we would still want to distinguish these traits from others that could be relevant, and thus "[w]e would find ourselves scrambling to invent a new term to distinguish 'individual skills and talents' (what used to be called 'merit') from other criteria a college might consider."[7] (Their discussion focuses on merit in the context of college admissions.) For McCrudden too, the conception of merit that he calls "general 'common sense' merit" is one in which the traits that make up merit must be ones that are socially useful.[8]

A conception of merit that uses a fairly narrow notion of the job or position in question also comports better the way we generally talk about merit, and so these two together (socially useful trait and narrowly defined description of the position) define what I am terming the commonsense conception of merit.[9] For example, when Johnny Damon played for the Red Sox in the 2004 season (the year the Red Sox won the World Series), he was noteworthy not only for his skill in baseball but also for his look. His long hair and long beard made fans either call him the "caveman" or say that he looked like Jesus. Red Sox fans wore T-shirts emblazoned with "WWJDD," meaning "What would Johnny Damon do?" a clear takeoff on the Christian fundamentalist "WWJD" ("What would Jesus do?"). Let us suppose, not unreasonably, that the Red Sox determined Damon's popularity was due in part to his look and that this popularity was responsible for an increase in ticket sales. If so, is his look an aspect of his merit as a baseball player? A commonsense conception of merit would say no. According to this conception, the job of a professional baseball player is defined as being able to hit, run, and field well (or pitch, if we are hiring a pitcher). Of course, questions remain about the appropriate balance among these skills (hitting versus fielding, for example). However, the job of a professional baseball player is not to increase box-office receipts, and thus Damon's look and its contribution to this end are irrelevant. His personal appeal is not an aspect of his merit as a baseball player, according to the commonsense conception of merit.

This conception of merit is unstable, however. It may be what we mean by *merit* but it is hard to see why the traits that can form merit must be ones that we *ordinarily* think of as socially useful or why we must limit job descriptions to their *conventional* boundaries. Perhaps thinking harder about merit will lead us to see how other characteristics are useful in some contexts and how the ways in which people perform may have significant impact beyond the narrow conception of their role.

Let us consider a few examples—cases in which the commonsense conception of merit initially might seem most sensible. Take, for example, a doctor. What ought to count as merit regarding who ought to be hired as a doctor or admitted to medical school? To ascertain what counts as merit for a physician, one must first determine what the goals of medical care are and what a good physician does. Merit is a relational concept in this way; there is not something that is merit plain and simple. Rather merit for a doctor is different from merit for a haircutter, for example (though not always—early physicians were often also barbers). The commonsense conception of the aims of a physician are to cure the sick and, at the least, to do no harm.[10] If the goal of medicine is to cure the sick and avoid medical error, then merit for the physician would consist of medical knowledge, technical skill (for surgeons or others called upon to physically manipulate their patients), and the sort of intelligence that allows a person to bring knowledge to bear in individual cases and to think creatively when diagnoses elude standard medical categories.

This straightforward account of the role of the physician and the conception of merit appropriate to it proves overly narrow on even a short reflection. While appropriate diagnosis and treatment of disease surely are central to the role of the physician, they are not the only functions she or he fulfills. Palliation, when appropriate, is also important. In addition, the physician must also be able to competently and compassionately explain treatment options to sick patients. Finally, even if the physician's role is limited to the diagnosis and treatment of disease, the merit triad of knowledge-skill-intelligence may not exhaust the qualities relevant to the attainment of that goal. The physician's personal style or manner may help or hinder her in eliciting the information relevant to a correct diagnosis. As Louis Lasagna, former Academic Dean of the School of Medicine at Tufts University, wrote in his modern version of the Hippocratic oath, the physician's role, properly conceived, includes the obligations to "remember that there is an art to medicine as well as science, and that warmth, sympathy, and understanding may outweigh the surgeon's knife or the chemist's drug," and that a good doctor "will not be ashamed to say 'I know not,' nor will [he or she] fail to call in . . . [his or her] colleagues when the skills of another are needed for a patient's recovery."[11]

This broader conception of the aims of medicine yields a broader conception of merit appropriate to it. Modesty and compassion are central. Nor can we necessarily stop with this broader conception of the physician's role, which still focuses on his or her functions in treating individual patients. It is not unreasonable to also include the willingness to provide medical care to underserved populations in the physician's role, especially in the context of medical school admissions, but also in the case of choosing which doctors to admit to residency training programs in various subspecialties, and even in the case of selecting doctors for staff positions in clinics or hospitals. Those physicians or would-be physicians who are more likely to practice in remote rural or underserved urban communities or in developing countries with fewer well-trained physicians would thereby have more merit than those who are less likely to do so. And who are the people who are more likely to fill these unmet medical needs and thus merit the positions in question in part for this reason? It may be difficult to identify people with this aspect of merit but there are strategies. A medical school or residency program could give preference to applicants who will commit to spending a particular number of years providing medical care to an underserved community. Alternatively, applicants who are from these communities could be given preference based on the theory that they are more likely than the average physician to return to these communities to practice. While this proxy is surely imperfect, so are other indicia of more traditional aspects of merit—MCAT scores as predictors of intelligence and knowledge, for example.

In sum, the commonsense conception of merit, in which only socially useful traits are considered as aspects of merit and in which the traits that make up merit are those that are useful in fulfilling a narrow conception of the position at issue, is unstable. Any conception of the position under consideration will be controversial. Does good doctoring reduce to diagnosing and treating disease or it does it also require compassionate interactions, attention to palliation, a manner likely to draw out truthful and fulsome medical histories, and a commitment to serve medically underserved communities? Does it include some, but not all, of these components? And how important is each component to good doctoring? The answers to these questions will determine which traits constitute merit for applicants for medical-training or physician positions. These are precisely the questions that medical school faculty, teaching hospitals with residency training programs, and clinics and hospitals hiring physicians will answer in choosing candidates. In other words, the question of what traits constitute merit for a particular position will replay any internal controversy about what the position or role *is* for which the person is being selected. Unless there is a way to settle the question of what being a physician entails, then most arguments that rely on the assertion that candidate A merits position B can be transposed into arguments about what is the best conception of the role of position B. Therefore, the merit argument is not doing any real work.[12]

This claim is stronger still in the case of jobs with less-developed role conceptions. After all, one might have thought that the role of a physician would be fairly uncontroversial. Consider next the position of a worker in a business. Is his or her role best conceived as being able to do the tasks that the job description entails, whether it be to make widgets, cook food, keep accurate accounts, or manage employees? Or, is his or her job best conceived as being a *productive* employee where productivity is defined by the business's bottom line? After all, a cheerful cook might have better interactions with the waiters, leading to less employee turnover, which in turn might help the restaurant's bottom line. Alternatively, the position may incorporate societal benefits as well as benefits that redound to the employer. For example, a manager of workers with family obligations who provides opportunity for part-time work or work-from-home may be thought more productive overall in that she serves the company's interests reasonably well while simultaneously enabling the important work of caring for children or dependent adults that is necessary in any society. If a business conceives of its function as socially responsible in this way, might it not then think of merit as incorporating a demonstrated commitment to social responsibility?

The entity—whether a business, hospital, or university—defines its role and function. Is it a purely profit-driven business or a socially responsible business? We may object to some ways that these entities define themselves, but that objection is then grounded in an argument about the entity's role, which has implications for merit, not the other way around. When the University of Tehran begins admitting students based in part on their revolutionary zeal, the claim that these students lack merit or that their intellectually talented competitors merit admission instead really adds nothing to the real argument, which is an argument about what a university *is*. In the view of Azar Nafisi, the values internal to a university (the pursuit of knowledge, teaching of students, etc.) are compromised by this new admissions criterion. In essence, she is arguing that university officials do not have free reign to adopt any admissions criteria without fundamentally altering the nature of a university. Nafisi's view can be interpreted as contending that being a university carries with it certain restrictions on which admissions criteria (and faculty hiring and retention criteria) are acceptable and unacceptable. By adopting the political-affiliation criterion, Nafisi would argue, the university alters its nature so dramatically as to become something other than a university, call it a *schmuniversity*. In fact, it ultimately becomes something so different from a university, as she knows it, that she feels compelled to resign her position as a faculty member.

The fact that arguments about merit are better conceived as arguments about the role or function of the position and of the institution of which it is a part has implications for what flows from the claim that X merits position Y in virtue of *m*. It is to the question of what entitlements, if any, merit arguments yield that we now turn.

Merit and Entitlement or Desert

If, as I have argued, discussions about merit (what it is and who has it in a particular context) are reducible to debates about the best way to conceive of the position in question, what follows regarding claims about entitlement or desert? In particular, if person X merits position Y in virtue of *m*, (1) is X entitled to Y?, (2) does X deserve Y?, and (3) is X having Y immune from moral criticism? Propositions 1 and 2 (X is entitled to Y; X deserves Y) are two forms of what I called the strong merit-based claim at the start of this chapter. Proposition 3 (X having Y is immune from moral criticism) is the weak merit-based claim. Let us consider 1 and 2 first.

It is important to identify what we mean by the terms *entitlement* and *desert*. At times the claim of entitlement is based on a claim that legitimate expectations entitle a person to be judged by a particular conception of merit. This sort of entitlement is important but it does not rely on an argument from merit. After all, hiring policies based on political affiliation that have been in place for a long time within a certain regime could also give rise to legitimate expectations. So long as the policies on which someone relies are not patently unjust, the factors that determine whether they would give rise to legitimate expectations would be very different from the factors that affect whether an individual merits the particular position. One would look at how long the current policies have been in place, how often hiring policies have changed in the past, what has been said regarding the institution's discretion in changing hiring criteria, what sorts of investments applicants must make in acquiring the qualifications that were relevant in the past, what are the background rules in that society regarding the freedom of institutions to change hiring criteria, and so on. These factors would affect whether the applicant has acquired an entitlement based in a claim of legitimate expectations to be judged by the old criteria governing hiring rather than the new. If she has, we may conclude that she is entitled to the position, but this entitlement does not flow from the fact that she merits the job. Rather, it flows from the fact that she has relied on the previously announced hiring criteria in a manner that entitles her to have the criteria maintained for some period of time.

Nor is a merit-based argument for entitlement an argument against rogue decision makers departing from the established criteria. One may well be entitled to be judged by the criteria that have been officially adopted. But again, this claim has nothing particularly to do with merit. The applicant with little merit (as defined by the entity in question) also may be entitled to be judged by the officially adopted hiring criteria. The entitlement to be judged by particular criteria of merit may arise from legitimate expectations or may arise from the commitments adopted by the entity and the role-obligations of the person administering the promulgated criteria. Thus institutions and procedures do, at times, give rise to entitlements. These entitlements may convert to an entitlement to be judged by a certain conception of merit but this does not mean that it is one's merit that entitles one to the position in question.

Can merit itself yield entitlement? Does the fact that X merits Y in virtue of *m* create an entitlement of X to Y? Suppose that Paul is a speedy widget-maker working in a widget factory. He is given a bonus because he is the fastest widget-maker on the factory floor. In other words, Paul merits the bonus by virtue of his speed. Does this mean Paul is entitled to the bonus? We are not asking whether Paul has a legitimate expectation that the bonus will be paid to the speediest widget-maker based on past practice. Nor are we asking whether the fact that the company announced it would pay a bonus to the speediest entitles Paul to the bonus. These are the forms of entitlement just discussed, from which the normative force of the entitlement does not derive from Paul's merit.

In addition, we must be careful to distinguish the question at hand from another important way in which a claim of entitlement is often asserted. Claims of entitlement are often offered as against claims made by the state that it may tax Paul on the money he makes from his skills and talents. The libertarian argues that if Paul is entitled to the bonus he is paid for his speedy widget-making, then the state acts wrongly in taking some of that money in income tax.[13] While this libertarian argument against taxation is itself interesting and has spawned an immense literature both defending and criticizing this position,[14] this entitlement-based claim is not our focus here. We are not examining whether the state may tax Paul but rather whether the company is morally required to reward him for his speed. Is he entitled to the bonus if his company decides it does not in fact value speed after all? Does his "merit" itself entitle him to the bonus?

Suppose the next year Paul is again the speediest widget-maker. However, this year the company decides to offer a bonus to the worker who is both fast and affable. This policy is announced far in advance thus weakening any claims of entitlement based on legitimate expectations and vitiating any claim based on entitlement to the application of the officially promulgated policies. In the intervening year, the company has hired a business consultant who has demonstrated that affable employees aid the company's productivity in ways that are less easily identified but nonetheless significant. Affable employees help others feel happy at work, which leads to lower worker turnover and better productivity from slower workers. In other words, although the affable employee may not be the speediest, she may help others work faster and thus may increase overall productivity as much as or more than the fastest employee. On the basis of these new criteria, Sue is awarded the bonus for the most productive employee. Does Paul have reason to complain? Is he entitled to the bonus? So long as Paul has no claim based on legitimate expectations that the criteria would remain the same, his claim that he is entitled to the bonus seems groundless, even silly. If the company has determined that speed and affability increase productivity more than speed alone, then Paul has no claim on the prize. He does not meet the criteria that the company adopts and he has no right to have the company use particular criteria in awarding bonuses. He may have a right to demand that the company refrain from using certain sorts of criteria (Part I of the book articulated a theory of what those are) but he has no right to demand that they use a criterion for granting bonuses that happens to reward his talents.

Note that Paul's failure to be entitled to the bonus does not stem from the fact that productivity really *is* better served by rewarding speed and affability combined rather than speed alone. Suppose that the business consultant turned out to be mistaken. While affable employees do help others to be productive, the practice of rewarding speedy employees induces all the employees to try to be as speedy as possible. If the company replaces the speedy bonus with a bonus for speed plus affability, it looses more than it gains in productivity (let us say). This is in part because affable employees are likely to be affable with or without a bonus while employees are motivated to be faster by the prospect of a bonus for speed. If so, then the company made the wrong choice—in terms of enhancing productivity—when it changed the criteria on which the bonus was awarded. Does this fact mean that Paul really is entitled to the bonus? No. The company is not under a moral obligation to be as productive as it can. It would be odd indeed to say that whenever managers make business decisions that are less than optimal, the workers who would have benefited by a better business decision are entitled to the rewards that they would have received had the ideal decisions been made. Workers are not entitled to be judged by ideal employment criteria. If business managers do stupid things, that is unfortunate but no more.

Moreover, if businesses choose to value things other than productivity alone, they ought to be free to do so. Just because one operates a business does not mean that one *must* be guided only by profit-making. The Business for Social Responsibility movement aims to convince business leaders to value things other than a company's bottom line. The claim that a productive employee is entitled to be paid what he would have been paid had the company only valued productivity would make the BSR's goals impermissible. Companies would be morally required to focus only on the bottom line. This seems a difficult argument to make. It is most plausible in the case of a publicly held company but even there a clearly articulated statement of the company's goals should put shareholders on notice that they are investing for a financial *and* a social return.[15] It is for the entity to decide what it values (within the limits articulated in Part I), and having done so it may reward employees in accord with those values. If X merits Y in virtue of *m*, this tells us no more than that the company values speed and so it awarded Paul a bonus. But the company is morally permitted to implement other values. In that sense, Paul is not entitled to the bonus.

Merit and Efficiency

What would be the counterargument? One might argue that companies and other entities ought to reward traits that enhance efficiency or productivity because enhancing productivity is itself a good thing.[16] If paying a bonus to the speediest widget-maker enhances worker productivity more than paying a bonus to the worker who is reasonably fast and affable, then the company ought to reward the speediest worker. The fact that his skills enhance productivity entitles him to the bonus. This is an argument that merit (defined as those traits that enhance efficiency) entitles an applicant to the position in question.

According to this argument, to say that a person merits the job is not merely to say she has the skills or abilities the entity seeks (the constructed sense of merit) but instead to say she merits the job because she is entitled to it. Why? The person who merits the job, where merit is defined as having those traits that most enhance productivity, is *entitled* to it because enhancing productivity is an important and worthy goal.[17] There are two important things to note about this argument. First, if efficiency is what matters and what explains and justifies why a particular candidate is entitled to a particular position, there is no reason to focus on the efficiency of the entity alone. As Norman Daniels explains, there is no reason to focus only on which candidate could add the most if selected for one particular job.

Rather, if productivity grounds the normative force of merit, why not ask which allocation of persons to positions as a whole would maximize overall productivity? Daniels calls this the "Productive Job Assignment Principle," or "PJAP."[18] Here is his explanation of PJAP:

> Jack and Jill both want jobs A and B and each much prefers A to B. Jill can do either A or B better than Jack. But the situation S in which Jill performs B and Jack A is more productive than Jack doing B and Jill A (S'), even when we include the effects on productivity of Jill's lesser satisfaction. The PJAP selects S, not S', because it is attuned to macroproductivity, not microproductivity, considerations. It says, "Select people for jobs so that *overall* job performance is maximized."[19]

In other words, if merit matters because productivity matters, then the merit that matters is not that of the person who could best perform this job but instead the set of job assignments that would maximize productivity overall. This sort of merit principle will legitimize some selections of employees for jobs that may seem counterintuitive, like the Jack and Jill example Daniels provides. Daniels recognizes the counterintuitive features of this conception of merit—in particular its *social* dimension: "We focus on the relevant abilities because of their utility, not because there is something intrinsically meritorious about having them."[20]

The second important feature of this efficiency-based argument for the claim that one is entitled to be judged according to merit (defined with reference to efficiency) is that it is only as valuable as efficiency itself. If other values would trump efficiency in some contexts, then in those cases the person whose skills and talents would most enhance efficiency is not entitled to the position in question. Consider the use of IQ testing of preschool-age children as an admissions criterion for elite public and private school programs, for example. Suppose that admissions officials at an elite private school were to defend their practice of using this as a major criterion (though surely not the only criterion) on the grounds that IQ test scores of 4- and 5-year-old children correlate well with SAT scores. Because colleges rely heavily on SAT scores, these are the kids who are most likely to get into the elite colleges in the country. In addition, attendance at elite colleges correlates well with leadership in a variety of fields—business, law, medicine, and public policy. I offer this story as a purely hypothetical justification. If so, the elite school or program argues, an admissions procedure that is substantially based on IQ test scores will succeed in selecting those kids who are likely to be the future leaders in many fields. The school believes its education is excellent and wants to ensure that its influence is brought to bear on these future leaders.

Now of course this story reveals problems with the conception of productivity used to justify the claim that merit (defined as those qualities that enhance productivity) yields entitlement. It is difficult to say what counts as enhancing productivity. If our country's future leaders can be made more knowledgeable, wiser, more humane, and more creative (assuming—and this is a big assumption—that the influence of an elite education are what determine *this*), then perhaps the school is right that choosing kids using IQ scores will enhance productivity, understood as macroproductivity in Daniels's terms. On the other hand, perhaps kids with high IQs are less in need of an excellent education than are their more-average peers or the large numbers of kids who would otherwise receive a poor education. Perhaps it would most enhance macroproductivity to admit kids with mediocre IQ scores or kids who would otherwise receive a terrible education (rather than those who would simply go to another fairly good school).[21] But let us put these worries aside for now.

Let us assume that the elite private school is right or at least reasonable in claiming that macroproductivity is enhanced by an admissions policy that, at least in part, selects students based on high IQ scores. Still, productivity is not all that matters, and if so then these students' "merit"[22] ought not to *entitle* them to school admission. Suppose, again hypothetically but not unreasonably, that the practice of testing small children has deleterious consequences for kids. Perhaps for some kids it is stressful because they understand they are being evaluated and that something that matters to their parents turns on how they do. Other parents may do a better job of shielding children from the knowledge that they are being evaluated, yet the testing may affect them still. When parents get the scores, these scores are likely to have an impact on the way the parents see their children. Despite the parents' best efforts to value their children for just being themselves, the parents may begin to value their children because the children are smart, have scored well, have great potential, and so on. In the case of the kids who do not score well, their parents may feel disappointed and lower their expectations. Sibling relationships and family dynamics may also be affected. The children who score better than their siblings may feel more valued by their parents and those that score less well, less valued. All this could happen without the kids or even the parents knowing or recognizing that it was caused by the test results. If testing yields these effects, perhaps schools ought not to test kids despite the increase in overall productivity that selecting kids based on test scores may produce. The relationship of parents and children and children's self-esteem matter too, surely. Moreover, as educators of young children, the school may even have a special obligation to do what is best for kids rather than what is best for society as a whole.[23]

The argument that other values could trump productivity is stronger still in the case of a public school. The public school has an especially clear obligation to value each child entrusted to its care. Though this mandate does not require that each child get the same education, it does mean that if testing children hurts kids, the fact that doing so increases the productivity of society cannot compensate for this harm to some of the children in its care.

Therefore, even if one were to define merit in terms of productivity enhancement such that the claim that merit yields entitlement has some moral appeal, this appeal will be limited. First, as the claim is appealing because enhancing productivity is important, this justification does not yield an entitlement to be judged according to whether an individual can be the most productive in a particular job, but instead an entitlement to the job the person would have if persons were allocated to jobs in a maximally productive way (Daniels's PJAP). Second, while productivity is important, it is surely not all that matters. Where other important values are at stake, productivity-based merit does not entitle a person to a position and must give way to the other values at stake.

Merit and Desert

The claim that the fact that someone merits a position means that she or he *deserves* it is even harder to justify. What distinguishes *entitlement* from *desert* is the sense that *desert* derives from some morally worthy action on the part of the person. So, for example, Paul, the speedy widget-maker, may be entitled to the bonus if his company announced it will pay a bonus to the speediest widget-maker. This is the entitlement that flows both from legitimate expectations and the entitlement that flows from the company's obligation to honor its commitments. But does he *deserve* it? Suppose he is naturally gifted in manual dexterity so that he can make widgets quickly without much effort. The fact that he has this natural ability is surely not something he deserves. From this claim, many philosophers have argued that he therefore does not deserve the rewards he is able to reap from this natural talent.[24]

On the other hand, he may be especially fast at making widgets because he makes an extraordinary effort to make them quickly. Even here, some philosophers have argued—John Rawls most notably—that the ability to make an effort is also something that is not deserved.[25] Others find this claim more controversial.[26] What is the basis of desert, one might argue, if not the effort expended by someone to achieve a particular result? In fact, I think it is the association of desert with effort that underlies the negative reaction that many people have to the IQ testing of young children. In theory and in practice the IQ test scores of 4- and 5-year-old kids do not reflect the effort these kids have expended to master a set of skills. Although the test score may reflect the richer educational environments of the more privileged test takers, it surely is not the effort of the children themselves that is measured or captured by the test. There seems to be something wrong with selecting children for a benefit purely on the basis of traits they are born with, rather than traits that they work to develop, at the least.

Even if we accept, contra Rawls, that making an effort does form the basis of a claim of desert, most (all?) of the instances in which a claim of merit is made rest on skills and abilities that result at least in part from a combination of effort and natural talents or brute luck. While Paul may be a speedy widget-maker in part because of the effort he expends to make the widgets quickly, he also succeeds in being the speediest because he is naturally dexterous enough that this effort yields him the top prize. Many others may expend as much or more effort than Paul but still succeed in being only average. Moreover, what determines which natural talents will be the ones that are valued by society is itself a product of luck. If speed alone in making widgets is valuable (and thus the basis of merit), because speed increases productivity more than some other trait or combination of traits (like speed plus affability), Paul is lucky. The skills he has are the ones that form the basis of merit rather than the skills someone else has. That fact is surely not one he deserves. Finally, the fact that some abilities have value is a function of their scarcity. Barbara Fried has argued—persuasively, I think—that because the value of certain talents is a function of their scarcity, the talented person does not own that part of the value of his talent that can be attributed to its scarcity.[27] Therefore he does not deserve the benefits that the scarcity-value of his talents make possible.

The Weak Claim—Merited Rewards Are Always Morally Permissible

Above I considered and rejected the claims that merit *entitles* a person to a position or that a person with merit *deserves* a position. Still, a weaker, but yet significant, claim about the relevance of merit to the allocation of positions is possible. In this section I consider the claim that the allocation of persons to positions based on merit is sufficient to establish its moral permissibility. In other words, even though the person with particular skills and abilities has no grounds for complaint if people with other traits are selected, if the position *is* allocated in accord with "merit"—some conception of the skills and abilities needed for the position—then perhaps no one else has grounds for complaint either. Does the fact that the hiring is merit-based insulate it from moral criticism?

This claim, too, is implausible for several reasons that replay much of the discussion above. First, in most contexts there is likely to be disagreement about what merit consists of and about how best to define the role of the entity or position involved. Suppose that two candidates, John and Jane, are being considered for a job at a law firm as a third-year associate. Both graduated in the top quarter of their class at top-ranked law schools. Both received glowing references from their current firms. John, however, billed 2100 hours per year in his previous job while Jane billed only 1800 hours per year. If the job of an associate at a law firm is to do high-quality legal work, then John and Jane equally merit the position. If, however, the job is defined more broadly as *generating income for the firm*, by completing as much high-quality legal work as possible, then merit-based hiring would suggest that John should be hired. So, to decide whether the candidates equally merit the job, or whether John merits it more, we would need to settle the question of how to best define the job of law-firm associate.

If we adopt the broader view that the job of an associate is to generate income, is there any reason to give a moral pass to the law firm's identification of what it values? John merits the job because he would bring in the most money but there is nothing morally important about this conception of merit. Here merit comprises simply those traits that the selecting entity wants—those that help it achieve its self-defined mission. As such, there is no reason to privilege this self-interested conception of merit. The more constructed the concept of merit becomes, the clearer this is.

One reason that merit-based hiring may seem to inoculate it from moral criticism is that it is often contrasted with some sort of inappropriate hiring criterion, such as cronyism or status-based selection. After all, historically, merit-based selection for jobs, schools, and so on replaced a system of selection that was based instead on wealth, family background, and privilege. If selection is merit-based, it insures that it is not based on wealth, family, and status. In that sense, it is good. However, just because merit-based selection may provide good evidence that the criteria used were not of this bad type, does not then mean there is something morally good about merit-based hiring in itself.

Let us return to John and Jane. Suppose the reason Jane bills fewer hours is that she is a mother with primary responsibility for the care of her children. John, by contrast, has no children. One might argue, as Joan Williams has, that jobs which reward the work patterns of people with no family-care obligations unfairly limit the work opportunities of workers with family-care obligations, mainly women.[28] Does the fact that the firm's choice of John over Jane is "merit-based" stop this argument in its tracks? The fact that the hiring is "merit-based" provides evidence that the criteria used are not of a special, bad sort (cronyism, etc.), but that is all. The firm's partners are trying to make more money. Is their desire to hire the worker who will help do that a desire that is entitled to deference or one that insulates it from moral critique? How so? There is nothing particularly good or valuable about making money such that actions that serve that goal are immune from criticism. I do not want to claim that Williams is ultimately right, though I am inclined to agree with her, but I do think that her claim deserves a hearing. The relevant issue is whether "ideal worker" norms, as she calls them, which are premised on the worker with no family-care obligations, unfairly disadvantage workers with care responsibilities. The fact that such hiring practices are "merit-based" should not end the inquiry.

This discussion of whether merit-based selection is always morally permissible (where merit is understood broadly as those traits desired by the selecting entity) overlaps the discussion in the next chapter. There we will look at whether the rationality of classifications is relevant to their moral permissibility. For that reason, I will not explore this point any further here.

Lastly, even cronyism is not always bad. Merit-based selection is supposed to be at least a step-up from status-based selection—selecting someone with the status of friend, relative, or insider, for example. But sometimes even status-based selection may be morally permissible, even desirable. Universities defend their practices of preferring legacies (the children or siblings of graduates) as necessary to their financial well-being. On the other hand, such practices contribute to the replication of wealth-based privilege. Let us leave that controversial practice aside for the moment and consider a similar practice that has not been the focus of a similar critique. Suppose the private school we looked at earlier has a sibling preference: once a child in a family has been admitted, a sibling has a much easier time getting in. This deviation from merit-based selection looks a lot like bad old cronyism but has a lot to be said in its favor. First, attending the same school may enhance sibling relationships. Second, it will be easier for families to send all their children to the same school, which would mean less time in the car (which is safer), fewer school meetings for parents to attend, less time away from work, and fewer school functions to attend. These are good reasons to deviate from merit-based selection in primary school admissions. This sort of nepotism is not morally equivalent to the bad sort of nepotism. There are many good reasons to deviate from merit-based selection—whether merit is defined narrowly or broadly.

Merit and Its Connection to Demeaning Differentiation

In this chapter, I argued against the claim that X is *entitled* to Y by virtue of his merit or that X *deserves* Y by virtue of his merit, which is what I term the *strong merit principle*. In addition, I rejected the *weak merit principle*, that selections made in accord with merit are immune from moral criticism. If so, then merit-based selection is neither necessary nor sufficient for a differentiation to be permissible. But is merit therefore irrelevant?

In this section, I want to suggest how merit may be relevant to determining whether a particular differentiation among people demeans. Merit refers to the constellation of traits that meet the needs, desires, or aims of the selecting entity. Merit-based selection—choosing those with the traits that serve an entity's ends—is *usually* not demeaning as it reflects the entity's self-understanding or goals rather than expresses something denigrating about the individuals who are passed over. For example, a college selecting students may consider high school grades an aspect of merit. This choice reflects the institution's self-understanding of its mission and so, in most instances, selection according to these criteria does not demean those who fail to get spots due to their low grades. This is true even if the college uses criteria not so clearly germane to its educational mission. Suppose it also considers athletic prowess to be an aspect of merit (which is common). Doing so expresses something about what sort of institution it is—not merely an institution of higher education but also one that values and promotes athletics. Valuing athletics is not itself problematic, nor is there any reason to criticize the institution for defining its mission thus (except from the inside), and so use of athleticism as a selection criterion does not demean those who fail to obtain spots at the school as a result. Of course, faculty, students, and alumni can themselves question whether the college should value athletics and how much it should count athleticism as an aspect of merit, but these objections are internal objections to the college's self-understanding of its aims and mission.

The prohibition on drawing distinctions among people that demean will, however, put limits on the selection criteria an institution may use and thus on the permissible conceptions of merit that can be implemented. Merit-based selection is *usually* not demeaning, but sometimes it is. For example, suppose the business leaders in a town decide to form a businessmen's club for which the membership criteria include being a man and owning a business in the town in question. Given the club's self-understanding as a busi-ness*men*'s club, it surely makes sense that it draws a distinction between male and female business owners when admitting new members. In that sense being a man *is* an aspect of merit. Nonetheless, if the club occupies a place of power or status within the town, its membership criteria may well demean women and women business owners in particular.[29] In this way, the prohibition on drawing distinctions that demean limits the conceptions of merit that can be used in selecting among people.

CHAPTER 5

Accuracy and Irrationality

In 2000, Harvard Business School Professor Myra Hart surveyed women alumnae from the classes of 1981, 1986, and 1991 and found only 38 percent worked full time.[1] Linda Hirshman's study of educated "elite" women yielded even fewer full-time employed women (less than 15 percent).[2] Suppose that Harvard Business and other graduate and professional schools decide that their admissions officers should give preference to men applicants in light of the waste of educating women who are less likely to put their knowledge and skills to productive use.

The intuition that the accuracy of classifications matters morally, and ought to matter legally, is common. For example, the requirement that one must pass the bar exam to practice law is relatively uncontroversial precisely because bar passage is thought to be a fairly good proxy for legal competency. To the extent that this requirement is controversial—when used to prohibit paralegal professionals or legal secretaries from fulfilling some functions of lawyers[3]—this is precisely because its critics object that as to some functions, filing for uncontested divorce, for example, bar passage is not well correlated with legal competency. So, as to complex legal cases and as to routine aid in form filing, critics and supporters of the differentiation between bar-passers and non–bar-passers agree that a relevant moral issue is whether bar passage is indeed a good predictor of legal competency. From the highly institutionalized to the relatively informal, this intuition is influential and persistent. When a 3-year-old complains that her preschool class is required to take naps while the 4-year-old group can either nap or play quietly, the answer that appears to satisfy her is that this is because most 3-year-olds need naps while most 4-year-olds do not. Similarly, in all fifty states the insurance business is governed by the principle of "actuarial fairness," which requires that insurers only set rates or levels of coverage for customers that are supported by data showing that such distinctions reflect actual differences in the likelihood that each customer will file a claim during the policy period.

This intuition is reflected in legal doctrine. To determine whether a classification violates the constitutional guarantee of equal protection, legal doctrine instructs that we must consider how well that classification achieves its end. Is the classification "narrowly tailored," "substantially related," or "rationally related" to its target? While each of these standards demands a different *degree* of classificatory accuracy,[4] even the most lenient—rationality review—requires that classifications be non-spurious.[5]

The term *fit* is familiar in constitutional law.[6] While it is often used loosely to mean simply a means-ends rationality, one important and pervasive meaning of the term is the narrower concept of classificatory accuracy. If a law or policy uses trait X as a proxy for trait Y, the fit requirement focuses on whether X is indeed a good proxy for Y.[7]

In this chapter I challenge the intuition that fit matters morally. To do so, I will argue first that many morally problematic classifications are fairly accurate. Second, I contend that some inaccurate classifications are not morally problematic. Third, I show that improving the degree of fit does not ameliorate the problematic nature of certain classifications. If proxies can be problematic despite their accuracy, then accuracy is not sufficient for permissibility. Moreover, if proxies can be permissible despite their inaccuracy, then accuracy is not necessary for permissibility. Finally, if tightening the fit of problematic classifications does not seem to render them less problematic, this suggests that there is no causal relationship between the accuracy and the permissibility of classifications.

Before beginning, it will be helpful to define some terms. So far, I have been using the terms *accurate, rational, non-spurious,* and *efficient* rather loosely and synonymously. It is time to be more careful. There is an important difference between the concepts of rationality and efficiency. A rational classification is one in which the proxy trait is positively correlated with the target trait. For example, the requirement that one must be at least 16 to drive is rational if and only if people 16 and older are more likely to be good drivers than people 15 and younger—or that requiring drivers to be at least 16 yields fewer accidents than not having an age requirement. To say that the classification is rational is not to say that it is accurate in all cases—there are doubtless many people 16 or older who are not good drivers and probably some kids 15 and younger who would drive quite well. A rational classification may be both over- and under-inclusive. All that is required is that it is accurate in more instances than it is inaccurate. I will use the terms rational and accurate interchangeably—rational discrimination rests on an accurate generalization.

The efficiency of a classification is a more composite idea. Some classifications are easy and relatively costless to use. Age is a good example. It is relatively easy to determine a person's age. It does not involve judgment calls and is fairly simple to verify with standard documents. Other traits that one could use to distinguish between people are more costly. Suppose one wants to hire sales personnel with good interpersonal skills because one believes that sales people with good people skills will sell more product. Determining who has good interpersonal skills may well be fairly costly. Interviewing candidates might be a good way to do it, but interviews take time and money. The efficiency of a classification takes into account these sorts of costs. A classification is efficient if the costs of employing the classification are outweighed by the benefits. If indeed sales people with good people skills are much more successful (the classification is strongly rational), it may well make sense to interview candidates before hiring them, even considering the costs.

The concept of an efficient classification can itself be ambiguous, however. At times the term *efficiency* is used to refer to an all-inclusive sense of efficiency, where the costs and benefits to society as a whole are included in the calculus. Other times, the term refers to efficiency as viewed from the perspective of the person or entity employing the classification. Though these two meanings will sometimes converge, more often they will not. For example, it might be efficient for a life or health insurance company to discriminate between insurance purchasers on the basis of genetic traits, where the traits in question are strongly predictive of disease, disability, or death. However, if prospective insurance purchasers are deterred from seeking genetic testing because they fear losing their health or life insurance and if this genetic testing could provide information that would allow more tailored health care, then the use of genetic information to distinguish between prospective insurance purchasers may not be efficient for society as a whole. Health may be compromised—a cost that would be counted if costs are viewed from the societal perspective, but that would not be relevant to the efficiency calculation of the insurer.[8]

We thus have three different concepts in play: rational/accurate classifications; efficient classifications, as viewed from the perspective of the person or entity employing them; and efficient classifications, as viewed from the perspective of society as a whole. The term *spurious*, which is usually used to refer to a generalization—discrimination being one manner of generalizing[9]—refers to those classifications that are not rational.

Perpetuating Inequality: Impermissible or Morally Troubling Rational Classifications

The first step of this argument is to show that many classifications that we would all recognize as morally troubling, if not outright impermissible, are rational, accurate classifications. For the argument presented in this chapter to be independent of the positive argument presented in Part I, I am not here claiming that the use of these classifications is wrongful because it is demeaning. Rather, I will refer to examples that I believe would be widely condemned as wrongful discrimination and easily accounted for on several different accounts. In this way, the reader can assess the strength of the argument against the moral significance of the accuracy of classifications on its own. However, acceptance of this argument strengthens support for the positive account of Part I by removing an important obstacle to its acceptance.

Today some of the clearest cases of wrongful discrimination—real and hypothetical—are (perhaps counter-intuitively) instances of rational discrimination. Despite the fact that courts have declared that race is rarely relevant to any legitimate governmental objective,[10] this claim is an aspiration rather than a reality. Unfortunately, race is often a fairly good predictor of many other traits, including whether the person was poor as a child,[11] whether the person received an adequate or inadequate education,[12] whether the person can expect to develop chronic disease or disability,[13] and whether the person is likely to have been incarcerated.[14] If any of these traits are relevant to legitimate purposes, then race may well be a rational means to achieve a legitimate end. Consider the following example: Suppose a large government employer needs workers with basic math and writing skills, for which a high school diploma should be a good predictor. Given that high school educations vary considerably in quality and thus that the diplomas they confer may differ in what they indicate about a graduate, the employer could—if the rationality of the classification were the only consideration—rationally decide to hire only white high school graduates but not African American high school graduates.

Of course in so doing the employer will miss out on many skilled African American job seekers and will end up hiring many unskilled white applicants because the proxy trait is under- and over-inclusive of its actual target group. Nonetheless, the use of the racial proxy is rational if racial categories are positively correlated with adequate and inadequate educational backgrounds. Moreover, the use of the proxy is not only rational but also efficient, as viewed from the perspective of the employer, if the cost of determining a person's race is substantially cheaper than the cost of using a more accurate proxy. For example, administering a test of basic skills to all job seekers may well more accurately predict which candidates have the necessary skills (though it too is likely to be both under- and over-inclusive with regard to the actual skills sought). However, it will be costly to use a test to screen job candidates. Although race may predict job skills less accurately than a skills test, if the costs of using the test outweigh the benefits to be gained in terms of better employees, it may make sense economically for the employer to stick with the less-accurate racial proxy.

This policy is clearly morally troubling and legally impermissible. Even to suggest that race may be a sound proxy for poor skills seems offensive. One wants to deny the *rationality* of the classification in order to emphasize and explain its wrongfulness. But doing so may merely deny important truths about our society, truths that may be important to highlight when designing social policy. Race may be a sound predictor of poor skills precisely because the schools many young African Americans attend offer an inadequate education. In other words, the fact that using a racial proxy is rational may well be the result of injustice. But the fact that the proxy's rationality results from injustice does not make it any less *rational* as a proxy, though it may make the discrimination wrongful.

Sex-based classifications are also often rational. Classifying on the basis of sex may well be supported by the data because there are "real differences" between men and women, because a history of limited opportunities for women has affected the traits they have developed, or because our society—particularly in the workplace—continues to be organized around an ideal worker who has no family-care responsibilities.[15] For example, suppose the military were to use sex as a proxy for "person with a dependent spouse" on the grounds that men are more likely than not to have dependent spouses, and thus the proxy *male* is positively correlated with the target *has a dependent spouse.* The military then might rationally adopt a policy of providing married male service members with additional benefits while requiring married female service members to establish the dependency of their spouses before providing benefits. Though use of this proxy may not be rational today, in 1973 when such a policy was challenged in *Frontiero v. Richardson*,[16] sex was likely quite strongly correlated with such dependency.

Interestingly, Justice Brennan, writing for the Court to invalidate the use of the sex-based classification, argued that the classification was invalid because it was not efficient. Taking issue with the finding of the district court that it would save administrative costs to simply assume that the spouses of male service members were dependent, Justice Brennan argued that because many of the wives of male service members were not in fact dependent, the military would save money by requiring all service members to prove spousal dependency before providing benefits.[17] Interestingly, the data Justice Brennan cites are not well chosen to prove his claim. Rather than look at whether the wives of most male service members are dependent on their husbands (and thus whether the proxy male is positively correlated with the trait of having a dependent spouse), Brennan cites data about the percentage of women in the labor market generally.[18] Perhaps the wives of male military members are more likely to adopt traditional gender roles than others. Perhaps their husbands' jobs require that the family move frequently, thus limiting their employment options. More significantly, he does not present data on *how much* money would be saved as compared to how expensive such a test would be to administer, which he must do if he is make the claim that the military would save money *overall* by testing all married service members.

These omissions are telling because they suggest that these facts would not have altered the outcome. If the wives of most male service members were in fact dependent such that the military would save money using the sex-based proxy for dependency rather than reviewing the cases of each of the married men, it hardly seems to render the use of this classification less objectionable. The wrong of *Frontiero* does not seem to lie in its irrationality or inefficiency, were the classification to be either. Catharine MacKinnon makes precisely this point when discussing the earlier sex discrimination case *Reed v. Reed*.[19] *Reed* examined an Illinois law that gave preference to male over female family members in determining which family member would serve as the administrator of an estate where the deceased had not indicated a preference. MacKinnon observes that "[i]t would have been considerably more rational, factually based, not arbitrary, and substantially related to the statutory purpose to presume that men would be the better administrators if most women were illiterate and wholly excluded from business affairs."[20]

As the above examples demonstrate, often differentiation that is clearly morally impermissible is in fact rational. American antidiscrimination law reflects this fact by forbidding rational as well as irrational discrimination. Samuel Bagenstos[21] stresses this point in explaining that the Americans with Disabilities Act [ADA] is not different in nature from other civil rights statutes. Part of the evidence Bagenstos marshals to debunk the difference between antidiscrimination law and accommodation mandates is the fact that much antidiscrimination law prohibits not merely irrational discrimination but also rational discrimination. Bagenstros emphasizes that "[i]mportant present-day problems of discrimination include rational statistical discrimination, in which employers rationally use protected-class status as a proxy for lower productivity."[22] But the law forbids the use of race and sex as proxies (and rightly so) for lower productivity, whether or not the generalization on which the proxy relies is accurate. This is so, not only in cases where the employer acts out of a desire to harm racial minorities or women or is inaccurately stereotyping but also when the employer simply wants to conduct his or her business most efficiently.[23]

The observation that much wrongful discrimination is rational is not controversial, though it is often overlooked. Because the use of race or sex, for example, as proxies for other traits can be irrational, and the disposition to use these classifications can be the product of either animus or flawed stereotyping, there is a natural desire to disapprove or disrupt these ways of thinking and acting. But these cases are over-determined. The fact that they are irrational and wrongful does not yet tell us whether they are wrongful *because* they are irrational.

Here Bagenstos provides an excellent analysis that bears repeating so that the argument of this chapter can build upon it. Focusing on the employment context, Bagenstos notes that no commentator actually defends an employee *right* to be treated as an employer's efficiency concerns would demand, and wisely so. If law required that employers treat employees in such a capitalist rational fashion, then "[a]t least where jobs are scarce, any number of exercises of corporate social responsibility would run afoul of such a right" and while "[w]e might expect the market to punish such transgressions against capitalist rationality," it would be odd to argue "that the law should do so where the *market* fails."[24] An employee does not have a claim of employment discrimination based on a deviation from the norm of capitalist rationality (efficiency as viewed from the employer's perspective) when the employer decides to hire workers from the local community, for example, nor should she.

To recap, Bagenstos emphasizes that constitutional and statutory antidiscrimination law currently forbid rational as well as irrational discrimination. This fact itself is not controversial, though there is disagreement about the centrality of prohibitions on rational discrimination. Do they constitute the "heartland"[25] of antidiscrimination law or exceptions at the periphery?[26] Moreover, and more importantly for our purposes, I do not believe there is a live controversy about the fact that such rational discrimination *ought* to be prohibited—though the reasons offered for this view may vary widely. The examples described above demonstrate that rational race and sex discrimination are often rightly prohibited. The accuracy of a classification is therefore not sufficient to establish its permissibility.

Incompetence and Stupidity: Inaccuracy Alone Is Not an Affront to Equality

That accuracy is not sufficient for the permissible use of classifications is not controversial. Most people readily admit there are instances of rational discrimination that are rightly prohibited. That other things besides rationality matter to the permissibility of using group-based generalizations may seem obvious. What is more controversial is the claim that the accuracy of classifications is not *necessary* to their permissibility or that inaccuracy or irrationality do not signal a moral problem. For example, equal protection doctrine treats rationality as a floor. Classification on the basis of suspect traits must be more than rational, but classification on the basis of non-suspect traits must be at least rational. But ought a classification's inaccuracy or irrationality alone to render it impermissible?

It is important to note at the outset that sometimes drawing a distinction among people on the basis of an inaccurate generalization is accompanied by some other feature that renders the discrimination wrong. I am not suggesting it is never wrong to use inaccurate classifications. Rather, I contend that their accuracy or inaccuracy is not why they run afoul of the requirement to treat people as moral equals. The way to test this claim is to examine cases in which there does not appear to be any other wrong-making feature at work.

For example, suppose a university adopts a policy requiring only math and science majors to complete a swimming class prior to graduation. Now it may be that there is something wrong with different graduation requirements for students in the first instance that derives from a commitment that university students ought to be treated the same with regard to such requirements. This is like the claim that everyone ought to have health insurance, regardless of health status. As such, it is an argument based on justice or on a conception of the university, but not on a concern with treating people as moral equals. The claim that all students ought to be subject to the same graduation requirements is unlikely to be defensible. Is there no reason to require that language majors take language courses, science majors take science courses, or that students with weaker writing skills complete an English composition class, and so on? Whatever the strength of such a claim, let us assume for now that different graduation requirements for students is generally permissible. Is the policy requiring only math and science majors to pass a swim test problematic?

Suppose that the generalization underlying this policy is that math and science majors are more likely to be poor swimmers than other students. Suppose, not unreasonably, that this generalization turns out to be false. Math and science majors are no more likely to be unable to swim than students with other majors. What is the nature of the complaint of the math or science major who swims well?

Although the generalization mischaracterizes her, this cannot be the basis of her complaint, as this claim would also be true of an accurate generalization.[27] After all, an accurate generalization will likely be both under- and over-inclusive. Even if a greater number of math and science majors cannot swim than social science and humanities majors, still some math and science majors swim well and some social science and humanities majors are unable to swim. Instead, she might say that because generalization is often unavoidable, the burden imposed by an accurate but somewhat over- and under-inclusive generalization is also unavoidable. However, the burden imposed by the inaccurate classification could be avoided—or at least minimized. If those in charge would simply verify their facts, she might not need to take a swimming class.

Is this a serious complaint—one that offends against the requirement that laws and policies treat people as of equal moral worth? To answer this question, let us examine what policies the university might otherwise have adopted. The university could instead have either (a) used an accurate proxy for non-swimmers or (b) treated everyone the same (by requiring that everyone take the swim class or by not requiring anyone to take it). I will consider each possibility below.

Failure to Use an Accurate Proxy

Let us suppose there is an accurate proxy for swimming ability that the university might have used instead—a swim test, for example.[28] First, it is important to remember that a swim test relies no less on a group-based generalization than does the use of a student's major to predict swimming ability. As Frederick Schauer explains when contrasting regulations prohibiting ownership of pit bulls with regulations requiring that all dogs be tested for dangerousness, any test will be based on a background assumption—"a generalization—about what is usually but not necessarily indicated about real-life aggressiveness by aggressiveness under test or clinical conditions."[29] So, the swim-test strategy is based on the generalization that people who pass the test are more likely to be competent swimmers, that swim test passage is an accurate proxy for swimming ability.

If the school had used a more accurate proxy like a swim test, this distinction (between test-passers and non–test-passers) would not *necessarily* have resulted in our student avoiding the burden of the swim class. The swim test itself is also likely to be imperfect—though accurate in the aggregate. People who pass the test are more likely (even far more likely) to be competent swimmers than people who do not. But a person must administer the test, and that person can make mistakes in judging who swims well enough to be exempted from the swim-class requirement. Moreover, our student might have been feeling unwell on the day of the test, though not so unwell that she asked to postpone the test. Perhaps she can only make it halfway across the pool before she must stop to rest. In other words, although the use of an accurate proxy by the school would have resulted in fewer people being burdened by having to take an unnecessary class, it would not have guaranteed that any particular person would not have been mischaracterized.

Second, there are good reasons for the university to use the math-and-science-major type of generalization, rather than the swim test. A swim test is costly. Someone has to evaluate each undergraduate as he or she swims across the pool. But, you might object, surely it is money well spent as a substitute for an *inaccurate* though cheaper proxy. The argument considering aggregate cost makes more sense when comparing two accurate methods of screening: one which is more costly but more accurate compared with an alternative that is less costly and less accurate. There, it is easy to see why a less-accurate but cheaper proxy might be preferred. If the cost of using the more-accurate proxy is likely to exceed the gain produced by using it, it makes sense to use the less-accurate predictor. For example, suppose that students' scores in a debating competition more accurately predict successful college performance than do students' SAT scores. Nonetheless, a college sensibly refrains from using the former, as the gain may not be worth the candle. The cost of setting up and scoring these debates is likely to be so high that they obscure the gains produced by better admissions decisions.[30]

If it often makes sense to choose a less-accurate but cheaper proxy, then it sometimes makes sense to choose an inaccurate but cheaper proxy *that the user does not know is inaccurate when it is adopted.* The inaccurate proxy may seem reasonable—either because it is based on a generalization that is supported by faulty data or because it is based on an untested generalization resulting from stereotype. In the case we are considering, it is likely to be the latter. Here is a common stereotype: Math and science types are awkward, unathletic nerds who are less likely to be competent swimmers than other college students. As stereotypes are usually condemned, it is especially interesting to see if this reliance on an untested, inaccurate stereotype renders the classification impermissible. If it does not, then the more innocuous-seeming case of reliance on flawed data is unlikely to be impermissible either.

Suppose that testing the accuracy of the proposed generalization is itself costly. If not a lot is at stake (after all it is not that terrible to be required to take a swimming class you do not need), then it may make sense for the college to continue to rely on its untested, possibly inaccurate generalization. I should note here that of course reliance on some stereotypes is morally problematic (women are bad at math and science, African Americans are more likely to be criminals than whites) but this is true whether these stereotypes are accurate or inaccurate—as discussed earlier in this chapter. If an employer were to refuse to hire women or African Americans on the basis of these generalizations, the fact that data supported the claim that there are fewer women who are exceptionally talented at math and science or that African Americans are disproportionately represented among convicted criminals would not provide a justification.

But what if the generalization on which the policy relies is not only inaccurate but also either easily testable (at little cost) or known to be inaccurate? These situations would seem to present the strongest cases on which to conclude that the person mischaracterized by this policy has a cause for complaint. But does she? In each of these cases, the university is doing something stupid or incompetent. Given the ease with which it could evaluate the policy, it should do so. Given that data already shows that math and science majors swim as well as anyone else, the university should revise its policy. But what sense of *should* is in play here? From the perspective of the university, given its aims, it makes sense to revise its policy. When the student complains, she is saying in part, "I'm harmed by this policy" and in part, "Given the university's goals, this is a silly policy." She is therefore saying that the university is making a blunder that unfortunately affects her, but this is not a complaint against the norm of fair treatment. After all, blunder-free policies are not possible, and being on the receiving end of a blunder is not the kind of harm we are entitled to avoid. Antidiscrimination is not a corrective for ineptitude.

The error at issue here is no different from errors that states, institutions, or individuals might make that can affect people adversely. Though such errors may at times give rise to a legitimate grievance, the grievance is not tied to equality. Suppose, for example, that a university (and its architects) neglect to consider the weight of the books when designing a new library.[31] As a result, the university must spend additional money to correct the library's structural design. To provide these extra funds, the university must either raise tuition or eliminate a program—both options would affect some students significantly. In this case, students are negatively affected by an error that was easily avoidable—a blunder. While the students should surely complain about the ineptness of those in charge and anyone with an interest in the university should seek to correct the decision-making process that allowed such a colossal error, I do not think that the adversely affected students have a complaint that we would recognize as a violation of rights, in particular the right to be treated as equally worthy of moral concern. Unfortunately, these are the sorts of errors we must live with—or attempt to avoid or remedy by working to insure capable people are making such decisions.

One difference between the library blunder and the swim-test blunder, however, is that the latter concerns a policy that distinguishes among people on its face (between math and science majors and other majors), whereas with the former, no such policy is at issue. This is surely true, but the question is whether that makes a difference. In drawing the analogy to the library blunder, I am trying to illustrate how the two cases are more similar than they might initially seem.

Consider another example that makes the same point—but in the context of distinguishing among students. Suppose that a university requires all students to pass a foreign-language proficiency exam prior to graduation. Most students are able to choose which language they will master. However, government department students are required to master either Chinese or Russian. These languages are harder than some of the alternatives (like French or Spanish), which makes this requirement a burden for government students. Moreover, government students have less choice about what languages will satisfy this requirement—also a burden.

The generalization on which this policy rests is that most government students will need Chinese or Russian in their work or for graduate study in the field. Suppose there is a government student who wishes to study Spanish (and wants to satisfy his language requirement by demonstrating proficiency in Spanish so that he does not have to take additional Chinese or Russian courses). He is interested in working on issues affecting Latin America. The generalization underlying the policy clearly mischaracterizes him. In addition, let us suppose (not unreasonably) that the policy rests on an error. The work of most government students does not require Chinese or Russian. Rather, to the extent that their future work or graduate study requires language proficiency, Spanish and Arabic are far more useful. Moreover, let us suppose that the fact that the policy continues to require Chinese and Russian is due to the fact that the professors in charge have simply neglected to note how the world has changed since they entered the field. The policy constitutes a blunder (based on an easily corrected inaccurate generalization). Though the students and university administrators should try to correct the policy and encourage these outdated professors to change, the students have not been treated in a way that violates a commitment to the equal moral worth of persons.

The government students are adversely affected by a policy that requires more of them than of others. In addition, it is a policy based on an inaccurate generalization—and one that could be verified fairly easily. It is a stupid policy and one that shows the government department to be rather weak and out of date. Yet something seems to be missing requisite to getting us roiled up about wrongful discrimination. We might be roiled up about ineptness (government professors should know which languages are most useful in the current political context), but unfairness or lack of equal treatment seems to require something more. Even the example of swim class requirement had a bit of a hook into the equality register. In my view, the hook lay in *the kind* of inaccurate generalization that was at work in that case. The claim that math and science majors are nerdy and unathletic seems insulting to math and science majors (perhaps even if it is accurate). It is this aspect of the generalization, I think, that makes it a possible claim of wrongful discrimination (though not a very strong one), which a claim about inaccuracy alone lacks.

Failure to Treat Everyone the Same

The university has two alternatives to continuing to use the inaccurate proxy—substitute an accurate proxy (discussed above) or treat everyone the same. Why not say that policies should always, to the extent possible, treat everyone the same? There is an extensive literature about the many ways in which same treatment policies can have extensive differential effects.[32] Much of that literature emphasizes the point that even when we decide to treat everyone the same, there remains a question about what that same treatment will be. For example, in the case of the swim-class requirement, the university could either require that all students take a swimming class or provide that no one be required to take one. Laws governing workers rights could require that all workers be permitted to take time off following the birth or adoption of a child or there could be no such requirement.[33] Feminist critics and others have emphasized that what sort of policy we adopt can have important consequences.

In addition, there are often good reasons to identify particular individuals for different treatment. Policies that treat everyone the same generally have costs. For example, in the swim-class context, if we require that everyone take a swimming class, some number of people (perhaps a very large number) will be required to take an unnecessary class. If instead we do not require anyone to take a swim class, then some number of students who could have learned to swim will not.[34] Where the costs of each of these alternatives are too high, then there are good reasons to opt for a policy of differential treatment—despite its own flaws.

Where the costs are not high, there may be a good reason for preferring same treatment. Frederick Schauer argues for such a preference, claiming that sometimes treating people as equals may require that we treat different cases the same. Schuaer commends the unlikely hero Procrustes, the road-side robber of Greek mythology who would stretch or cut passing strangers to whom he offered a bed so that everyone would fit into the one bed he had. As Schauer relates, to be "procrustean" is therefore to be "irrationally committed to uniformity, seeking to make every situation fit the same mold, just as Procrustes made every passerby fit the same bed."[35] Schauer argues that just because like cases ought to be treated alike does not thereby entail that different cases ought to be treated differently. Rather, he wants to argue—with Procrustes—that sometimes different cases should be treated the same. Part of his argument consists in showing the reader that much of antidiscrimination law does just this. The part of antidiscrimination law that forbids rational race and sex discrimination, for example, actually requires that we treat different cases the same.[36]

The need to balance these concerns is particularly relevant in the context of screening at airports, for example. On the one hand, travelers may present varying danger risks and thus there are good reasons to treat them differently. Travelers of particular ages flying between certain cities, who have previously traveled to certain countries, and so on, may be more likely to be terrorists or drug couriers. On the other hand, there are impor-tant reasons to treat all travelers the same by subjecting all to the same screening procedure. By requiring all travelers to remove their shoes and jackets and put hand luggage through an X-ray machine, we eradicate the stigma attached to being singled out for screening. After all, the burden of screening is only partly a function of the inconvenience and invasion of privacy. The stigmatic harm of being singled out for screening in cases where only some are searched is no doubt one of its most troublesome aspects.

There are often significant costs to treating everyone the same, however. Because it is impractical to search all air travelers closely, treating everyone the same (i.e., not singling any passengers out for in-depth screening) en-tails not closely searching those who are most likely to be dangerous. Be-cause the judgment about which passengers are most likely to be dangerous is based on generalizations that are almost certainly both over- and under-inclusive, some closely searched passengers will not be dangerous. Perhaps most. Nonetheless, if we do not make use of the information we have about which passenger traits are strongly correlated with dangerousness, we are likely to pay a real cost. Our current hybrid policy (searching everyone a bit, a random number a lot, and a few intensely) presumably attempts to balance these concerns. It does not eliminate them by doing a bit of each—rather it adopts a middle course by presumably setting the bar for different treatment fairly high.

A more prosaic example in which the costs of treating everyone the same outweigh the benefits of doing so are the laws that require drivers to be over a minimum age and pass a basic-skills test. These laws distinguish between people who are the minimum age or older (16, for example) and pass the test and those who are either below that age or fail the test. Rather than drawing this distinction among people (discriminating on the basis of age and test passage), we could adopt a policy that would treat everyone the same. The two alternatives in this context that would treat everyone the same would have unacceptable costs. First, we could allow everyone to drive—that is, abolish all age and skill requirements. Alternatively, we could forbid driving altogether. As neither alternative is appealing (though with the rise of global warming, road rage, and stress-related illnesses that may be attributable to commuting, one might question this conclusion), it is easy to see why we quickly migrate to a regime that attempts to treat different cases differently rather than one that treats different cases the same. However, doing so requires classification, which runs the risk of being inaccurate.

Last, there are some situations in which it is not possible to treat everyone the same—even if that were desirable. Where there are more applicants than openings, in a school or a company, for example, it is just not possible to treat everyone the same. If more people apply for jobs than there are job openings to fill, then not everyone who applies can get a job. Ditto regarding admissions to schools or universities. Judging everyone by the same criteria—those with the highest grades will be admitted, for example—is not the same as treating everyone the same (everyone gets the job). Rather, judging everyone by the same criteria is instead to distinguish among them, in this case between applicants with high grades and those without. This policy rests on the generalization that students with high grades are more likely to do better (in school or work) than others. In situations of scarcity, we may therefore simply be unable to treat everyone the same. If we must distinguish among people on the basis of attributes they have or lack, we must address the question of when or whether it is permissible to do so.

This chapter addresses the relevance of the accuracy of classification in answering this question.

Prophylactic Reasons to Consider Accuracy

Perhaps the accuracy of the generalizations is important to consider not because accuracy is itself morally relevant but instead because an accuracy requirement serves a prophylactic purpose. It may be that by mandating accuracy and forbidding irrational distinctions, we thereby do a fairly good job of blocking distinction drawing that is wrong for other reasons. Why might this be so? To achieve their objectives, the classifying person or entity has every reason to insure that the classification is an accurate proxy for the traits being sought. Sometimes the actor will fail to do so due to carelessness or ineptitude. At other times, the inaccuracy will remain because the generalization that underlies it tracks familiar stereotypes that hamper people who are already disadvantaged in our society. There is abundant evidence that people tend to overvalue observations that confirm their beliefs and undervalue observations that challenge them.[37] For example, if a supervisor holds the view that women usually stop working or cut back considerably after their children are born, he is likely to notice when a woman does precisely this and see it as confirmation of his view. However, when another woman continues working after her children are born, this case is less salient to him and to the extent that he notices it, he sees it as anomalous. An accuracy requirement helps to resist this so-called confirmation bias and helps to challenge erroneous stereotypes that may persist despite their inaccuracy. Of course, we need a theory of which instances of distinction drawing are wrong in order to assess whether this prophylactic argument for the importance of accuracy is solid. But it might turn out that accuracy is important for prophylactic reasons; in other words, forbidding inaccurate generalizations may help prevent instances of distinction drawing that are wrong for other reasons.

This argument supporting an accuracy requirement may go some way toward explaining why rationality and irrationality *seem* important. That said, the first point to note about this argument is that it is based on the desirable consequences that are predicted to flow from this prophylactic rule. Because it is not based on the claim that inaccuracy offends against the norm of treating people as moral equals, this justification for requiring accuracy does not challenge my claim that accuracy is irrelevant to the moral permissibility of a classification. Rather, prophylaxis is an argument for a particular doctrinal implementation of the norm of treating people as equals or for a prudential guide to decision makers.

Second, the claim that accuracy is important for prophylactic reasons rests on empirical assumptions that are hard to evaluate. Does a doctrinal scheme that requires accurate classifications succeed in blocking more cases that are *really* wrong than does an alternative that focuses directly on wrong-making features? We can only speculate. Moreover, the fact that this scheme would block cases that are not wrong (it will be over-inclusive) may not be troubling because only inaccurate classifications are at issue. However, the doctrinal schema may work to mask consideration of questions and issues that *are* relevant to whether a differentiation wrongfully discriminates.

Consider the following example: In *Nguyen v. I.N.S.*,[38] the Supreme Court upheld a law requiring that children born out-of-wedlock to citizen-fathers meet a higher standard of proof than those born to citizen-mothers in order to establish citizenship. The law provides that children born to citizen-mothers are automatically considered citizens as long as the mother meets minimum residency requirements, whereas those born to citizen-fathers must provide evidence that the father formally acknowledged paternity before the child became 18.[39] The law was defended on the grounds that the sex of the citizen-parent is a good proxy for two desired characteristics about the child. First, the state asserted an interest in insuring that the child be biologically related to the citizen-parent. Second, the state asserted an interest in insuring that a relationship had been formed between the child and the citizen-parent. In upholding the law, Justice Kennedy stressed that the sex of the citizen-parent was a good proxy for these traits.

As *Nguyen* involves a sex-based classification, it had to pass a heightened standard of review, one that requires more than rationality, but the point I want to make here is not affected by this fact. Justice Kennedy's opinion for the majority and Justice O'Connor's dissenting opinion focus almost exclusively on how tight is the fit between the sex-based proxy and the purported targets. If the fit between the proxy and its targets were not treated as the indispensable element in the determination of whether a sex-based discrimination is permissible, the opinion would presumably focus on other features. Kennedy's opinion stresses that "the recognition that at the moment of birth . . . the mother's knowledge of the child and the fact of parenthood have been establish in a way not guaranteed in the case of the unwed father" is "not a stereotype"—by which he presumably means an inaccurate generalization—rather it is "real"[40] and therefore permissible. O'Connor's rebuttal points out that the law condemns rational generalizations as well as inaccurate ones: "This Court has long recognized . . . that an impermissible stereotype may enjoy empirical support and thus be in a sense 'rational.' "[41] But she does not offer a coherent alternative basis for judging which accurate stereotypes are problematic and which are not.

On the one hand, O'Connor rejects the idea that "only of those overbroad generalizations that the reviewing court considers to 'show disrespect' for a class"[42] are prohibited. On the other hand, she unhelpfully suggests that "the hallmark of a stereotypical sex-based classification under this Court's precedents is not whether the classification is insulting, but whether it relies upon the simplistic, outdated assumption that gender could be used as a proxy for other, more germane bases of classification."[43] But has not O'Connor merely restated the question: *When* is it that gender can be used as a proxy? She acknowledges that rational discrimination is sometimes forbidden, but hesitates to offer alternative criteria—other than tighter fit, which most of her opinion stresses is lacking here. Notwithstanding her explicit rejection of respect as the touchstone, she closes her opinion with a comment about the majority's opinion that comes close to endorsing this idea. She find the majority's discussion "may itself simply reflect the stereotype of male irresponsibility that is no more a basis for the validity of the classification than are stereotypes about the 'traditional' behavior patterns of women."[44] But if the generalization of male irresponsibility and female responsibility for biological offspring are indeed not simply accurate but strongly accurate (so that the classification would pass even a heightened standard of fit), what is it exactly that makes this generalization problematic? O'Connor appears to suggest that it is the generalization's *content* rather than its *accuracy* that is key. However, the focus on accuracy obscures this fact—even for her.

Tightening the Fit

The discussion so far has aimed to show that accuracy is neither necessary nor sufficient to establish the permissibility of classifications. But perhaps it is a relevant factor nonetheless. In this section, I use examples, which I hope we will agree constitute wrongful discrimination, to show that tightening the fit does nothing to ameliorate their problematic features. But why think it would? So far I have said little about why accuracy has been so prominent a feature in antidiscrimination law and in our common understanding about when and whether it is morally acceptable to distinguish among people. While I am only speculating here, I believe this focus on accuracy stems from the fact that the history of racism and sexism (quintessential instances of wrongful discrimination and thus the moral lessons from which we all learned) is a history of irrational discrimination. Laws that forbid blacks from voting or sitting on juries, for example, rest on the mistaken view that blacks, as a group, lack the capacity for self-government or thoughtful deliberation. Laws that forbid women from practicing professions or owning property likewise rest on inaccurate views of women's ability to function outside the home. (Laws that disable both groups can also be viewed as intended to keep blacks and women from these spheres, whatever their abilities.) The inaccuracy of the generalizations underlying these laws is salient and thus appears to pertain to what makes them wrong.

But correlation is not causation: Three men go into a bar. One orders scotch and water, the second orders vodka and water, and the third orders gin and water. They each imbibe many of their preferred drinks. At the end of the night, they are all drunk. Not understanding much about how people become drunk, we conclude that it must be the water. After all, they all drank water and they all got drunk. So it is with the early days of antidiscrimination law. Responding to the fact that prominent instances of wrongful discrimination were based on inaccurate generalizations about racial groups and women, we have made the mistake of taking this inaccuracy to be the cause of what makes such discrimination wrong.

Let us look at two instances of wrongful discrimination—one real, one invented—to see whether increasing the accuracy of the generalization underlying a classification makes the distinction-drawing seem any less wrong. If not, this will suggest that accuracy is not *causally* related to the wrongfulness of discrimination.

In 1995, the public, bar, and legislatures began to respond to information that insurers were charging higher rates for health and life insurance for battered women. This practice was rational, as women who are being beaten by their husbands or boyfriends are more likely than the average insurance purchasers to be hurt or even killed. In fact, the insurers did not distinguish between abuse victims who had left their abusers and those who had not because the data indicated that women are most in danger of being attacked just after leaving.[45]

In my view, which I hope is shared, this practice is wrong. Insurers ought not to use a person's status as a victim of domestic abuse as a criterion in determining whether to insure her or at what rate. This is so notwithstanding the fact that the generalization underlying the discrimination is accurate. Will tightening the fit—increasing the accuracy of the generalization—ameliorate what we find troubling about this practice? I think not. Suppose that abuse victims are dramatically more likely to draw from insurance pools, especially after leaving their abusers, than are average insurance purchasers. This increase in accuracy just does not seem to matter. Rather, if anything, it highlights the need to not pile on by refusing to sell insurance to victims of injustice and cruelty. But the basic point is that increasing the accuracy does not seem to help justify the practice.

Second, imagine that a business school has conducted a survey of graduates ten years out of school and found that 60 percent of women were not in the paid labor force. Given the school's mission of training business leaders, it decides to favor men in its admissions policy. In my view this policy would be wrong. Now suppose the survey data instead revealed that 80 or 90 percent of women were no longer in the paid labor force. What does this tell us? Does it increase the justification for distinguishing between men and women applicants, as a causal relation between fit and permissibility would suggest? I think not. It would, I hope, leave us scrambling to find out why women are leaving paid employment, rather than find us endorsing policies that would block women's opportunity at the front end.

These two examples suggest that accuracy is not causally related to the permissibility of classifications. Increase the water and the fellows do not get more drunk. It must not be the water that is the problem.

Pure Arbitrariness

In Chapter 1, I began with the following example: An employer decides not to hire anyone whose last name begins with the letter A. As a result Adams is not hired. One might wonder whether our discussion in Chapter 5 has addressed the irrationality or arbitrariness of this sort of case. In this chapter, I have argued that the rationality or irrationality of a distinction (and the accuracy or inaccuracy of the generalization on which it relies) is immaterial to whether drawing such a distinction is morally permissible or impermissible. But even irrational discrimination (math and science majors must pass swim tests) is based on some reason, even if a bad one (in the sense of being inaccurate). The *no A names* criterion seems different in that it seems not based on any reason at all, not even a bad reason. What should we say about *pure arbitrariness* of this kind? Is it wrongful discrimination, and if so, does it provide a counterexample to the thesis that wrongful discrimination is differentiation that demeans, because pure arbitrariness does not seem to demean?

To say that a decision is arbitrary could thus be (a) to say that it is based on a faulty generalization, or that is it based on no reason in two distinct ways: (b) in the way a lottery is, or (c) it is based on no reason, not even a bad one, and does not result from a lottery. The reason for this disjunctive in describing the third choice is that it is difficult to capture what it is, except by saying what it is not. As (a) is discussed above, this section will focus on (b) and (c)—what I am calling "pure arbitrariness."

Let us begin with the sort of arbitrariness at play in a lottery. If there is a limited number of something to distribute and many people want it, sometimes it makes sense to use a lottery. The people whose names are selected from the hat (or whatever procedure is used) are the ones to whom the benefit is given. In other words, we distinguish among people on the basis of whether their name is arbitrarily selected or not. While lotteries are arbitrary in that there is nothing about the person playing that determines whether he or she is selected, lotteries do not fail to treat people as moral equals. In fact, a lottery by definition affords each person an equal chance to be selected. In that sense, a lottery is often said to instantiate fairness.

What about the third sense of arbitrariness—a decision based on no reason, but not resulting from a lottery? Is this sort of arbitrariness morally problematic? While the example with which I began this book—failing to hire Adams because his last name begins with A—seems to fit this description, it is hard to grasp exactly what is the nature of such an arbitrary decision. If indeed it is based on no reason at all, then it begins to approach the arbitrariness of a lottery. We are talking about a selection procedure (no As) that just happens to pop into someone's head at the moment. If certain ways of distinguishing among people randomly pop into the decision-maker's head more than others, then the choice of Baker over Adams is in fact based on a policy (prefer Bs over As)—albeit subconsciously. But if not, if the decision to forgo A names is *truly* random, then it would be just as likely to be no Bs, Cs, Ds, and so on, and thus to be equivalent to a lottery.

This method of selection is criticizable—as is a lottery—when there are reasons to apply particular criteria rather than random selection. Take, for example, the ubiquitous law student complaint that "grades are arbitrary." Sometimes lotteries are fair, indeed they are the very model of fairness, but they are not fair when there are important moral reasons to use particular criteria to draw distinctions. So William Burroughs's quip "As one judge said to another, 'Be just and if you can't be just be arbitrary' "[46] is funny precisely because a judge's arbitrary decision is unjust, even if not unfair, given the criteria a judge ought to apply. Were a law school professor to use a lottery to assign students grades (the first two selected get As, the next ten get A-minuses, the next fifteen get B-pluses, etc.), the students would have a legitimate complaint. Note however the source of the complaint. The problem is not that drawing distinctions among students in this way fails to treat the students as moral equals. Rather the problem is that the internal values of a university require that student grades be awarded in way designed to reflect student achievement and that the students have been told that this will occur and have relied on these assurances.

The students would have a similar complaint against the professor who decided which students to award A grades to on a whim, so to speak. If the decision is really arbitrary in the sense of based on no reason at all, the professor acts wrongly in that she is required by her role as a professor not to assign grades for no reason and instead to assign grades in a manner designed to fulfill some plausible educational goal.

This sort of arbitrariness is not always forbidden, however. Many roles and contexts do not require using particular criteria. Moreover, as discussed in the previous chapter, institutions are free (within the limits provided by the prohibition on drawing distinctions that demean) to adopt whatever internal values they see fit. So, for example, a university could decide to use a lottery to determine which students to admit rather than choosing on the basis of grades and test scores. Doing so would no doubt change its character (from an elite institution to something else), but it is free to do so. In fact, some magnet public high schools do use lotteries to select among the many students wishing to enroll. In doing so, they define themselves as institutions of a particular sort.

Conclusion

In this chapter I have argued that sometimes it is rational to distinguish among people on the basis of particular traits (race, sex, age, disability, etc.) but—as is reflected in antidiscrimination law in the United States and elsewhere—such differentiation is sometimes wrongful despite its rationality. To the extent that wrongful discrimination has had an effect in the world, it is likely that there will be lingering effects on the capacities of actual people here and now. Moreover, the commitment to the equal moral worth of persons covers others who are clearly "differently-abled." Distinction drawing that affects children, the disabled, and others may well be rational, but that does not yet tell us whether it comports with the commitment to honor the equal moral worth of persons. Moreover, and perhaps more controversially, drawing irrational and arbitrary distinctions among people does not, by itself, fail to treat people as moral equals. For the person affected, it is bad luck but no more. Sometimes institutions or actors have special obligations that derive from their mandates or their roles that require them to employ particular criteria in differentiating among people. Failing to comply with these norms is wrong, but is not the wrong of wrongful discrimination.

CHAPTER 6

Is It the Thought that Counts?

Women employees of Wal-Mart are suing that company for sex discrimination. They claim the company policy of allowing managers wide discretion regarding whom to ask to apply for promotion is problematic. The managers are likely to rely on stereotypes regarding the abilities of women and especially regarding whether women would be willing to relocate (as is often required for promotion). The women and their lawyers do not claim that Wal-Mart managers intentionally discriminate against women. Rather they claim that the promotion system allows unconscious stereotypes to play a role in decision making.[1]

Some commentators argue that the Americans with Disabilities Act should not be described as an antidiscrimination statute. If an employer fails to hire a disabled employee who could do the job in question because doing so would require the employer to make costly modifications to the workplace, this should not properly be described as "discrimination" (by which these commentators mean wrongful discrimination) because the employer intends only to make the most cost-effective hiring decision.

Many people believe that the intention of the person or people who enact a law or policy is crucial to determining whether the resulting law, policy, practice, or action constitutes wrongful discrimination. An actor's intention is certainly significant *legally*. But should it be? In the context of discrimination, is it the thought that counts?

To address this question, we must first separate two different ways in which the actor's intentions could be relevant. First, one might think that the intentions of the person drawing the distinction determine whether or not she is in fact distinguishing among people on the basis of a particular trait. For example, if Wal-Mart supervisors do not intend to treat women differently from men and indeed if sex-based stereotypes are operating only unconsciously, if at all, does this mean that Wal-Mart cannot be engaging in a practice that treats employees differently on the basis of sex?

Second, one might think that intentions are relevant to determining whether distinguishing among people on a particular basis is wrong. If one does treat people differently for a good reason, this is quite different than if one does it for a bad reason—or so one might think. This view underlies American constitutional doctrine's focus on what it terms *invidious intent* as the touchstone for a violation of the constitutional guarantee of equal protection. As Justice Brennan remarked in *U.S. Department of Agriculture v. Moreno*, "if the constitutional conception of 'equal protection of the laws' means anything, it must at the very least mean that a bare congressional desire to harm a politically unpopular group cannot constitute a legitimate governmental interest."[2] Though that may be so, does that illegitimate interest undermine the legitimacy of the action done for its sake? And what of the converse? Does the absence of an invidious intent insulate the action from moral criticism on grounds of equality? For example, does the fact that an employer refuses to hire a disabled employee because doing so will be costly render that action morally permissible? These questions and others relevant to these central concerns will be the focus of this chapter.

In what follows, I argue that an actor's intention does not determine whether he or she in fact distinguishes on the basis of a particular trait. We may need to understand the psychology of Wal-Mart supervisors, to get inside their heads if you will, to determine whether they distinguish among employees on the basis of sex, but we do not need to consult their intentions to reach this conclusion. The sex of the employee may be relevant to the supervisor's decisions without his even being aware of it, let alone intending that it play a role. Second, the actor's intention does not determine whether or not distinguishing on a particular basis in a particular context is in fact wrong. Here I take a strong stand against the importance of intention in two respects. I argue that a "bare desire to harm" a particular group is neither necessary nor sufficient to make an action that flows from this intention wrong. In addition, I argue that the intent to target a particular group as a means to a benign end is not morally significant either.

What Is an Intention?

As I will use the term, the actor's intention is what he or she is *aiming at*. This is the third of the three senses of intention that G.E.M. Anscombe noted in her classic treatment: "Very often, when a man says 'I am going to do such-and-such,' we should say that this was an expression of intention. We also sometimes speak of an action as intentional, and we may also ask with what intention the thing was done."[3] The first sense of intention identified by Anscombe focuses on the way in which intentions direct and constrain future action. The second contrasts intentional action with unwitting or involuntary action. The third sense identifies the aim or goal of the actor in so acting. Although sometimes these senses of intention become confused and interrelated, it is the third sense that will be our focus here. This chapter looks at the question whether what the actor aims to do matters in determining whether an action discriminates and, if so, whether it discriminates wrongfully.

Intentions as aims are different than motives as well, though I also believe that the motives of the actor are not relevant to the moral permissibility of an action. Though the terms *intention* and *motive* are often used synonymously in court decisions, *motive* refers to a desire-state—that which actually moves the actor to act.[4] Or as Anscombe put it, "A man's intention is *what* he aims at or chooses; his motive is what determines the aim or choice."[5] The question thus is whether the actor's aim—what he seeks to do—matters in assessing whether the actor distinguishes among people at all or whether it matters in assessing whether this distinguishing is morally permissible or not.

I argue that the actor's intention neither determines whether she distinguishes among people on the basis of a particular trait nor whether doing so is wrong. I am not thereby claiming that whatever goes on inside the head of the actor is irrelevant. My claim is narrower. The actor's intention, his aim or goal, is what is irrelevant, his mental processes are not. This more circumscribed claim is quite controversial nonetheless.

Intention and Identification

In an oft-quoted passage, Justice Holmes asserts that "even a dog distinguishes between being stumbled over and being kicked."[6] The passage appears to suggest that it is the intention of the actor that determines what sort of action takes place. The actor's intention has the power to transform the action from an instance of tripping to an instance of kicking. And because we assume that kicking is, generally speaking, morally wrong whereas tripping is, generally speaking, not morally wrong, this transformation is important. But this common understanding of the meaning of that passage[7] may be mistaken. After all, Holmes only needs to bother with the assertion that *even* a dog can discern the kick from the trip, unless what matters is how the *recipient* is likely to interpret the action. The logic of the passage actually works in the opposite way: If even a dog knows the difference, then a fortiori a person can be expected to know as well. Holmes therefore concedes that the way an action is likely to be perceived matters to the determination of what sort of action it is and how we ought to judge that action.

Do we need to know the actor's intentions in order to *identify* whether a law, policy, or action classifies on the basis of some particular trait? The idea behind the claim that intentions are determinative is that drawing distinctions is itself an intentional act; one can only classify or distinguish if one acts with that intention. Is that so?

There is a large body of psychological scholarship[8] that suggests that it is not. As Linda Hamilton Kreiger explains, "because race, ethnicity, and gender have been made salient by our history and by observable patterns of economic, demographic, and political distribution, people will continue to categorize along these lines," and therefore, "we can expect the resulting categorization-related distortions in social perception and judgment to bias intergroup decisionmaking."[9] While the extent of cognitive bias may be subject to dispute, it is hard to imagine that someone could deny the possibility of this sort of unconscious classification. But let me be clear about what I mean by the term *unconscious bias*—as the psychological studies relied on by Kreiger and others have recently aroused controversy.[10] A person acts with unconscious bias if she treats one group differently than another without any intent to do so, without any desire to harm either group, and without harboring any negative feeling about one group vis-à-vis the other. Unconscious bias—as I use the term—is merely the unwitting use of a trait to classify or distinguish among people.

And, if unconscious bias is possible, what ought we to say about it? If a stereotype about gender, for example, affects the way an employer makes sense of data about a particular employee, then gender is—almost by definition—affecting the decision-making process. So if Wal-Mart managers—women as well as men—unconsciously overlook women employees when considering whom to encourage to apply for promotions to jobs that require relocation, then the sex of the employee is playing a role in the manager's decision process—whether he intends it or not, or indeed whether he is aware of it or not. The employer is classifying on the basis of sex, just not consciously or deliberately. Once we strip the normative evaluation from our understanding of the descriptive inquiry, it is clear that the unintentional use of a trait to distinguish among people is not only possible but is likely to be prevalent.

Another way to approach the question of whether one can distinguish among people on the basis of particular features without aiming to do so is to ask a more general question about what sorts of actions can only be done with an intention to do that action. After all, the claim that the actor's intentions determine if she is classifying on the basis of a particular trait amounts to the claim that classification is the sort of action that can only be done when one aims to classify. First, we should note that the claim that there is a gap between intentions and actions is uncontroversial. The fact that one intends to do a particular action does not guarantee that the intended action will occur. This is true of mundane actions: The fact that I intend to write a persuasive book surely does not ensure that this book will indeed be persuasive. And it is true about classification. I may intend to classify on the basis of ability, let us say, but may not succeed in doing so for any number of reasons.

But what of the opposite direction? Here too, it is commonly the case that the nature of the action does not depend on the intentions of the actor. I can kill someone without intending to. I can shoot a basket or hurt your feelings without intending to. However, there are some actions where the actor's intentions seem constitutive. Perhaps one can only murder intentionally. But even this is not quite right. My action has to be intentional in the sense of voluntary but I need not intend to kill. And Holmes's kick distinguishes itself from the trip by virtue of the actor's intentions. Is classification like either of these examples? I think not. Murder is a moralized concept; it is to kill wrongfully where part of what makes it wrongful derives from the culpable mental state of the actor. Kicking is also a misleading example. Sometimes kicking means no more than to "strike out with the foot or feet (as in defense or bad temper or in effecting a swimming stroke)."[11] This sort of kicking need not be done with these aims or intentions. However, when what we mean by *kick* is to strike with the foot intentionally, then this is just part of the way we are using the word—as a sort of short-hand for "kick with the foot intentionally." If so, this does not suggest anything deep about kicking, it is just to say that we can use the word *kick* to mean intentionally striking.

There may well be other sorts of actions that depend on the actor having a specific intention, but why think classification is one of them? Rather, there are good reasons to think it is not. Orchestras use a screen to audition musicians to protect against the cognitive bias that Krieger describes. If you are the orchestra director and aware of the phenomenon of cognitive bias, and thus on guard against it, why still use a screen? A well-motivated director might choose to use a screen because it is so hard to avoid these errors in perception and judgment. Cognitive bias is hard to root out because it is easy to classify without intending to do so. Classification is often and easily done unintentionally.

Why Think Otherwise?

Larry Alexander argues against the view I present above. He believes that the actor's intention determines whether an action distinguishes on the basis of trait X or trait Y. His complex article *Rules, Rights, Options and Time*,[12] in which he lays out this argument, presents a useful foil. In what follows, I briefly describe Alexander's argument and then reply to it.

Alexander argues that there are many constitutionally permissible rules that have the effect of excluding people.[13] For example, the rule "the pool is now closed," excludes those who want to swim now.[14] In addition, he argues that it is also permissible for a state actor to change his or her mind about which of these constitutionally permissible rules to adopt. For example, "pool open" and "pool closed" are both constitutionally permissible rules. However, if different rules impact certain groups of people adversely, then switching between constitutionally permissible rules in a *calculated* manner may produce troubling results. Though Alexander presents his argument in terms of *constitutionally* permissible rules, it could be extended to apply to morally permissible rules. A town is morally permitted to open and close its swimming pool. But closing the pool in order to keep certain people out seems morally troubling.

For example, suppose the person in charge of determining when the town pool is open or closed opens the pool when he sees a group of white patrons approaching and closes the pool when he sees a group of black patrons approaching. Alexander argues that here the *real* rule is that whites may swim and blacks may not. In his view, "[i]t is the operative rule for constitutional [or, we could add, moral] assessment."[15] And, here is the key claim, the only way to fix the real rule is by looking to the actor's intention: "the purpose essentially defines the real rule that must be constitutionally evaluated."[16] Although the term *purpose* itself may be ambiguous—*purpose* may refer to the person's aim as he conceives it or it may refer to the best understanding of the policy's aim, viewed objectively—Alexander is clear that it is the internal motivation or aim of the actor that for him is key. He says repeatedly that it is motivation that matters and emphasizes the reasons *for which* a policy was adopted.[17]

This is an important argument. If indeed intention is necessary to distinguish this case from instances of benign switching between constitutionally permissible rules, then Alexander is right and it is the thought that counts. But it is not. Below I present two arguments against Alexander's contention that intention analysis is necessary to identify cases like the one described above.

Before doing so, however, it is important to distinguish Alexander's claim from two related claims that are significantly more modest (and more plausible). Alexander claims that the "purpose essentially defines the real rule."[18] In other words, we need to look to purpose to know what the rule is because intentions are constitutive of the action. This view should not be confused with a more modest epistemological claim. Someone might believe that whether or not a person classifies on the basis of race, sex, or some other trait is determined independently of that person's intentions and yet believe that consulting the actor's intentions is a fairly good way to find out about the real nature of the action. If people generally do what they intend to do, this may well be reasonable. Nor should Alexander's view be confused with a claim about what legal doctrine ought to require for a showing of illegal discrimination: that an intent-based test reaches the right result (where rightness is defined independently) more often than any plausible alternative.[19] Alexander's claim about the relation between intentions and classification is far more basic and constitutive.

Neither Necessary Nor Sufficient

The intention to distinguish on the basis of trait X is neither necessary nor sufficient to establish whether an actor does distinguish on the basis of that trait. Alexander argues that we need intention analysis to *determine* what he terms the *meta-rule* (here, that whites may swim but blacks may not). The first point to note about Alexander's argument is that it is circular. He assumes that the real rule *is* what the actor intends. That is why he tells the reader that the lifeguard has been instructed to display the Pool Open sign when whites arrive and the Pool Closed sign when blacks arrive. But if the example is offered as an *argument* for why intentions are relevant, we must *start* from a place that does not yet make any assumptions about what the real rule is.[20] A fairer way to present the issue would be to consider the following three scenarios and then ask oneself whether intentions matter as Alexander supposes.

> *Scenario 1:* A lifeguard on duty displays the Pool Open sign when whites arrive to swim and the Pool Closed sign when blacks arrive to swim.
>
> *Scenario 2:* Same as above, plus the lifeguard is switching the rule in order to keep blacks out.
>
> *Scenario 3:* Same as 1, plus the lifeguard is not switching the rule in order to keep blacks out.

If no other plausible explanation is offered (as Alexander's example assumes), the rule in all three cases may be the same. There are two points here. First, we do not need to know the actor's intentions to define the meta-rule. Sometimes it is determined from what takes place. Second, the *real rule* can be different from what the actor intends. In Scenario 3, notwithstanding the fact that the actor may not intend to keep blacks from swimming, if he consistently opens the pool for whites and closes it for blacks, then the real rule is that the pool is open for whites but not for blacks. Of course, this scenario is puzzling. We want to ask, but then why *is* he opening the pool when whites arrive and closing it when blacks arrive? It could be that he intends to close the pool when he believes it is getting too crowded and does indeed close it when blacks arrive to keep it from getting too crowded. However, subconsciously, he perceives the pool as too crowded when a group of exclusively black patrons arrive and perceives it as not too crowded when a group of white patrons arrive (and perhaps when a group of blacks and whites arrive at the same time).

In making this claim, am I thereby endorsing "disparate impact"[21] as the test for what the rule is—and thus for what counts as wrongful discrimination? Yes and no. Yes, in that in the analysis I offer it is the features of the action, law, or policy that matter and the disparate impact is one such feature. But no, in that this approach does not commit me to the view that disparate impact is the *only* or even the *central* feature that matters.[22] If race played a role in the actor's decision without his being conscious of it, then this establishes the real rule, notwithstanding the lack of intention to distinguish on the basis of race. In addition, even if race played no role in the decision, at either the conscious or unconscious level, if the pool is consistently open when whites arrive to swim and closed when blacks arrive to swim, and there is no apparent good reason for this pattern, then the "real rule"—to use Alexander's term—is that the pool is open for whites but not for blacks.

Alexander might respond to this critique by pressing a more ambiguous case. Consider the following example, drawn from another thought-provoking article by Larry Alexander (here with Kevin Cole).[23] A hypothetical state-supported law school in the Plains states adopts a policy favoring regional applicants. It does so, however, because this policy will decrease minority enrollment, which the school would like to do because it turns out that the LSAT overpredicts the performance of minority applicants (these are the, admittedly bizarre, facts assumed by Alexander and Cole in their article). By decreasing the number of minority students admitted, the law school will thereby enhance the performance of its students.[24]

Two questions are raised by this hypothetical. First, is Alexander right that the *real rule* here is "limit minority applicants" (as an intent analysis might suggest) rather than "prefer local applicants"? If we do not *assume* that the intention defines the real rule, it is not at all clear that the real rule is "limit minorities." It is important to distinguish the rule from the reason for adopting the rule. A more natural way to describe this case would be to say that the rule is "prefer local applicants" but that the intention in adopting the rule is to limit minority applicants (to boost overall student performance). Where the external features of the policy do not manifest the intention, to say that the real rule is defined by the goal for which it is adopted is to merely assert his view and at the cost of some fairly counterintuitive formulations.

The second question raised by this example is more serious. If the rule "prefer local applicants" is adopted to limit the enrollment of minority students, does this reason itself provide grounds for holding the policy impermissible? This issue—whether problematic intentions are relevant to the *evaluation* of a law, policy, or decision—will be considered later in this chapter.

Facial Discrimination, Disparate Impact, and Intent

Intention matters, for Alexander, in order to determine the real rule. By this he means that intention is necessary to determine whether a law or policy classifies on a suspect basis or not (i.e., on the basis of race, sex, or something else that the law requires courts to scrutinize). Alexander is not interested in the motive for classifying (in the way that affirmative action is often described as benign discrimination). Rather he is only interested in using intention to determine whether the real rule is one that classifies on a suspect basis or not (for whatever reason). As a result, for Alexander there is a fairly firm line between cases that in legal doctrine are called "disparate treatment" and "disparate impact."[25] Disparate treatment cases are those in which the law, policy, or action explicitly draws a distinction on the basis of a characteristic legally recognized as suspect. Disparate impact cases are those in which the law, policy, or action does not explicitly classify on the basis of a suspect trait but in which the effect of the law, policy, or action is felt disproportionately and negatively by disadvantaged groups.

Disparate treatment cases are not Alexander's focus, presumably because in these laws or policies the fact that the law classifies on the basis of a suspect trait is obvious and thus inquiry into intent unnecessary. But can Alexander distinguish between disparate impact and disparate treatment cases in this hard-and-fast way and cabin the use of intent analysis to disparate impact cases? If not, this may reveal something problematic about Alexander's argument for the claim that the actor's intention determines what the real rule is.

Let us begin by looking a bit more closely at how Alexander detects the "real rule" at work in disparate impact cases. In discussing policies adopted at California universities to promote diversity in the wake of proposition 209 (which prohibits race-based affirmative action), Alexander says the following:

> Administrators who select facially nonracial admissions criteria "in order to promote racial diversity" are not avoiding the law but are violating it. They are choosing close proxies for race for racial reasons, and we must assume that if the reasons remain constant over time, the proxies will change if necessary. . . . The real rule is "admit so as to promote racial diversity," which is forbidden.[26]

To determine the real rule, Alexander looks to the actor's intent. If a university wants to admit some percentage of minority applicants but is forbidden from explicitly classifying on the basis of race, the school might instead adopt a facially neutral policy like "admit the top 10 percent of all high school graduates." Alexander claims that this policy *is* a racial classification itself. This is the odd and strongly counterintuitive implication of his view that I highlighted in the previous section. On what *basis* does he determine that this is the real rule, notwithstanding the evidence provided by the policy itself? He determines that the real rule is "admit so as to promote racial diversity" because over time the proxies used to achieve this goal will change. In other words, because the top 10 percent rule is likely to be retained only so long as it serves the diversity goal, we ought to conclude that the real rule is "admit to promote racial diversity" rather than "admit top 10 percent."

However, this analysis can also be used to show that rational race or sex discrimination is not actually race or sex discrimination at all. So-called rational race or sex discrimination refers to using race or sex as a proxy for some other trait where race or sex correlates positively with that other trait. For example, suppose a state employer refused to hire women because in general women decline to work the long hours that are required by the jobs in question. Here sex is being used as a proxy for willingness to work long hours.[27] Is this policy an instance of distinguishing among job candidates on the basis of sex? Alexander's analysis would seem to suggest that the answer is no. As in the Proposition 209 example, Alexander would have to say that one cannot simply look at the face of the rule or policy, rather, one must discover the "real rule." To do so, according to Alexander, one looks at the actor's intent. In particular, one looks at whether "the proxy will change as necessary" to accommodate the underlying purpose. In the case of rational sex discrimination (or rational race discrimination), the underlying purpose is to hire the most cost-effective worker. Alexander's analysis would therefore imply that the real rule is "do not hire people unwilling to work long hours" rather than "do not hire any women." As such, this is simply not a case of picking candidates on the basis of sex at all, following the logic of Alexander's argument.

The problem here is that Alexander's analysis fuses the normative question of whether the discrimination is permissible with the interpretive question of what sort of classification is being used (i.e., what the "real rule" is—to use his term). Alexander would have to conclude that the employer who refuses to hire women because they generally will not work long hours does not distinguish on the basis of sex. This seems just plain wrong. If the rationality of the classification matters—which it does to some commentators and not to others—surely it relates to the moral or legal permissibility of the classification, not to whether this is a gender classification at all.

To summarize the points discussed thus far: First, intention is not necessary to identify the *real* rule at work in a law. Evidence about the action itself will suffice to identify troubling cases. Neither is intention sufficient. The pattern of rule switching that is motivated by an intent to keep blacks out is not necessarily different from one that is not. To insist that it is different is not really to make a claim about the need to consult intentions to *identify* the rule at work but instead to make a claim about how one ought to *evaluate* a rule that is motivated by bad reasons—a claim that will be explored below. Second, the claim that one needs to look at the actor's intent to discover the "real rule" leads to the counterintuitive conclusion that facially discriminatory laws that discriminate rationally (and perhaps others) do not really classify on the basis of sex or race (or whatever else). On this view, the real rule is defined by the proxy's target (hire the most productive employee, for example). This account seems wrong. Either the actor's intent matters in disparate treatment and disparate impact cases in determining what the real rule is, which leads to unsupportable conclusions, or evidence about the action itself determines the real rule in both types of case.

Private Bias

One kind of case continues to be troubling to the account I have provided—that in which the actor uses race or sex (or something else troubling) as a criterion in a way that eludes detection. Imagine that an employer follows a policy of hiring the candidate she judges to be the best qualified but in the case of a tie, she hires the white job seeker. Because the employer uses race only to break ties, the manifestation of this policy may not suggest that race has played a role. Another employer for whom race was not a factor could easily have chosen to hire the same applicants as the first employer, but for other reasons. It seems that what we should say about this example is that the "real rule" is that race plays a role in the selection process. To do so, however, must we consult the actor's intentions, as Alexander supposes?

To answer this challenge, consider two different employers, A and B. Employer A decides that where two job seekers have equivalent relevant credentials, she will favor the white job seeker. In adopting this policy, she makes a deliberate choice that race will play a role in her employment decisions. B, by contrast, chooses the candidate he thinks is best qualified. However, he consistently devalues the accomplishments of non-white candidates and is unaware that he does so. The bias is small (which partly explains why it continues, unrecognized by B), and leads to the same employees being selected over time as by employer A. In these cases, I think it is fair to say that A intentionally uses race as a factor in decision making while B does not. B is not even aware of the fact that race is relevant to his decision making process and he surely has not adopted the preference for non-whites as a reason for action. If, following Alexander, we say that the "real rule" in the case of employer A is "choose the best candidate, but in case of ties choose the white person" *because* this is what employer A intends, then what must we say about employer B? It seems we must say that the "real rule" used by B is "choose the best candidate"—as that is what he intends. Yet, that does not seem right.

The real rule in both cases uses race as a factor that is relevant to the decision-making process. Though we might blame employer A and not B, as the actor's intentions may be relevant to a judgment of the actor (about this issue I take no stand), that does not mean that the actor's intentions determine what *action* the actor has indeed taken. Both A and B use the race of the job seeker as a factor in their decision making. To determine what the real rule is we need to know whether race was a factor, not whether the employer intended race to be a factor. Race was a factor for B as it was for A, notwithstanding the lack of B's intention to make it so.

This example raises the question of whether there is a difference between a rule such as *pick the best candidate but in the case of a tie, choose the white candidate* and a biased application of the rule *choose the best candidate*. I am not sure that there is. If the biased application is a one-time occurrence (due to a substitute decision maker, for example), we are more apt to describe it as a biased application of the rule *choose the best qualified candidate*. But if the decision maker is routinely biased, then it makes more sense to say that the rule is *choose the best candidate, but in the case of a tie, choose the white candidate*. The concept of a rule itself requires some regularity. This discussion does raise one further point. If the racial criterion plays an especially small role, at some point its role will become de minimus.

In sum, an approach that privileges intentions allows the actor's conscious choices to be determinative of the real rule, to use Alexander's term. However, because what an actor does can be different from what she intends (as in the pool-closing case) and because cognitive bias can affect perception and judgment, an actor's intentions do not determine the real rule she follows.

Now of course there remains an important practical problem. How should a court (or anyone else judging another's action) determine what the real rule is? How is anyone to know that race was a criterion in the decision making for both A and B, because the criterion is private, even obscure to the person using it? The first thing to note about this issue is that it presents a question at the level of doctrinal implementation only, not about what factors *really* matter to a determination of what the real rule is. As the aim of this chapter has been to argue against the claim that intentions *really* matter, establishing this much is sufficient to the philosophical issue addressed here.

That said, let me offer some brief thoughts about the question of doctrinal implementation. Someone might argue that a doctrinal approach that focuses on intentions is the best approximation of the factors that really determine what the real rule is—after all in many cases what that actor intends and what she does will be the same. Although this approach may initially seem plausible, it is far less so than it initially seems. First, intentions themselves are non-public and thus difficult for a challenger to establish. Therefore, this approach does not have even the legal virtue of administerability. Second, there are good reasons to think that the intended act and the actual act will often come apart—either because cognitive bias is pervasive or because the social context in which people act has a powerful impact on what that action actually is.

Intention and Evaluation

If the actor's intentions do not determine whether a law, policy, or decision *classifies* on the basis of a particular trait, perhaps the actor's intentions determine whether a classification is wrongful. This claim seems more promising. To address it, I start by examining a related debate. The claim that an actor's intentions can affect whether or not an action is permissible or impermissible plays a prominent role in what is known in the philosophical literature as the Doctrine of Double Effect (DDE). This doctrine—and the claim that underlies it—has generated significant controversy. Because much of the debate focuses on whether the actor's intentions can determine the wrongfulness of the action, a closer look at that debate may be useful here.

According to the Doctrine of Double Effect, actions that will cause harm are sometimes wrong and sometimes not depending on whether the harm is intended or instead merely foreseen. The DDE originates in the Catholic Just War doctrine, and thus the example most often used to illustrate it is the wartime contrast between the strategic bomber and the terror bomber.[28] The strategic bomber intends to bomb a legitimate military target (a munitions factory, for example) but foresees that in doing so nearby civilians will also be killed. The terror bomber, by contrast, intends to kill civilians. To make the cases equivalent except for the actor's intentions, the example generally requires that we suppose that the war is a just war, the same number of civilians will die in each case, and the probability that the civilians will die is also the same in both cases. According to the DDE, the strategic bombing is morally permissible whereas the terror bombing is not—an intuition that is supposed to be widely shared—*because* the strategic bomber does not intend for the civilians to die, he merely foresees that they will, whereas the terror bomber intends the death of the civilians. As Judith Thomson restates the doctrine (which she calls the Principle of Double Effect [PDE]), "PDE tells us that if the good effect of the act is proportionately good enough, then an agent may morally permissibly perform the act if, while foreseeing the bad effect, he intends only the good effect and does not intend the bad one, either as an end (i.e., for its own sake) or as a means to the good effect."[29] Because the strategic bomber does not intend for the civilians to die either as an end in itself or as a means to some other end, bombing the munitions factory is permissible. The death of the civilians is truly collateral damage—a regrettable side effect of a legitimate aim. The terror bomber by contrast aims to kill the civilians. Because his intention is to bring about their deaths, his action is impermissible.

A second and more controversial sort of case in which the DDE is used to explain and justify a supposed moral difference between a pair of cases can be found in the area of physician-assisted suicide. Here critics of assisted suicide insist on the importance of the distinction between injecting drugs to hasten death and injecting drugs to provide sufficient palliation, where death will be the predictable result (often called "terminal sedation"). To those for whom these cases are meaningfully morally different, this difference seems to be accounted for by using the DDE. In the case of injecting drugs to bring about death, the actor's intention is to kill the patient. By contrast, in the terminal sedation cases, the aim of the actor is to relieve the patient's suffering. The death of the patient, while a foreseeable consequence of injecting the palliative drug, is thus merely a consequence of a legitimate goal.

Justice Rehnquist relied on precisely this account in explaining why the decision in *Vacco v. Quill*,[30] sustaining the New York law forbidding assisted suicide, would not thereby make terminal sedation illegal. He began by asserting that the legal system in general uses an actor's intentions as a way to distinguish between actions.[31] In support of this claim, he relied on examples from criminal law in which the actor's state of mind determines the level of offense and, perhaps because *Vacco* was an equal protection case, on that doctrine's insistence that drawing distinctions among people is only impermissible when a policy is adopted "because of" and not merely " 'in spite of' their unintended but foreseen consequences."[32] Drawing explicitly on the DDE, Rehnquist argued that terminal sedation is meaningfully different from assisted suicide because the state "may permit palliative care related to that refusal [of medical treatment], which may have the foreseen but unintended 'double effect' of hastening the patient's death."[33]

Critics of the DDE object to this account of the moral difference between pairs of cases by pointing out that it seems odd, if not outright absurd, to insist that it is the actor's intentions that make the moral difference. The objection runs something like this.[34] Suppose a doctor is considering giving her patient a high dose of painkiller and comes to you for advice (in your capacity as a member of the hospital ethics committee). The doctor tells you the patient has requested the drug and the patient recognizes that giving sufficient medicine to provide palliation will likely cause his death. The doctor also relays that the patient's condition is terminal and there are no alternative treatments available (and any other relevant information about the patient and his condition). Before giving your opinion about the case, should you ask the doctor a further question about her intentions? Should you say, well, it depends on what you intend; if you intend to bring about the death of the patient, then you may not administer the drug but if you intend merely to provide pain relief, then you may go ahead?

This objection is powerful because the permissibility of providing the drug seems to turn on factors outside the head of the person administering it. What matters instead are factors about the patient and his situation: has he requested the drug, is his condition terminal, is he in terrible pain, and so on. Asking the doctor about her intentions seems superfluous.

This is a compelling objection to the claim that the actor's intentions are relevant to the moral permissibility of assisted suicide. Still, the point seems at first hard to transfer to the discrimination context. Discrimination is different in that it often occurs in situations where the actor has *discretion* about which of several possible people to choose or policies to adopt. There is often no single right outcome (analogous to giving the patient the drug) that is morally required or forbidden. Rather, several policies or decisions are permissible. Moreover, what is forbidden is not a particular outcome but the use of particular criteria in decision making.

This fact need not indicate that the actor's intentions determine whether an action is wrongful, however. Tim Scanlon's account of where the DDE goes wrong is useful in explaining why. For Scanlon, a moral principle contains within it a specification of the reasons that count as exceptions to it. If we follow the principle, we take the reasons that count as exceptions to the general statement as our guides to action. If we fail to take these reasons as guides to our actions (i.e., if we act with different intentions), we act wrongly. But, as Scanlon explains, "what makes our action wrong is not the reason on which we acted (i.e., our intention) but, rather, *the features of the action and its circumstances* that the principle identifies as decisive reasons against it."[35] Scanlon provides the following example, which clarifies the rather subtle distinction he is making.

> Suppose that I have promised to do something, and that under the circumstances this counts as a decisive reason for doing it. In particular, the fact that I could benefit financially from breaking the promise is not a sufficient reason to fail to keep it. But suppose I break it anyway, in order to get this benefit. In describing what was defective about my action, you might say that I acted wrongly in taking my own advantage as sufficient reason to break my promise. But, at a more fundamental level, what made my action wrong was not the reason I acted on but the reason counting against so acting. The act was wrong because the fact that I promised made it the case, under the circumstances, that I should do the thing in question.[36]

An analogous account can explain the wrongfulness of wrongful discrimination cases as well. Suppose an employer prefers white candidates. He consciously and deliberately chooses white candidates over candidates of color. Following Scanlon's account, what makes this wrong is not the fact that the employer *intends* to hire whites. Rather, what makes the action wrong is that skin color ought not to be a factor affecting the hiring decision. It is not the intention that is relevant, rather it is the fact that the race of the job candidate affects a decision when it should not.[37]

Now pair this account with the fact of cognitive bias. In the above section, we established that people classify on the basis of race, sex, or other traits without intending to. In other words, race- or sex-based traits can influence decision making without cognitive awareness. And, if what makes an action wrong is the fact that race is playing a role it ought not to play, then what makes such an action wrong is not the actor's intentions but the fact that racial categorization played a role in the decision making that it ought not to have played.

It is important to pause over this point because it is this sort of case that inspires the view that intention must be relevant to the evaluation of claims of wrongful discrimination. Most people agree that where an action is morally required, tossing the life preserver to the drowning person, for example, the action is right whether one does it to save the person or to get a hoped-for reward. Drawing distinctions among people seems different however. This is because wrongful discrimination often occurs in contexts where no one particular action is required. In the employment context, often no one particular person is clearly the best qualified, nor is the employer required to choose the best-qualified candidate. In such cases, it often seems that what is forbidden therefore is acting with a particular intention (hire only whites) or from a particular motive (racism). Scanlon's insight—although it does not deal with a context in which there are multiple permissible actions—exposes the confusion behind this intuition. Although multiple actions are permissible, some actions—properly described—are forbidden, such as, for example, using race as a criterion in selecting employees (except under well-defined and limited circumstances).

Steven Sverdlik disagrees.[38] He argues that discrimination presents one of the kinds of cases in which motivation has moral significance. He uses the example of a seller who refuses to sell his house to a prospective buyer because the buyer is black. Sverdlik believes that because the seller could refuse to sell to the buyer for other reasons (lack of credit worthiness, for example) or could simply take his house off the market altogether (because he has second thoughts and decides to keep the house) and thus is not obligated to sell his house to this would-be buyer, it must be the case that the actor's motives make the moral difference—turning a morally permissible action (refusing to sell for the two latter reasons) into a morally wrong action (refusing to sell because the buyer is black). But is it really the actor's motives (as Sverdlik thinks) or intentions that matter?

Where multiple actions are permissible—selling or refusing to sell to this buyer, for example—reasons do matter, but let us look more closely at how they matter. It is morally impermissible for the race of the buyer to affect the seller's decision. Thus the seller may decide to sell or not to sell for a myriad of permissible reasons, but he may not refuse to sell to the buyer because of the buyer's race. If the buyer's race affects the seller's decision, a wrong has occurred. Neither motives nor intentions matter in that it does not matter whether the actor desires or is motivated by race nor whether his goal is to refuse to sell to a black buyer. What matters is whether indeed the race of the buyer was a factor in his decision, whether he wanted it to be or intended it to be or not. If race played such a role, the action is wrongful.

The claim that one must intend to wrongfully discriminate in order to do so is based on the claim that to classify wrongfully one must intend to do so. But if one can *classify* unintentionally, why think that *wrongful* classification requires an intent to classify on a particular basis? The argument against the importance of the actor's intentions breaks the link between the actor's autonomy and the wrongfulness of the action. Sometimes we treat people unfairly even though we do not mean to do so. Often, it is not the thought that counts.

The Relevance of Invidious Intent

There is an important ambiguity in the claim that intentions matter to whether discrimination is wrongful. Often when we distinguish among people on the basis of a particular trait, we use that trait as a proxy for another trait, which I call the *target*. We could say that the actor's intention in classifying on the basis of trait X is to identify people with trait Y (the target). The actor's intention then is to select people with the target trait, Y. In addition, there is a reason that the actor aims at Y. That reason could also be described as the aim of the actor. He intends to classify on the basis of X trait, in order to pick out people with Y trait, for Z reason.[39] For example, if a state law school adopts a regional preference in order to reduce the number of black students admitted, in order to raise student performance, the school uses the *proxy* "local" to aim at the *target* "non-black" because it wants to raise student performance (the purpose or goal).[40] If an employer refuses to hire a disabled job candidate in order to avoid hiring an employee who will have high medical costs in order to increase the firm's profitability, the employer uses the proxy "disabled" to aim at the target "employee with high medical costs" in order to increase firm profitability (the purpose or goal). If the actor's intention matters to the moral permissibility of the action, is this because the intended target matters[41] or because the purpose or goal matters? Below, I will consider each possibility in turn.

The Target

To isolate whether aiming at a problematic target is relevant to whether a law or policy is permissible, let us begin with an example in which the law uses a benign proxy to aim at a problematic target for a good (or at least permissible) reason. Alexander's regional law school provides an apt example. In that case, as you will recall, the school authorities decide to adopt a regional preference in order to decrease the number of black students admitted. This is the problematic target: local student is used as a proxy for the target non-black. The reason that motivates this decision, however, is benign. The school has found (through the experience of a law school in a nearby state) that the LSAT over-predicts the performance of black students as compared with white students. Though these facts present an unlikely scenario, it is a useful hypothetical to test our intuitions about whether and how the use of a suspect target matters.

If we are trying to assess whether the intention to exclude blacks matters to the determination of whether the policy is wrongful, we should first assume that the policy does not have its desired effects. Suppose it is adopted for the reasons specified, but the demographics of the two states are sufficiently different so that this regional policy does not in fact have a negative impact on blacks. Here, to hold that the proxy's target renders the law impermissible would seem to fetishize the purity of the actor's motive. If we are not in the business of judging the virtue of policy makers, this ineffectual attempt to exclude blacks seems irrelevant. More interesting and troubling is a case in which the proxy does reach the desired target—fewer blacks are admitted. In such a case, does the intent to raise student performance via reducing the number of blacks matter to assessing the permissibility of this policy?

Alexander and Cole believe that intent is crucial in such a case because without looking at intent we are unable to distinguish this policy from the benign adoption of a local preference. In other words, Alexander and Cole believe that an intent standard is required to support what they term the "anti-discrimination principle" by which they mean the rule that some rational race and sex discrimination is forbidden.[42] If one can *get around* the prohibition on rational race and sex discrimination by substituting a close proxy for race or sex, then the prohibition is useless, or so they argue. Thus, Alexander and Cole argue that the intent principle "is necessary to prevent easy circumvention of the Anti-Discrimination Principle."[43]

But is this right? The only way to know whether the school is classifying on the basis of residency to restrict the number of blacks (to raise student performance) *is* to consult intentions. But this merely states the obvious. The only way to know the school's intentions is to look at the school's intentions. As an argument for why these intentions are relevant, it is a nonstarter.

To begin to think about whether this intention ought to be relevant to the permissibility of this policy, consider the following variation on Alexander's example. Suppose that the school adopts the preference for local applicants in order to enhance student performance but without recognizing why this works. After the fact, however, studies demonstrate that the reason the local preference enhances student performance is because it lowers the number of minority candidates admitted, which in turn enhances student performance. Now what? Should the school repeal the policy? If you are the school official responsible for deciding what to do, how should you think about this question? If Alexander and Cole are correct that it is the intent to use locality as a proxy for race that is problematic, then it would seem that the administrator need not worry in this case. The policy of her school was adopted without this intention and so is not wrongful. Remember, I am not considering the issue of what sorts of actions might make one vulnerable to suit in the real world or what prophylactic or defensive actions might well be prudent. Rather, the aim is to consider when drawing distinctions among people is or is not wrongful.

Instead, and taking a page from Scanlon, the school administrator should think about the question in this way: Is enhancing student performance an adequate reason to prefer local applicants when this policy works by lowering the number of minority candidates admitted? Now, of course, a school administrator who does not know that the policy works this way will only be able to ask herself this question: Is enhancing student performance an adequate reason to prefer local applicants? Her lack of knowledge may well be relevant to our assessment of praise or blame of her, but it is not relevant to our assessment of the policy itself. If the policy works to enhance performance by limiting minority enrollment, this is a feature of the policy that must figure in our assessment of its permissibility whether it is known or intended by the actor or not. Thus, when this fact comes to light, the administrator judging the permissibility of the policy ought not consult her (or the school's) intentions to determine whether she ought to repeal the policy. Rather, she ought to ask the first question posed above: Is enhancing student performance an adequate reason to prefer local applicants when this policy works by lowering the number of minority candidates admitted?

Is it not worse to reduce minority enrollment *deliberately*? That depends what is meant by "worse." If the answer to the above question is that it *is* wrong to enhance student performance via a local preference that lowers minority enrollment, then to try to evade the law (assuming it is unlawful as well as wrong) reveals something vicious in the character of the actor. She acts in a way that shows she thinks she is above the law. However, if it is wrong to enhance student performance via a local preference that lowers minority enrollment, then it is wrong to do it unintentionally as well as intentionally—and neither *action* is worse than the other. Similarly, it if is permissible to do so, then it is permissible to do so intentionally.

Alexander and Cole fuse the questions of how we ought to judge the actor and the action by using the term *circumvention*. The term suggests a crafty evasion of the law that reveals something distasteful in the actor. If we are careful not to let this distaste for the actor bleed into our judgment of the action, we can address the question of circumvention more carefully.[44] Whether or not the use of locality as a proxy for race, which is a proxy for student performance, is indeed a circumvention of the prohibition on rational race discrimination, depends on what it is, exactly, that is forbidden by a prohibition on rational race discrimination.

At least two possibilities come to mind—each of which would have different implications for the question whether the use of locality as a proxy for race, which is in turn used as a proxy for performance, ought to be forbidden. Before I discuss them, I want to pause to emphasize that although this example and discussion focuses on rational race discrimination, the same observations and inquiries would apply to rational sex, disability, or other forms of rational discrimination. For ease of exposition, I will focus on rational race discrimination. The prohibition on rational race discrimination forbids generalizing over race even when the generalization is supported by available data. Thus, though race may be as good a proxy for a desired outcome (school or job performance, for example) as other indicia like grades or experience, we forbid the use of race as a proxy in most instances. In doing so, however, what exactly do we forbid? At least two possibilities come to mind: Perhaps we forbid (a) the use of race as a proxy to disadvantage or (b) the explicit or near-explicit use of race as a proxy to disadvantage.

The choice between these two conceptions of what rational race discriminations forbids will depend on why one believes rational race discrimination itself ought to be forbidden. If the problem with rational race discrimination is that it tends to support and entrench the racial hierarchy of our society—an anti-caste understanding of antidiscrimination norms[45]—then the prohibition on rational race discrimination forbids (a). If instead the problem with rational race discrimination is that generalizing over race tends to reify racial categories or expresses denigration of racial minorities,[46] then the prohibition on rational race discrimination may forbid something more narrow, something like (b). These are not meant to be exhaustive formulations or explanations, just exemplary.

If the prohibition on rational race discrimination forbids (a), then the use of locality as a proxy for race as a proxy for performance ought also to be forbidden. Intending to use locality as a proxy for race in this way would indeed be an attempt to circumvent the prohibition on rational race discrimination by carrying it out in a manner that is hard to detect. But, it is not the intent to circumvent that makes it wrong. On this understanding of what makes rational race discrimination wrong, the use of locality as a proxy for race is wrong, whether it is intended or unintended.

On the other hand, if the prohibition on rational race discrimination forbids (b), then the use of locality as a proxy for race as a proxy for performance is not wrong. A policy that privileges local applicants as a way to enhance student performance does not express denigration of racial minorities or reify racial categories because race is not used explicitly and because a local preference is not understood in a racialized manner. On this understanding of what makes rational race discrimination wrong, enhancing student performance is an adequate reason to prefer local applicants even when the policy works by lowering the number of minority applicants.

Perhaps a few more examples will make this point clearer. Consider the practice of redlining, in which a mortgage lender refuses to lend money to homebuyers in specific neighborhoods. Suppose that this practice increases loan performance overall and does so because neighborhood is well correlated with race, which, in turn, is correlated with loan performance. I do not mean to assert that this is true. Rather, I use this example, and assume the truth of these suppositions. In rejecting an approach that makes the actor's intentions relevant, I argue that we need not ask whether the lender, in adopting the neighborhood exclusions, intends to exclude buyers of color. Instead the relevant question is this: Is enhancing loan performance an adequate reason to refuse loans to people buying houses in certain neighborhoods when this practice succeeds in improving loan performance by limiting the number loans offered to non-white home buyers? Using this approach, the moral permissibility of redlining does not depend on the actor's intentions.

The objective approach I advocate here also does a better job of making sense of the sort of case in which it is unlikely that the actor specifically intends the proxy/target relationship that is supposed to be troubling. Consider exclusions of persons capable of becoming pregnant. Suppose an employer were to exclude persons capable of becoming pregnant from certain jobs because that trait is well correlated with susceptibility to injury in the workplace. If persons who are capable of becoming pregnant are more likely than the average worker to be injured by the hazardous work environment, or, if injured, more likely to suffer a serious injury (miscarriage or impairment of the developing fetus, for example), then the proxy *person capable of becoming pregnant* may well be correlated with the target *likely to be injured in the workplace*. If we simply ask the question whether limiting the number and seriousness of workplace injuries is a sufficient justification for refusing to hire persons who are capable of becoming pregnant, we miss something important about this practice. In truth, it is hard to really miss it as we cannot comprehend the classification *persons capable of becoming pregnant* without recognizing its overlap with the category *women*. But if we could somehow see it as just that—persons capable of becoming pregnant— we would miss something that is relevant to its permissibility. What we ought to ask, in considering its moral permissibility, is this: Is limiting the number and seriousness of workplace injuries a sufficient reason to refuse to hire persons capable of becoming pregnant when that proxy works by excluding women? Whatever one's resolution of the question, the fact that it is women only who are capable of becoming pregnant is surely a central factor. And what is more, it is central whether or not the employer enacted the pregnancy exclusion to target women (which it most likely did not) or not.

To summarize the argument here: The fact that an actor intentionally uses a trait in a law or policy as a proxy for another more-suspect trait—like race or sex—is not relevant to the moral permissibility of the law or policy. While it surely matters that the policy is successful or efficient because the trait works via a proxy to reach its target, that fact is relevant whether it is intended or not. In reviewing a law, policy, or decision, we need not ask whether the actor had the right intentions, but rather whether the action is justified given the manner in which it operates.

The Purpose

The second sense of intention that might be relevant to the evaluation of whether a law, policy, or decision constitutes wrongful discrimination is the ultimate *purpose* for which the law or policy is adopted. In this section, we will examine whether the fact that a law or policy is adopted for a bad reason is sufficient to render that law or policy impermissible. *Purpose* is often used interchangeably with *motive*. By purpose, I mean the end at which the actor aims. Motive, by contrast, relates to the reason that actually moves the actor. But I do not want to make too much of that distinction here. The view I endorse here is that the intention of the actor is not relevant to the moral permissibility of an action that distinguishes among people. Though I contend his motives—the desire states that actually move him to action—are similarly irrelevant, that claim will follow from the argument presented here. In passages from cases cited below, these two terms—*purpose* and *motive*—are often used interchangeably and without careful attention to whether it is what the actor aims at or what the actor desires that is thought to be central. As I want to argue that neither ought to be morally relevant to the evaluation of whether laws or policies wrongfully discriminate, I ask the reader to treat them interchangeably in the passages below.

   The view that a bad purpose is relevant to whether a law violates the constitutional guarantee of equal protection seems to be the claim underlying Justice Brennan's claim in the 1973 case *U.S. Dept. of Agriculture v. Moreno* that "if the constitutional conception of 'equal protection of the laws' means anything, it must at the very least mean that a bare congressional desire to harm a politically unpopular group cannot constitute a legitimate governmental interest."[47] This equal protection minimum is reiterated in *Romer v. Evans*.[48] There the Court explains that one of the reasons in support of holding Colorado's Amendment Two (which forbade local governments in Colorado from enacting laws to prohibit discrimination on the basis of sexual orientation and made it more difficult for such protections to be enacted at the statewide level) in violation of the Equal Protection Clause "is that laws of the kind now before us raise the inevitable inference that the disadvantage imposed is born of animosity toward the class of persons affected."[49]

Some scholars similarly endorse the view that animus is at the heart of what makes wrongful discrimination wrong. For example, Richard Arneson argues that "Discrimination that is intrinsically morally wrong occurs when an agent treats a person identified as being of a certain type differently than she otherwise would have done because of unwarranted animus or prejudice against persons of that type."[50] But is bad purpose or motive—a bare desire to harm—relevant to whether a classification wrongfully discriminates or does it just seem so because the cases in which it is cited are over-determined? Perhaps there are other wrong-making features present that confuse the issue in these cases.

To test the claim that invidious purpose or motive is relevant, we need to examine cases in which that bad motive is not accompanied by other wrong-making properties, else we will not know if it is the motive that is really doing the work. Consider the following case: The orchestra of a large city is hiring new musicians. The musical director aims to keep as many Asian and Asian Americans out of the orchestra as possible. Unfortunately for her, the orchestra auditions musicians behind a screen, to protect against this and other kinds of bias. To achieve her aim, the musical director picks musicians by preferring passion over technique, an approach she believes (mistakenly) will screen out as many Asian musicians as possible. As it turns out, the musical director bases her action on an inaccurate generalization. Asian musicians are not less passionate and more technically skilled than other musicians. As a result, the orchestra selected is one in which passionate musicians outnumber highly technical ones, but one that has the same racial composition (let us suppose) as would have been the case had the director adopted a different hiring policy. Ought her bare desire to harm invalidate the hiring procedure?

My intuition, which I hope is shared, is that it ought not. If the desire or motive is not actualized in any way, it is hard to see what makes the action wrong—though the desire surely reveals something unsavory about the musical director's character. Of course, her desire or motive is actualized in some way, in that *different* musicians have been chosen by valuing passion over technique than would have been chosen using other selection criteria, but the intention to keep Asians out has not been actualized in the form of a policy that distinguishes among people on the basis of being Asian, nor has the intention been actualized by producing an orchestra with fewer Asians that would otherwise have been selected.

Perhaps saying that there is nothing wrong with the director's action is too strong. There is something wrong about the actions of the orchestra director but it is not the wrong of wrongful discrimination. As was discussed in Chapters 1 and 4, there are often constraints on the criteria that people may use in making decisions that derive not from the moral demands of equality but instead from the internal goals of the institution involved. Here, the orchestra director is no doubt subject to standards of practice that derive from her job description—either explicitly or implicitly. The orchestra director's job is to create the best orchestra, for example. If she also attempts to affect the racial composition of the orchestra, she acts outside of her role, abuses her discretion, or something of that nature. In other words, her role obligations as an orchestra director may forbid attempts to wrongfully discriminate. Thus the action itself is not wrongful discrimination but because the orchestra director attempts to wrongfully discriminate,[51] she has violated the obligations defined by her job, as it is surely plausible to suppose that her employment contract explicitly or implicitly forbids her from trying to wrongfully discriminate.

If bad purpose or motive is insufficient to render a law, policy, or decision wrongful, perhaps it is relevant nonetheless. Does not a bad intention contribute to making the use of a classification wrongful? The sort of case that tests this issue is one in which there is a bad intention and a bad effect but the effect, standing alone, would not render the classification wrongful. For example, suppose an employer decides to hire only those employees who are willing to work seventy hours per week. Further, suppose, not unreasonably, that this selection criterion has the effect of rendering the workforce almost all male. Women, particularly women with children, are simply less willing to work the long hours the employer demands. Suppose one believes that this policy does not wrongfully discriminate against women or mothers. Does that judgment change if the employer adopts the policy deliberately in order to keep women out of his employ? At first blush, it does seem that this intention matters to whether the policy is wrong. It seems to turn a permissible or ambiguous case into an instance of wrongful discrimination. Does this mean the actor's intention really is relevant?[52]

This example is analogous to one discussed in the philosophical literature on intentions, particularly that literature focusing on the DDE. For example, Alec Walen discusses the example of the constrained terror bomber. His goal is to bomb civilians but for self-interested prudential reasons, he has decided only to bomb legitimate military targets, some of which afford him the opportunity to bomb civilians. When this constrained terror bomber bombs a legitimate military target, acting on the intention of bombing civilians whenever permitted by independent criteria of legitimate action, has he acted impermissibly? Walen argues no, and I agree. So long as the constrained terror bomber only bombs legitimate targets and is committed to doing so, his aim to terrorize civilians does not taint the moral permissibility of his action. Walen explains:

> if an intention directs an agent to perform only independently permissible acts, then it seems intuitively that the worst we can say is that he deserves criticism for performing those acts for a bad reason. It seems overly demanding to require, at least as a general matter, that an agent do what, in some sense he *has* good reason to do *for* a good reason.[53]

The terror-bomber example and the long-hours example may seem different, however, in the following way. A military target's legitimacy is partially a function of the other targets available. If bombing a military target will likely cause civilian deaths and another target will provide the same military gain with substantially fewer civilian deaths, the first may not qualify as a legitimate target. As a result, the limits the constrained terror bomber accepts are quite substantial. In the context of distinguishing among people, this comparative element is not always present. And where it is not, the intentions of the actor may *seem* more relevant.

First, we should note that sometimes the permissibility of drawing a distinction among people does involve a similar comparative element. In the case of the long-hours example discussed above, presumably what makes the policy legitimate despite its negative effect on women and mothers is the fact that it serves valid business needs. If the policy does not demean women and mothers, this is due, at least in part, to the fact that the business in question needs employees who are available to work such hours. If this is not the case, if the business could effectively staff and meet its goals with a less-demanding workload policy that does not affect women so dramatically, then perhaps the long-hours policy is demeaning (and therefore not permissible). In other words, the analysis of when drawing distinctions among people is or is not morally (and legally)[54] permissible sometimes depends on a comparative analysis.

But not always. Sometimes ill fit between means and ends expresses disregard for the interests of those affected, but not always. If not, does the fact that a decision maker has discretion about which selection criteria to adopt make intentions relevant? Still, I think not. If the actor has discretion, he has discretion—discretion to exercise wisely and well or stupidly and spitefully. Arneson considers an example of such acts of discretion outside of the discrimination context. He asks what we should say about his failure to share his ice cream with his little brother, who really wants some, when he refuses to share out of spite. Arneson thinks that his brother has no right to the ice cream and thus that Arneson has no duty to share. However, he thinks that he acts wrongly in refusing to share because he does so out of spite.[55] I disagree. Arneson does not *act* wrongly in refusing to share out of spite, but he does show himself to be a mean-spirited person by so doing.

Translating this point to the discrimination context would yield the following: Where an employer adopts a policy for choosing among applicants that is independently morally permissible (is not demeaning considering effect, alternatives, social meaning, etc.), but does so for bad reasons (to keep women or minorities out, for example), this bad intention does not thereby render the policy impermissible. However, the fact that the action is permissible does not stop it from reflecting something morally bad about the actor. The employer who adopts a legitimate policy *because* of its negative effect on a group is surely shown to be a bad person.

Demeaning and Intending

The reader may be wondering about the connection between the discussion here and the book's core thesis that wrongful discrimination is differentiation that demeans. In this chapter I have argued that the intention of the person differentiating among people is irrelevant to whether the differentiation distinguishes on the basis of any particular trait *and* that the intention of the person differentiating among people is irrelevant to the moral assessment of this action. Therefore, whether or not a person differentiates on the basis of a trait that has significant demeaning potential (like race or sex) is not determined by his intentions. One can differentiate on the basis of race or sex (as well as other traits) without intending to do so. Similarly, one can fail to do so despite one's intentions. More controversially, differentiating among people on the basis of a trait for benign reasons does not insure that the action *is* morally permissible. Finally, and perhaps most controversially, a bad intent—including animus toward a group and even an intention to demean a group—does not insure that the action itself is morally wrong. If the action itself—described without reference to the intentions it springs from—is permissible, the intention to demean or to harm will not change its moral valence.

Conclusion

Imagine posing the following question to the people affected by the laws, policies, or decision at issue: When is it wrong to distinguish among people on the basis of possessing or lacking some trait? Focusing on this perspective shows that it makes sense to be concerned with *how people are treated* rather than with passing moral judgment on the agents who draw the distinctions. To know how people are treated, we must focus on the features of the laws and policies themselves, rather than on the intentions (or motives) of the actors that adopt or enact these policies and laws. And Holmes would, most likely, agree. At the end of Lecture I of the Common Law, titled "Early Forms Liability," in which the aphorism about dogs appears in the early part of his discussion, Holmes has this to say:

> It remains to be proved that, while the terminology of morals is still re-
> tained, and while the law does still and always, in a certain sense, measure
> legal liability by moral standards, it nevertheless, by the very necessity of its
> nature, is continually transmuting those moral standards into external or
> objective ones, from which the actual guilt of the party concerned is wholly
> eliminated.[56]

As the last part of his sentence makes clear, for Holmes, the "moral" refers to a judgment about the "actual guilt of the party." In other words, Holmes too thinks that we often wrongfully confuse judgments about the moral character of the actor with judgments about the moral permissibility of the action. In assessing the wrongfulness of discrimination, it is not the thought that counts.

This view has an important practical virtue as well. Wrongful discrimination need not spring from culpable acts of racists, sexists, or others. In recognizing that laws and policies may wrongfully discriminate inadvertently, we can disentangle the important work of providing a remedy for those who are treated unfairly from the finger-pointing involved in finding a wrongdoer to blame. It is hard work to change the deeply ingrained social meanings that attach to traits in our culture. If we only take steps in that direction when we have concluded that someone is culpable for acting badly, we set the bar too high.

Conclusion

This book addresses the question of when it is morally wrong to draw distinctions among people on the basis of any traits. The first point of departure is the premise that people are of equal moral worth. The second point of departure is factual rather than moral. It is sometimes necessary and often desirable to draw distinctions among people and treat them differently as a result. This practice of differentiating between people risks, at the least, treating people in a way that runs afoul of the commitment to honor their equal moral worth. The theory advanced in this book aims to provide a response to this moral concern. Given that differential treatment is necessary and that people are of equal worth, how and when is differentiation morally permissible?

The answer provided here is that drawing distinctions among people is morally permissible when doing so does not demean any of those affected. We can treat people differently if, in doing so, we do not demean them. Many answers to the question of what sorts of differentiation (on the basis of what traits, in what contexts) do demean will be controversial. In discussing the examples used in this book, I do not claim to be right in my own interpretations about whether particular practices demean. Rather, I only claim and defend the position that this is the right question to ask.

This approach to what I have called the *discrimination puzzle*—the question of when differentiation offends against the moral equality of persons—is inspired by an empirical observation. Drawing distinctions on the basis of certain traits and meting out different treatment matters to people because of the social significance of some traits or some treatment. In other cultures, traits might be invested with a meaning that they lack in ours. This is deeply important because if we are morally required to treat one another *as equals*, what that imperative will require will depend on context, including culture.

This does not make the view I endorse a relativist one—quite the contrary. The claim I present is that distinction drawing is morally wrong when it is demeaning—this is a claim that asserts a moral truth that is applicable everywhere. But because drawing distinctions on the basis of some characteristics will demean in some contexts and cultures but not in others, my theory is sensitive to the conventional nature of social practices that demean. Which practices demean depends on the social conditions in which they operate.

This empirical observation is related to a moral claim as well. This book is fundamentally concerned with the moral question of when drawing distinctions among people comports with the moral obligation to treat each other as of equal moral worth. As such, it relates to more general arguments about the nature of equality and to views about what a commitment to the equal moral worth of people requires in terms of just political and economic arrangements. While this book does not address these more general issues about equality and justice, the view of wrongful discrimination endorsed here has affinities with a particular way of answering the question of what justice requires.

A commitment to the equal moral worth of persons commits one to the view that people are equally entitled to *something*[1]—freedom, resources, welfare, capabilities, or something else. So-called egalitarians have focused on the latter of these: resources, welfare, capabilities, or something else of this nature. As that view has evolved, particularly in response to critics, it has come to focus on the need to distinguish which welfare, resources, or capabilities are the result of individual effort or freely chosen risks versus which are the result of luck or something outside of the individual's control. This distinction needs to be made in order to avoid taking from the industrious while providing benefits to the lazy or imprudent—and to answer critics who worry that equalizing welfare or resources or whatever else the egalitarian view proposes would lead to unfair results. So, for example, if a hard-working person forgoes spending money on restaurants and clothes in order to purchase health insurance, it seems unfair for her to subsidize the person who chose not to buy health insurance in order to have more money to go out and party. Thus, the egalitarian would equalize only when the lack of equal X results from luck rather than choice.[2]

To draw these distinctions, these so-called luck egalitarians must determine which people are poor, say, due to lack of talent or lack of opportunity (bad luck) and which are poor due to lack of effort (a choice). Recent critics of luck egalitarian political theory find this feature of these views disturbing. For example, Jonathan Wolff argues that it is demeaning to condition access to resources on the identification of a person as lacking talent.[3] Similarly, Elizabeth Anderson argues that these egalitarian theories require moral agents to act out of pity or condescension to those less fortunate—an attitude at odds with the moral requirement that we treat others as persons of equal moral worth.[4] Instead, both of these critics of luck egalitarianism argue that a guaranteed minimum welfare payment of sorts ought to be accorded to all, irrespective of whether one is poor due to luck or choice. In addition, Anderson in particular is not disturbed by differences in income, wealth, or welfare among people above some minimum threshold.

My point in discussing these critics of the luck/choice distinction in egalitarian moral theories is not to endorse them but rather to note some similarities in approach and outlook between these recent critics of egalitarianism and my own view. These views as well as my own emphasize that differences among people *in themselves* are not what is problematic with respect to the commitment to the equal moral worth of persons. Rather the problem is the social significance these differences can come to have. Anderson argues that some people may have fewer talents or abilities than others but we ought not to therefore assume their lives are less fulfilling and they therefore need or are entitled to compensation.[5] It is not the differences among people that matter. Rather a moral problem arises when these differences give rise to domination or subjugation. The crux of similarity between this approach and my own is that it is the political or social dimension of difference that is significant. According to my conception of wrongful discrimination, drawing distinctions among people is morally wrong when doing so demeans any of those affected. Otherwise, it is simply good business (when it is efficient) or in line with the goals of an institution (when it is based on merit) or bad business or simply dumb (when it is irrational).

Secondly, these views, and my own, see bad luck not as the fundamental concern of the norm of equality. Samuel Scheffler, one critic of luck egalitarianism, rejects the view that the aim of the ideal of equality is to "compensate for misfortune" and instead suggests that it is "a moral ideal governing the relations in which people stand to one another."[6] The conception of wrongful discrimination I defend in this book similarly treats the bad luck of being judged by irrational criteria or having a silly distinction applied to oneself as bad luck but nothing more. If someone does not get a job or place at school or something else because the selection criteria used are unrelated to the institution's goals, this is bad luck, but no more. This bad luck is not the sort of thing that offends against the requirement that we treat each other as equals. If the selection criteria are just irrational or silly but not demeaning, then being on the receiving end of such criteria is just a piece of bad luck and nothing more.

This rejection of bad luck as morally relevant to the requirement that we treat one another as equals is analogous to Anderson's insistence that the bad luck of not having traits that are valued by the market is not, itself, morally relevant either. So long as one is not exploited or made to be a second-class citizen as a result, this bad luck ought not to be the focus of egalitarian concern, or so she argues.

What does matter is whether, in drawing distinctions among people, we treat some in a way that puts them down. When discrimination demeans it is wrong, as it then conflicts with the moral norm that we treat each other as equals. To paraphrase Anderson's insistence on asking, "what is the point of equality?" I say, the point of prohibiting discrimination is not to forbid distinguishing between people—differentiation is important and even necessary in some instances. Neither is it to insure that we always act efficiently and sensibly. Stupid or careless judgment, without more, is not of particular concern from the perspective of equality. Rather the point of equality is to treat one another as equals, and thus the wrong of discrimination is to fail to treat people as equals. We do that when we differentiate among people in a manner that ranks some as less morally worthy than others. This is the concern that fuels our worries about classification and differentiation. To forbid such subjugation is the point of antidiscrimination prohibitions, and therefore the act of demeaning is the wrong of wrongful discrimination.

NOTES

ACKNOWLEDGMENTS

INDEX

Notes

Introduction: The Discrimination Puzzle

1. Actually, skin color might be relevant to what clothes it would make sense for a person to wear—a white person ought to cover her skin more carefully with clothes or sunblock than a black person. Noting this fact shows right away a bit of the problem in relying on relevance.

2. The phrase "equal concern and respect" is from Ronald Dworkin. See Ronald Dworkin, *Taking Rights Seriously* (Cambridge, Mass.: Harvard University Press, 1977), 273. The idea it expresses—that each person is worthy of concern and respect merely by virtue of being a person—is widely shared. Some, notably Joseph Raz, have argued that nothing significant is added to the claim that each person is entitled to concern and respect by saying that each person is entitled to *equal* concern and respect. See Joseph Raz, *The Morality of Freedom* (New York: Oxford University Press, 1986), 228. About this, I disagree with Raz. To say that we are each entitled to respect is inadequate. What would it mean to show someone the respect she deserves by virtue of being a person? The best way to cash this out is to say that each person is entitled to be treated *as equally worthy as any other*. In other words, it is the comparative aspect that puts meat on the bones of the concept of treating a person with the respect that personhood requires.

3. City of Cleburne v. Cleburne Living Center, 473 U.S. 432, 468–469 (1985) (Marshall, J., concurring in the judgment in part and dissenting in part).

1. The Basic Idea

1. Owen Fiss, "Groups and the Equal Protection Clause," *Philosophy and Public Affairs* 5 (1976): 107–177. Cass R. Sunstein, "The Anticaste Principle," *Michigan Law Review* 92 (1994): 2410–2455, 2411 (defining "the anticaste principle" as one which "forbids social and legal practices from translating highly visible and morally irrelevant differences into systemic social disadvantage, unless there is a very good reason for society to do so"). Sunstein notes that the Civil War amendments were originally enacted with the intent of making Congress "the

principal institution for implementing the Fourteenth Amendment," but in the twentieth century the principle "transformed from an anticaste principle into an antidifferentiation principle" due to the amendment being enforced case-by-case in the courts, rather than by broad legislative attempts to eliminate second-class citizenship. *Id.* at 2439–2440.

John Hart Ely, *Democracy and Distrust: A Theory of Judicial Review* (Cambridge, Mass.: Harvard University Press, 1980).

2. This hypothetical is adapted from Zadie Smith's *On Beauty.* See Zadie Smith, *On Beauty: A Novel* (New York: Penguin Press, 2005).

3. Azar Nafisi, *Reading Lolita in Tehran: A Memoir in Books* (New York: Random House, 2003).

4. Amnon Reichman makes a similar argument about professions. He argues that at Common Law, members of professions were required not to discriminate on the basis of group-based characteristics of individuals seeking service because being a *professional* requires one to provide service to all comers. *See* Amnon Reichman, "Professional Status and the Freedom to Contract: Toward a Common Law Duty of Non-Discrimination," *Canadian Journal of Law and Jurisprudence* 14 (2001): 79–132.

5. Of course, one might argue that distinguishing among insurance applicants on the basis of genetic traits is meaningfully different from distinguishing among such applicants on the basis of health status more generally and thus that genetic discrimination in insurance is wrongful discrimination. I explore the arguments one could make for this position. See Deborah Hellman, "What Makes Genetic Discrimination Exceptional?" *American Journal of Law and Medicine* 29 (2003): 77–116. In addition, this position may be the impetus for legislation forbidding genetic discrimination in health insurance, which has been adopted in numerous states and is currently under consideration in Congress (see H.R. 493 and S. 358, "Genetic Information Nondiscrimination Act of 2007," proposed). Interestingly, the proposed legislation cites (finding 2) the history of sterilization of those with genetic "defects" as one of the reasons why the proposed law is necessary.

6. In an article noting that law professors whose last names begin with letters earlier in the alphabet are more likely than other professors to visit another law school, the author notes that "the alphabetic bias in visits seems more curious than disturbing—even to one whose name falls on the wrong side of the alphabetic mean." See Deborah Jones Merritt, "Calling Professor AAA: How to Visit at the School of Your Choice," *Journal of Legal Education* 49 (1992): 557–563, 561–563. The presumed explanation for this disparity is that associate deans trying to cover courses simply work their way through lists of acceptable candidates that are presented in alphabetical order.

7. Whether in fact courts do invalidate classifications on the basis of irrationality alone is, I think, debatable.

8. In fact, the admissions policies of Ivy League institutions changed in the 1920s from using criteria that tested intellectual ability alone (high school grades and

standardized test scores) to criteria meant to assess other more intangible qualities. These criteria were adopted in reaction to the fact that the proportion of
Jewish students was rising to a level seen as unacceptable and were used to limit
the number of Jewish students admitted. See Malcolm Gladwell, "Getting In: The
Social Logic of Ivy League Admissions," *The New Yorker*, Oct. 10, 2005, 80–86.

9. Exponents of this position include Owen Fiss and Glenn Loury. See Fiss, "Equal
Protection Clause," 107–177; Glenn C. Loury, *The Anatomy of Racial Inequality*
(Cambridge, Mass.: Harvard University Press, 2002).

10. Owen Fiss uses the concept of a social group in his articulation of his Group-
Disadvantaging Principle, see Fiss, "Equal Protection Clause," 125–126. Fiss's
understanding of equal protection is an example of an anti-caste approach.

11. For example, according to Fiss's conception of the Equal Protection Clause, the
clause protects groups not individuals: "Blacks are what might be called a spe-
cially disadvantaged group, and I would view the Equal Protection Clause as a
protection for such groups." Fiss, "Equal Protection Clause," 132.

12. This understanding of why and how history matters is clearly inspired by John
Hart Ely's influential account of how best to understand the animating principle
of the Equal Protection Clause. Ely was concerned that isolated minority groups
would be unable to influence the political process in an adequate way such that
the resulting legislation would not treat their interests fairly. Ely, *Democracy and
Distrust*, 135–179. For a more recent discussion of a similar view, see Kasper
Lippert-Rasmussen, "Private Discrimination: A Prioritarian, Desert-
Accommodating Account," *San Diego Law Review* 43 (2006): 817–856, 836
(noting that "the harm involved in disadvantageous differential treatment
based on membership of socially salient groups is likely to spread across individual acts and to accumulate across individual acts" and that "the same is not
true of disadvantageous differential treatment based on membership of socially
nonsalient groups or individual properties").

13. Mathias Risse and Richard Zeckhauser use an argument of this sort in their defense of racial profiling, see Risse and Zeckhauser, "Racial Profiling," *Philosophy
and Public Affairs* 32 (2004): 131–170 at 157–59.

14. Loury, *Racial Inequality*, 113, 117.

15. *Utterance* is the term philosophers of language commonly use to refer to a group
of spoken or written words—so that it does not prejudice the account of those
words by characterizing them in any particular way.

16. François Recanati, *Literal Meaning* (Cambridge; New York: Cambridge University
Press, 2004), 5–6.

17. Paul Brest, *Processes of Constitutional Decisionmaking* (Boston: Little, Brown,
1975), 489. Ely, *Democracy and Distrust*, 148.

18. Ronald Dworkin offers a defense of the Supreme Court's decision in Regents of
the University of California v. Bakke, 438 U.S. 265 (1978), in his essay "Bakke's
Case: Are Quotas Unfair?" in Ronald Dworkin, *A Matter of Principle* (Cambridge,
Mass.: Harvard University Press, 1985), 293–303. In Dworkin's view, denying
admission to Allan Bakke, in part because of his race, is meaningfully different

from denying admission to an African American because of his race because in Bakke's case "race is not distinguished by the special character of public insult." *Id.* at 301. This view builds on the argument in defense of *Brown v. Board of Education,* made by Charles Black in the 1960s. Black emphasizes that it is only by looking at the social meaning of segregation that one can assess it—that its meaning if you will is in part determined by context. See Charles L. Black, Jr., "The Lawfulness of the Segregation Decisions," *Yale Law Journal* 69 (1960): 421–430. Interestingly, Rae Langton provides a related account of how pornography may constitute subordination in her "Speech Acts and Unspeakable Acts," *Philosophy and Public Affairs* 22 (1993): 293–330. Building on J. L. Austin's distinction between locutionary, perlocutionary, and illocutionary speech acts, Langton argues that the feminist claim that pornography subordinates is philosophically coherent when one interprets it as a claim about the illocutionary act that pornography is.

19. 347 U.S. 483, 494 (1954).

20. Erving Goffman, *The Presentation of Self in Everyday Life* (Garden City, N.Y.: Doubleday, 1959). Loury, *Racial Inequality,* 67.

21. Many accounts of when discrimination is wrong, or when it violates the Equal Protection Clause, emphasize the effect of classification—that it is likely to make the people affected feel stigmatized. Matthew Adler emphasizes this in his article voicing skepticism about whether there are any genuinely expressive accounts of law. See Matthew D. Adler, "Expressive Theories of Law: A Skeptical Overview," *University of Pennsylvania Law Review* 148 (2000): 1363–1502, 1428–1438. But, as Elizabeth Anderson and Richard Pildes point out in their reply to Adler, language has illocutionary as well as perlocutionary force. See Elizabeth S. Anderson and Richard H. Pildes, "Expressive Theories of Law: A General Restatement," *University of Pennsylvania Law Review* 148 (2000): 1503–1575, 1571.

22. Nelson Mandela, *Long Walk to Freedom: The Autobiography of Nelson Mandela* (Boston: Little, Brown, 1994), 334–335, 338–339.

23. Of course *sinister* means both "suggesting or threatening evil" and on the left side or left. See *The American Heritage Dictionary,* 2nd College Edition (Boston: Houghton Mifflin, 1985), 1143.

24. Jean Hampton, "Forgiveness, Resentment and Hatred," in Jeffrie G. Murphy and Jean Hampton, eds., *Forgiveness and Mercy* (New York: Cambridge University Press 1988), 35–87, 52.

25. *Id.* at 44–45.

26. See, for example, Peter Westen, "The Empty Idea of Equality," *Harvard Law Review* 95 (1982): 537–596.

2. Demeaning and Wrongful Discrimination

1. Jespersen v. Harrah's Operating Co., Inc., 444 F.3d 1104, 1107 (9th Cir. 2004) (en banc).

2. 447 F. Supp. 1346 (D. Del. 1978), aff'd, 591 F.2d 1334 (3rd Cir. 1979). Robert Post discusses this case in his article "Prejudicial Appearances: The Logic of American Antidiscrimination Law," *California Law Review* 88 (2000): 1–40, and it is this article which brought it to my attention.

3. Whether or not my action demeans also does not depend on whether the person affected recognizes it as demeaning. An action is demeaning if the best understanding of the action is that it is demeaning and thus if the person affected *should* recognize it as demeaning whether or not she actually does.

4. Suppose I spit on someone who appears to be homeless but is really pretending to be homeless. He is actually a university student trying to get a better sense of the life of the homeless. Have I demeaned him? Yes and no. I have demeaned homeless people in spitting on the person who seems to be homeless but I have not demeaned the actual human being before me because he is not really homeless. My action is wrongful as it demeans homeless people even though it does not succeed in demeaning the actual person I spit on.

5. For an interesting discussion of the moral significance of manners that derives from their function as a means of showing respect, see Sarah Buss, "Appearing Respectful: The Moral Significance of Manners," *Ethics* 109 (1999): 795–826.

6. Amnon Reichman, "Professional Status and the Freedom to Contract: Toward a Common Law Duty of Non-Discrimination," *Canadian Journal of Law and Jurisprudence* 14 (2001): 79–132.

7. See, for example, Austin's famous account. J. L. Austin, *How to Do Things with Words*, 2nd ed., eds. J. O. Urmson and Marina Sbisà (Cambridge, Mass.: Harvard University Press, 1975).

8. For an extended discussion of the illocutionary act of promising, see John R. Searle, *Speech Acts: An Essay in the Philosophy of Language* (London: Cambridge University Press, 1970), 54–71. Searle claims that the speaker's intention is relevant—in particular the intention "that the utterance of T will place him under an obligation to do A," *id.* at 60, to making an utterance a promise. That may be right—I do not express a view one way or the other about this here. In the same chapter, Searle points out that for some illocutionary acts, sincerity is not at issue: "One cannot, for example, greet or christen insincerely, but one can state or promise insincerely." *Id.* at 65. As I argue in Chapter 4, demeaning is more like greeting or christening in that one can demean insincerely and thus unintentionally.

9. Here I am talking about promising, not contracting. In order to contract rather than simply to promise, more is generally required—consideration, for example.

10. Glenn C. Loury, *The Anatomy of Racial Inequality* (Cambridge, Mass.: Harvard University Press, 2002), 58.

11. Justice Brown, writing for the majority in Plessy v. Ferguson, 163 U.S. 537, 551 (1896) held that the Louisiana law requiring separate seating for white and "colored" passengers by an interstate railroad company did not stamp either group with a "badge of inferiority" (these are his words). Justice Harlan, writing

in dissent, rebuked Brown's reading of the cultural significance of the practice as the "real meaning" of the law is "that colored citizens are so inferior and degraded that they cannot be allowed to sit in public coaches occupied by white citizens." *Id.* at 560 (Harlan, J., dissenting).

12. A hair-length policy is not without problems, however. Such a policy forbids men from having long hair. This policy reinforces a conception of masculinity that may demean men who do not fit this conception of what a "real" man looks and acts like.

13. I say that this policy likely demeans because I can only offer my view of the best interpretation of the meaning of this practice. What I defend in this book is that I have identified the right questions to ask about policies that distinguish among people, not that my particular views about or interpretations of these policies are necessarily right.

14. In the next chapter concerning disagreement about the social meaning of practices that distinguish, I consider whether sex-segregated bathrooms demean transgendered or ambiguously gendered persons.

15. Post, "Prejudicial Appearances," 34 (noting that courts generally uphold dress codes that reflect community standards—but not all conventional practices, like sex-segregated privacy concerns—and emphasizing that courts never confront the "fundamental question" of why some conventional practices should be upheld and others rejected).

16. *Id.* at 36–37.

17. Post's own answer is also unsatisfying. He notes that a court's rejection of this claim would be *proper* but does not explain why. Indeed, his account is more descriptive than normative: "This [hypothetical court response to a *Fesel*-like case based on race rather than sex] is because antidiscrimination law seeks to exercise a far more sweeping transformation of race than of gender." *Id.* at 37.

18. Kimberly A. Yuracko, "Sameness, Subordination, and Perfectionism: Toward a More Complete Theory of Employment Discrimination Law," *San Diego Law Review* 43 (2006): 857–897.

19. *Id.* at 869.

20. Peter Westen, "The Empty Idea of Equality," *Harvard Law Review* 95 (1982): 537–596.

21. See Harry G. Frankfurt, "Equality and Respect," in Harry G. Frankfurt, *Necessity, Volition and Love* (New York: Cambridge University Press, 1999), 146–154.

22. *Id.* at 149.

23. *Id.* at 150.

24. *Id. at 149*, explaining that it "may well be that the entitlements of all people to certain things are in fact the same [but that] it is not because equality is important" rather it is because "all people happen to be the same, or are necessarily the same, with regard to the characteristics from which the entitlements in question derive—for instance, common humanity, a capacity for suffering, citizenship in the kingdom of ends, or whatever." Joseph Raz also shares this view. Raz, *The Morality of Freedom.*

25. This view was suggested to me by Connie Rosati, Associate Professor of Philosophy, University of Arizona.

26. Avishai Margalit, *The Decent Society*, trans. Naomi Goldblum (Cambridge, Mass.: Harvard University Press, 1996), 125.

27. Sarah Buss argues that manners are morally significant because their function is to allow people to directly recognize the equal dignity of others. Buss, "Appearing Respectful," 795.

28. Robert H. Frank, *Luxury Fever: Why Money Fails to Satisfy in an Era of Excess* (New York: Free Press, 1999). Frank documents a pattern of escalating spending driven by a desire to keep up with the Joneses.

29. Frank describes the story of Aristotle Onassis and Stavros Niarchos in which each tried to have a yacht bigger than the other. The end result was that both had yachts far bigger than they would have otherwise chosen and which were difficult to use as there were few ports that could accommodate them. Frank, *Luxury Fever*, 5–6, 9.

30. Contract law does not enforce promises to make gifts, for example.

31. Jean Hampton, "The Moral Education Theory of Punishment," *Philosophy and Public Affairs*, 13 (1984): 208–238.

32. As Michael Moore explains, "retributivism is the view that we ought to punish offenders because and only because they deserve to be punished." Michael Moore, *Placing Blame: A General Theory of the Criminal Law* (New York: Oxford University Press, 1997), 153.

33. *Id.* at 165.

34. George P. Fletcher, "Disenfranchisement as Punishment: Reflections on the Racial Uses of *Infamia*," *UCLA Law Review* 46 (1999): 1895–1907.

35. Some psychologists and parenting gurus argue against punishing children because it is demeaning and because it is thereby unhelpful to the moral education of children. See, for example, Alfie Kohn, *Unconditional Parenting: Moving from Rewards and Punishments to Love and Reason* (New York: Atria Books, 2005); Haim Ginott, *Teacher and Child* (New York: MacMillan, 1972). Jean Hampton takes the opposite view, arguing that punishing criminals is justified as good for them in the same way that punishing children is good for them. Hampton, "Moral Education."

36. *Canadian Charter of Rights and Freedoms*, Part I of the Constitution Act, 1982, being Schedule B to the Canada Act 1982, ch. 11 (UK).

37. For an excellent analysis of the evolution of the Canadian Supreme Court's equality jurisprudence, see Denise G. Réaume, "Discrimination and Dignity," *Louisiana Law Review* 63 (2003): 645–695.

38. [1995] 2 S.C.R. 513.

39. *Id.* at 36.

40. [1999] 1 S.C.R. 497.

41. *Id.* at 51.

42. Réaume, "Discrimination and Dignity," 673.

43. Gosselin v. Québec (Attorney-General), [2002] 4 S.C.R. 429.

44. This analysis may provide support for the fundamental-rights strand of American equal protection doctrine.

45. This is not the same as the analysis provided by Réaume, *supra* note 37, as she argues that failing to provide a basic level of resources itself offends the dignity of those welfare recipients.

46. Charles L. Black, Jr., "The Lawfulness of the Segregation Decisions," *Yale Law Journal* 69 (1960): 421–430.

47. *Id.* at 427.

48. *Id.*

49. Ronald Dworkin adopts a similar view in his 1985 essay defending the decision in The Regents of the University of California v. Bakke, 438 U.S. 265 (1978). Dworkin, "Bakke's Case: Are Quotas Unfair?" in Dworkin, *A Matter of Principle* (Cambridge, Mass.: Harvard University Press, 1985), 293–303.

50. Charles R. Lawrence, "The Id, the Ego, and Equal Protection: Reckoning with Unconscious Racism," *Stanford Law Review* 39 (1987): 317–388.

51. Lawrence explains his proposal for a cultural-meaning test in the following way: "this article proposes a new test to trigger judicial recognition of race-based behavior. It posits a connection between unconscious racism and the existence of cultural symbols that have racial meaning. It suggests that the 'cultural meaning' of an allegedly discriminatory act is the best available analogue for, and *evidence of*, a collective unconscious that we cannot observe directly. This test would thus evaluate governmental conduct to determine whether it conveys a symbolic message to which the culture attaches racial significance. A finding that the culture thinks of an allegedly discriminatory governmental action in racial terms would also constitute a finding regarding the beliefs and motivations of the governmental actors." *Id.* at 324 (emphasis added).

52. There are other differences as well. He focuses on whether the cultural meaning is racially tinged. I focus on whether it demeans. My focus is both narrower and broader. It is narrower in that in my view any racially tinged meaning is not problematic, only those that demean. It is broader in that in my view any distinction that demeans is morally problematic, not merely those that demean on the basis of race. Moreover, for Lawrence the cultural meaning of an action is determined empirically by looking at whether "a significant portion of the population thinks of the governmental action in racial terms," *Id.* at 356. In my view, the cultural meaning of a law or policy is determined interpretively.

53. Catharine A. MacKinnon, *Feminism Unmodified: Discourses on Life and Law* (Cambridge, Mass.: Harvard University Press, 1987), 42. As she explains:
    If gender were merely a question of difference, sex inequality would be a problem of mere sexism, of mistaken differentiation, of inaccurate categorization of individuals. This is what the difference approach thinks it is and is therefore sensitive to. But if gender is an inequality first, constructed as a socially relevant differentiation in order to keep that inequality in place, then sex inequality questions are questions of systematic

dominance, of male supremacy, which is not at all abstract and is anything but a mistake.

54. I have found inspiration for my view of wrongful discrimination from the work of Rae Langton on pornography (Rae Langton, "Speech Acts and Unspeakable Acts," *Philosophy and Public Affairs* 22 [1993]: 293–330) and Andrew Altman on hate speech (Andrew Altman, "Liberalism and Campus Hate Speech: A Philosophical Examination," *Ethics* 103 [1993]: 302–317). Both Langton and Altman analyze speech acts to explore the reasons pornography or hate speech may be legitimately banned in a liberal political community. Langton and Altman see pornography and hate speech, respectively, as not only speech but also speech acts that warrant legal restriction. Like a threat or harassment—which are both speech and speech acts that warrant prohibition—Langton sees pornography as subordination and Altman sees some hate speech as treating another as a moral subordinate. Both Langton and Altman are careful to distinguish the harm that pornography or hate speech causes from the wrong that pornography or hate speech is—subordination. It is the fact that pornography and hate speech subordinate that makes them wrong for both Langton and Altman.

55. Kenneth L. Karst, *Belonging to America: Equal Citizenship and the Constitution* (New Haven, Conn.: Yale University Press, 1989), 3.

56. *Id.* at 4.

57. Margalit, *Decent Society*, 1.

58. *Id.*

59. *Id.* at 85.

60. *Id.* at 88.

3. Interpretation and Disagreement

1. This example describes the familiar pattern of challenges raised by transgendered or transsexual individuals against dismissals for refusing to use the bathroom that conforms with their biological sex. Thus far, no court has upheld the employee's claim of wrongful discrimination based either on Title VII or the Equal Protection Clause. See, for example, Etsitty v. Utah Transit Authority, 2005 WL 1505610 (D. Utah 2005 WL 1505610); Johnson v. Fresh Mark, Inc., 337 F. Supp. 2d 996 (N.D. Ohio 2003), aff'd by 98 Fed. App'x 461 (6th Cir. May 18, 2004); Sturchio v. Ridge, 2005 WL 1502899 (E.D. Wash.).

2. Stephanie Saul, "Maker of Heart Drug Intended for Blacks Bases Price on Patients' Wealth," *New York Times*, July 8, 2005, C3. The BiDil example was suggested to me by Dorothy Roberts.

3. Rob Stein, "FDA Approves Controversial Heart Medication for Blacks," *Washington Post*, June 23, 2005, A15 (quoting Bloche).

4. Carolyn Johnson, "Should Medicine Be Colorblind? Debate Erupts over Drug that Works for Blacks," *Boston Globe*, Aug. 24, 2004, C1 (quoting Kahn).

5. *Id.*

6. If it is obeyed, this is its effect, but we do not need to know whether it was obeyed or not to know whether it was an order.

7. The FDA originally denied a new drug application (NDA) for BiDil when it was presented without regard to race because the data on which the NDA was based were not focused enough to support the conclusion that the therapy was better than standard alternatives. The study on which the NDA relied, which was from the 1980s, was not designed with FDA approval in mind and so was not directed to providing the sort of data that FDA approval requires. Reanalysis of the old data, looking only at the African American patients in the study, showed a more pronounced benefit from BiDil. It was on that basis that a new patent for the drug was issued (as a method for treating heart failure in African American patients), that a new study was conducted (which showed a statistically significant benefit from BiDil in African American patients), and ultimately that FDA approval was based. The path to approval has been criticized on the ground that BiDil may be beneficial for all heart failure patients regardless of race, particularly those who do not tolerate alternative therapies well, and that it is just a fluke that the old study showed a stronger benefit for black patients. The new study—designed with FDA approval in mind—tested only African American patients and thus does not address the question of whether there is in fact a racial difference in response to this drug. For an account of the history of BiDil, see Jonathan Kahn, "How a Drug Becomes 'Ethnic': Law, Commerce, and the Production of Racial Categories in Medicine," *Yale Journal of Health Policy, Law and Ethics* 4 (2004): 1–46.

8. In the case of BiDil, even this aspect is of far less significance than it might seem, as BiDil is made from two generic drugs: hydralazine and isosorbide. As Jonathan Kahn explains, "BiDil was a breakthrough of convenience . . . [because] a doctor only had to write one prescription and the patient only had to take a total of six pills (two pills three times a day) instead of sixteen (four pills four times a day)." Kahn, "How a Drug Becomes 'Ethnic,' " 30.

9. Drug manufacturers are prohibited from advertising the off-label uses of their drugs. For a description of the regulations governing off-label use of drugs, see generally, Ralph F. Hall and Elizabeth S. Sobotka, "Inconsistent Government Policies: Why FDA Off-Label Regulation Cannot Survive First Amendment Review Under *Greater New Orleans*," *Food and Drug Law Journal* 62 (2007): 1–48, 3–10.

10. While one study did try to rule out environment causes of the observed racial difference, the study was limited to two factors—education level and financial distress. Kahn, "How a Drug Becomes 'Ethnic,' " 18–19.

11. It could be morally problematic as well because it leads to bad consequences.

12. Glenn C. Loury, *The Anatomy of Racial Inequality* (Cambridge, Mass.: Harvard University Press, 2002), 70.

13. Kahn, "How a Drug Becomes 'Ethnic,' " 43.

14. See, for example, American Medical Association, "Subject Selection for Clinical Trials," *Code of Medical Ethics.* Op. No. E-2.071, issued June 1998; Council for In-

ternational Organizations of Medical Science, "Equitable Distribution of Burdens and Benefits in the Selection of Groups of Subjects in Research," *International Ethical Guidelines for Biomedical Research Involving Human Subjects*, Guideline No. 12 (2002), available at http://www.cioms.ch/frame_guidelines_nov_2002 .htm; and Barbara A. Noah, "The Participation of Underrepresented Minorities in Clinical Research," *American Journal of Law and Medicine* 29 (2003): 221–245.

15. For a survey of views about what objectivity in law and morals requires, see Brian Leiter, ed., *Objectivity in Law and Morals* (New York: Cambridge University Press, 2001).

16. Gerald J. Postema, "Objectivity Fit for Law," in Leiter, *Objectivity in Law and Morals*, 99–143, 111.

17. *Id.* at 112.

18. Jules L. Coleman and Brian Leiter, "Determinacy, Objectivity, and Authority," *University of Pennsylvania Law Review* 142 (1993): 549–637, reprinted in Andrei Marmor, ed., *Law and Interpretation: Essays in Legal Philosophy* (New York: Oxford University Press, 1995).

19. Coleman and Leiter, "Determinacy, Objectivity, and Authority," 608 (explaining minimal objectivity in this way: "what seems right to the majority of the community determines what is right" and thus "individuals are not the measure of all things, but their collective or convergent practices are").

20. *Id.* at 608–609.

21. Brian Leiter, "Objectivity, Morality, and Adjudication," in Leiter, *Objectivity in Law and Morals*, 66–98.

22. Plessy v. Ferguson, 163 U.S. 537, 551 (1896).

23. *Id.* at 562 (Harlan, J., dissenting).

24. Bradwell v. Illinois, 83 U.S. 130 (1873) (restricting women from practice of law).

25. International Union v. Johnson Controls, Inc., 499 U.S. 187 (1991) (rejecting employer's "fetal protection policy" of restricting women of child-bearing age from positions involving lead exposure).

26. Sarah Buss has a similar conception of manners. In her view, the point of manners is to directly recognize the moral worth of others. Therefore, if a code of manners fails to do so, it can be criticized as a bad code of manners: "from the point of view of manners, we can criticize a code of manners for failing to appreciate that all persons are intrinsically valuable." Sarah Buss, "Appearing Respectful: The Moral Significance of Manners," *Ethics*, 109 (1999): 795–826, 809.

27. Connie S. Rosati, "Some Puzzles about the Objectivity of Law," *Law and Philosophy* 23 (2004): 273–323, 307–308 (footnote omitted).

28. Coleman and Leiter, "Determinacy, Objectivity, and Authority," 607 ("According to the strong metaphysical objectivist, what is the case about the world never depends on what humans take there to be (even under ideal epistemic conditions").

29. Connie Rosati makes a similar point about the inadequacy of Coleman and Leiter's strong conception of objectivity to law: "like other rule-governed

systems or activities, such as chess (to use a familiar example), law is something we make, and the conventional origins of law seem terribly at odds with the idea that legal facts are utterly independent of our beliefs, judgments, attitudes, or reactions concerning what the law is." Rosati, "Objectivity of Law," 303.

30. Coleman and Leiter, "Determinacy, Objectivity, and Authority," 620.

31. Philip Pettit, "Embracing Objectivity in Ethics," in Leiter, *Objectivity in Law and Morals*, 234–286, 244.

32. Coleman and Leiter, "Determinacy, Objectivity, and Authority," 630.

33. She also challenges the criterion that the judge should "be fully informed" about "all relevant information." Coleman and Leiter, "Determinacy, Objectivity, and Authority," 630. Rosati thinks no one has adequately described how one would determine what information is relevant and thinks that the idea that an ideal judge would have all relevant information is incoherent. Rosati, "Objectivity of Law," 318–319.

34. Coleman and Leiter, "Determinacy, Objectivity, and Authority," 630.

35. I see this "resolution," such as it is, as in tune with Joseph Raz's "long route" to a conception of objectivity. See Joseph Raz, "Notes on Value and Objectivity," in Leiter, *Objectivity in Law and Morals*, 194–233.

36. Ronald Dworkin, "Bakke's Case: Are Quotas Unfair?" in Ronald Dworkin, *A Matter of Principle* (Cambridge, Mass.: Harvard University Press, 1985), 293–303, 301.

37. The named plaintiffs in challenges to affirmative action in higher education are generally whites from the lower socioeconomic classes. See, for example, Grutter v. Bollinger, 539 U.S. 306 (2003) and Gratz v. Bollinger, 539 U.S. 244 (2003). These choices are likely informed by the inchoate intuition that the claims of lower-class whites have more appeal than of a white plaintiff qua white. However, because affirmative action policies do not distinguish among people on the basis of socioeconomic status (at least not in the negative sense), this will be a much harder claim to defend.

38. This objection was raised by an anonymous reviewer for Harvard University Press.

39. This phrase comes from the book by Robert Hughes with that title. Robert Hughes, *The Culture of Complaint: The Fraying of America* (New York: Oxford University Press, 1993).

40. Raz, "Notes," 226.

41. Thomas Nagel, *The View from Nowhere* (New York: Oxford University Press, 1986).

42. Postema, "Objectivity Fit for Law," 111–112.

43. The idea that one might instruct decision makers to follow a test that merely approximates the real criteria is familiar. For example, a rational decision maker might decide to set the minimum age for driving at 17 on the grounds that using the bright-line rule will better identify the group of young drivers responsible and skilled enough to drive safely than would allowing the staff at the registry of motor vehicles to directly apply the criteria of responsibility and skill.

4. Merit, Entitlement, and Desert

1. Azar Nafisi, *Reading Lolita in Tehran: A Memoir in Books* (New York: Random House, 2003).
2. Business for Social Responsibility, available at http://www.bsr.org/Meta/About/index.cfm.
3. For example, many selective private schools in Washington, D.C. (as elsewhere), use the Wechsler Preschool and Primary Scale of Intelligence, 3rd ed. (known as the WPPSI-III).
4. John Rawls makes this claim. John Rawls, *A Theory of Justice*, rev. ed. (Cambridge, Mass.: Harvard University Press, 1999), 104. But see George Sher, "Effort, Ability and Personal Desert," *Philosophy and Public Affairs* 8 (1979): 361–376 (arguing that the claim that people do not deserve their attainments does not follow from the premise that they do not deserve their natural abilities).
5. See Christopher McCrudden, "Merit Principles," *Oxford Journal of Legal Studies* 18 (1998): 543–579, 545–546 (arguing that "the concept of 'merit' and 'the merit principle' are contested concepts, in that there are various competing conceptions which usually point in different, and sometimes incompatible, public policy directions" and thus that "those who currently use merit arguments, particularly those who use them approvingly" should "conclude that such arguments are more trouble than they are worth, and stop using merit as a basis of argument").
6. *Id.* at 554.
7. Robert K. Fullinwider and Judith Lichtenberg, *Leveling the Playing Field: Justice, Politics, and College Admissions* (Lanham, Md.: Rowman and Littlefield, 2004), 27.
8. McCrudden, "Merit Principles," 557–558 (defining his second model of merit as "the 'possession of qualities that are thought to be of general value and are reasonably likely to prove useful in carrying out a specific function,'" relying on (and citing) Richard H. Fallon, Jr., "To Each According to His Ability, From None According to His Race: The Concept of Merit in the Law of Antidiscrimination," *Boston University Law Review* 60 (1980): 815–877, 826.
9. McCrudden picks out the necessity for only a loose fit between the traits that can make up merit and the description of the job in question as the second key aspect of his second model of merit which he labels "general 'common sense' merit." McCrudden, "Merit Principles," 557.
10. The classical version of the Hippocratic oath provides that "I will apply dietetic measure for the benefit of the sick according to my ability and judgment; I will keep them from harm and injustice." See "Hippocratic Oath: Classical Version," *Nova Online*, available at http://www.pbs.org/wgbh/nova/doctors/oath_classical .html. The modern version, written in 1964 by Louis Lasagna, academic dean of the School of Medicine at Tufts University, provides, "I will apply, for the benefit of the sick, all measures which are required, avoiding those twin traps of overtreatment and therapeutic nihilism." Louis Lasagna, "Hippocratic Oath:

Modern Version," available at http://www.pbs.org/wgbh/nova/doctors/oath
_modern.html.

11. *Id.*

12. This is McCrudden's view as well. See generally Christopher McCrudden.

13. Robert Nozick argues that because the skills and talents of the worker are his,
he is entitled to the money he is paid for using those skills and talents. See
Robert Nozick, *Anarchy, State and Utopia* (New York: Basic Books, 1974).

14. See, for example, Barbara Fried, "Wilt Chamberlain Revisited: Nozick's 'Justice
in Transfer' and the Problem of Market-Based Distribution," *Philosophy and
Public Affairs* 24 (1995): 226–245. Fried explains that the principle of "justice in
transfer" does not work to justify why Wilt Chamberlain is entitled to keep the
money fans are willing to pay. She argues that Nozick's argument depends on
the claim that Chamberlain owns his talent. But Nozick does not provide an argument explaining why Chamberlain owns the scarcity-value of his talent as
well. Without such an argument it is not clear that Chamberlain does. If Chamberlain does not own the scarcity-value of his talent, then society has a lien on
his worth, which it can collect when Chamberlain gets paid.

15. The concept of a "social return" on an investment refers to the non-monetary
benefits that may accrue as a result on the investment—less pollution, better
working conditions for workers, and so on.

16. Norman Daniels explores the implications and limitations of such an argument.
See Norman Daniels, "Merit and Meritocracy," *Philosophy and Public Affairs* 7
(1978): 206–223.

17. As Daniels explains, efficiency is a good thing in itself, unless other considerations override it. *Id.* at 209 (arguing that the PJAP "seems desirable because, in
the absence of arguments showing that justice or other considerations or right
demand some array other than a maximally productive one, there is good
reason to seek productivity in social arrangements").

18. *Id.* at 209.

19. *Id.* at 210.

20. *Id.*

21. Robert Paul Wolff and Tobias Barrington Wolff similarly challenge our intuitive
conceptions of merit in the education and health care contexts using the following hypothetical. They ask the reader to imagine another society that allo-
cates health care in the emergency room not on the basis of need but instead
on the basis of who among those presenting for treatment could most easily be
made to be in excellent health. The same society uses need as the basis on
which to allocate limited spaces for students at an elite research university. In
the university context, participants in this imaginary society argue, it makes
sense to admit those students who most need an excellent education rather
than those who are likely to succeed in life and educate themselves no matter
where they go to school. See Robert Paul Wolff and Tobias Barrington Wolff,
"The Pimple on Adonis's Nose: A Dialogue on the Concept of Merit in the Affirmative Action Debate," *Hastings Law Journal* 56 (2005): 379–440.

22. I put "merit" in quotes here because "merit" in this discussion refers to those traits that enhance overall productivity—itself a controversial conception of merit.

23. It is possible that these negative consequences will result in lower productivity overall so that the increase in productivity that comes from selecting kids with high IQs is offset by the lower productivity overall that testing itself produces. If so, then a macroproductivity principle forbids testing. However, the fact that the facts may turn out this way does not mean that they must. Poor self-worth could motivate kids to overachieve, increasing productivity at the cost of happy, well-adjusted individuals. The point here is that when making educational choices for kids, surely we ought to consider what is good for kids and helps them develop into happy, emotionally stable adults and not just productive members of society.

24. Rawls, *Theory of Justice*, 310–315.

25. *Id.*

26. See, for example, Sher, "Personal Desert," 361–376.

27. Fried, "Wilt Chamberlain Revisited," 228. While her argument is meant to answer the claim that persons are entitled to the rewards they receive from the use of their talents, it would apply as well to the claim of desert. Notably, even Robert Nozick—who powerfully defends the claim that people are entitled to the benefits they gain from the use of their talents—does not think that the talented therefore *deserve* these rewards. See Nozick, *Anarchy, State and Utopia*, 159.

28. Joan Williams, *Unbending Gender: Why Family and Work Conflict and What to Do about It* (New York: Oxford University Press, 2000).

29. A similar line of argument could be used to defend the Supreme Court's decision in Roberts v. United States Jaycees, 468 U.S. 609 (1983), in which the Court held that the Jaycees, a men's civic organization, could not refuse admission as regular members to women.

5. Accuracy and Irrationality

1. This data was cited in Linda Hirshman's provocative essay in the *American Prospect* (advocating that women ought not to leave the workforce to stay home with children). See Linda Hirshman, "Homeward Bound," *American Prospect,* Dec. 2005, 20, available at http://www.prospect.org/cs/articles?article=–homeward_bound (requires sign in).

2. *Id.*

3. Lawline v. American Bar Ass'n, 956 F.2d 1378, 1385 (7th Cir. 1992) ("The prohibition against the practice of law by a layman is grounded in the need of the public for integrity and competence of those who undertake to render legal services. . . . [T]he public can better be assured of the requisite responsibility and competence if the practice of law is confined to those who are subject to the requirements and regulations imposed upon members of the legal profession."); Sussman v. Grado, 746 N.Y.S.2d 548, 552 (N.Y. Dist. Ct. 2002) ("[T]he guid-

ance of an attorney and his or her professional staff seems much preferable to an 'independent paralegal' who has not gone through law school, has not passed the bar exam and who is not licensed in New York State.")

4. Whether tighter fit ameliorates the problematic nature of certain classifications is an issue I will turn to later in this chapter.

5. While some cases employing *rationality review* in a fairly demanding way have been characterized as requiring more than mere rationality—often termed *rationality review with bite*—even where rationality review is easy to pass, some kinds of classifications are ruled out. In principle, the cases that are ruled out are those in which the trait used in the classification is not positively correlated with its purported target.

6. For example, in Nguyen v. INS, 533 U.S. 53, 77 (2001), the Court explained: "The most important difference between heightened scrutiny and rational basis review, of course, is the *required fit between the means employed and the ends served.* Under heightened scrutiny, the discriminatory means must be 'substantially related' to an actual and important governmental interest. Under rational basis scrutiny, the means need only be 'rationally related' to a conceivable and legitimate state end" (emphasis added and citations omitted).

7. See Joseph Tussman and Jacobus tenBroek, "The Equal Protection of the Laws," *California Law Review* 37 (1949): 341–381. Tussman and tenBroek's analysis has set the dominant conception of equal protection for years—it ranks among the top-twenty law-review articles in number of times cited. See Fred R. Shapiro, "The Most-Cited Law Review Articles Revisited," *Chicago-Kent Law Review* 71 (1996): 751–779, 767; but see James E. Krier and Stewart J. Schwab, "*The Cathedral* at Twenty-Five: Citations and Impressions," *Yale Law Journal* 106 (1997): 2121–2147, 2139, critiquing Shapiro's method and proposing an alternative method in which the Tussman and tenBroek article falls to 103. As Tussman and tenBroek analyzed the problem that I am here calling the discrimination puzzle, the answer lay in the concept of "reasonable classification"; Tussman and tenBroek, "Equal Protection," 344. Reasonable classification is classification in which the proxy trait is positively correlated with the target trait, i.e., the classification is rational.

8. See Deborah Hellman, "What Makes Genetic Discrimination Exceptional?" *American Journal of Law and Medicine* 29 (2003): 77–116; Henry T. Greely, "Genotype Discrimination: The Complex Case for Some Legislative Protection," *University of Pennsylvania Law Review* 149 (2001): 1483–1505.

9. See Frederick Schauer, *Profiles, Probabilities and Stereotypes* (Cambridge, Mass.: Harvard University Press, 2003), which discusses the moral issues raised by generalization. Schauer explains that a generalization is non-spurious (and thus statistically sound and rational to use in drawing distinctions) when the following obtains: The generalization "bulldogs have bad hips" is non-spurious "[a]s long as the probability of a dog's having hip problems given that the dog is a bulldog is greater than the probability of a dog's having hip problems given no information about the breed of the dog." *Id.* at 11.

10. See, for example, City of Cleburne v. Cleburne Living Center, 473 U.S. 432, 440 (1985) (White, J., for the Court) (explaining that because the traits of race, alienage, and national origin are "so seldom relevant to the achievement of any legitimate state interest that laws grounded in such considerations are deemed to reflect prejudice and antipathy—a view that those in the burdened class are not as worthy or deserving as others" and are thereby subject to strict scrutiny).

11. U.S. Dep't of Health and Human Services, "Long Term Poverty," *Indicators of Welfare Dependence: Annual Report to Congress 2003* (2003), iii–14, Tbl. Econ6, available at http://aspe.hhs.gov/HSP/indicators03/ch3.htm#econ6 (showing that black children have been much more likely to live in poverty for longer periods; in 1967, for example, *thirty times* as likely as non-black children to live in poverty for ten years).

12. Jonathan Kozol, *The Shame of the Nation* (New York: Crown Publishers, 2005), (describing the intense racial segregation in inner-city schools in the United States).

13. U.S. Dep't of Health and Human Services, *Indicators of Welfare Dependence: Annual Report to Congress 2006* (2006), iii–32, Fig. WORK7, available at http://aspe .hhs.gov/hsp/indicators06/report.pdf (showing that black adults are 30 percent more likely to have a disability than members of the general population).

14. Paige M. Harrison and Allen J. Beck, "Prisoners in 2005," *Bureau of Justice Statistics Bulletin*, Nov. 2006, 1, available at http://www.ojp.usdoj.gov/bjs/pub/pdf/p05 .pdf ("About 8.1% of Black males age 25 to 29 were in State or Federal prison, compared to 2.6% of Hispanic males and 1.1% of White males in the same age group."). For a comprehensive account of race and criminal justice, see Randall Kennedy, *Race, Crime and the Law* (New York: Pantheon Books, 1997).

15. *See* Joan Williams, *Unbending Gender: Why Family and Work Conflict and What to Do about It* (New York: Oxford University Press, 2000). Williams argues that the workplace is structured around the worker with few outside obligations, in particular no child-care or elder-care obligations, and thus the workplace systematically disadvantages workers—largely women—who fulfill these important caring functions.

16. 411 U.S. 677 (1973).

17. *Id.* at 681–682, and at 689–690.

18. *Id.* at 689 n. 23.

19. Catharine A. MacKinnon, *Sexual Harassment of Working Women: A Case of Sex Discrimination* (New Haven: Yale University Press, 1979), 107–116 (discussing Reed v. Reed, 404 U.S. 71 [1971]).

20. *Id.* at 108.

21. Samuel R. Bagenstos, " 'Rational Discrimination,' Accommodation, and the Politics of (Disability) Civil Rights," *Virginia Law Review* 89 (2003): 825–923.

22. *Id.* at 849.

23. From this observation, Bagenstos argues that antidiscrimination prohibitions and accommodation requirements are normatively equivalent—both require

accommodation by the employer, subordination by her of her desire to save money to the social goal of a more just and equitable community.

24. *Id.* at 878.

25. *Id.* at 833–834.

26. See Mark Kelman, "Market Discrimination and Groups," *Stanford Law Review* 53 (2001): 833–896 (arguing that antidiscrimination law [as compared with accommodation requirements] for the most part merely requires that employers act rationally in choosing employees).

27. See Schauer, *Profiles*, 55–78 (arguing that non-spurious generalizations are often over- and under-inclusive and unavoidable).

28. Many colleges and universities do require students to pass a swim test prior to graduation—Dartmouth College, for example. See Douglas Belkin, "Time to Sink or Graduate," *Boston Globe,* May 8, 2006, A1.

29. Schauer, *Profiles,* 66.

30. Of course, this method might be efficient when viewed from the perspective of the university if the applicants will bear the costs of the debate-style screening. Nevertheless, the university still might judge that the cost is not worth the increase in accuracy. There is no reason that university officials cannot count the cost to prospective students as relevant to their determination of what tests to require.

31. I believe this actually happened at the University of Edinburgh.

32. For a good description of the debate in the feminist literature between "sameness" and "difference" approaches to eradicating inequality between the sexes, see Martha Albertson Fineman, "Feminist Legal Theory," *American University Journal of Gender, Social Policy and the Law* 13 (2005): 13–23, 15–19.

33. The Family and Medical Leave Act (FMLA), 29 U.S.C. §§ 2601–2654 (2000), which requires that workers of medium and large employers be allowed to take up to twelve weeks of unpaid leave following the birth or adoption of a child or to care for a sick relative, is an example of a policy that treats everyone the same. However, it is an entitlement that is likely to be used more by women than men just as the previous norm of no-entitlement-to-leave likely disadvantaged women far more than men. Although neither option picks out particular workers for particular treatment (both opt for same-treatment regimes), the choice of the norm has dramatic and differential results.

34. Obviously these students could themselves choose to take a swim class. But there are likely to remain some who either are fearful of swimming, feel reluctant to self-identify as non-swimmers, fail to recognize the importance of learning to swim, etc., who will not sign up for the class on their own.

35. Schauer, *Profiles,* 200.

36. *Id.* at 199–223 (Chapter 8: "Two Cheers for Procrustes"). This is also the argument of some critics of Peter Westen's provocative thesis that equality is an empty idea. See, for example, Kenneth W. Simons, "The Logic of Egalitarian Norms," *Boston University Law Review* 80 (2000): 693–771 (arguing for a comparative conception of the norm of equality such that if A is entitled to x, so is B,

despite the differences between A and B). Simons's article is one of many responses to Peter Westen's "The Empty Idea of Equality," *Harvard Law Review* 95 (1982): 537–596, (arguing that the idea of equality expressed by the commitment to treat "like cases alike" is empty).

37. The tendency to do so is known as confirmation bias. See Raymond S. Nickerson, "Confirmation Bias: A Ubiquitous Phenomenon in Many Guises," *Review of General Psychology* 2 (1998): 175–220. See also Mark Schaller, "Social Categorization and the Formation of Group Stereotypes: Further Evidence for Biased Information Processing in the Perception of Group-Behavior Correlations," *European Journal of Social Psychology* 21 (1991): 25–35.

38. 533 U.S. 53 (2001).

39. The law provided that the child must show that either legal legitimation, the father's declaration of paternity under oath, or a court order of paternity took place before the child becomes 18. 533 U.S. at 62.

40. *Id.* at 68, 73.

41. *Id.* at 89.

42. *Id.* at 90.

43. *Id.* (internal quotation marks omitted).

44. *Id.* at 94.

45. For a detailed analysis of the moral permissibility of charging higher rates or refusing to insure victims of domestic abuse, see my article, "Is Actuarially Fair Insurance Pricing Actually Fair? A Case Study in Insuring Battered Women," *Harvard Civil Rights–Civil Liberties Law Review* 32 (1997): 355–411.

46. William Burroughs, *Naked Lunch*, available at http://www.brainyquote.com/quotes/authors/w/william_s_burroughs.html.

6. Is It the Thought that Counts?

1. Dukes v. Wal-Mart Stores, Inc., 222 F.R.D. 137 (N.D. Cal. 2004) (certifying the women employees of all domestic Wal-Mart stores as a class, based in part on the evidence presented by sociologist William T. Bielby that unconscious bias plays a large role in decision making when not constrained by explicit criteria or other methods that restrict its reach).

2. 413 U.S. 528, 534 (1973).

3. G.E.M. Anscombe, *Intention*, 2nd ed. (Ithaca, N.Y.: Cornell University Press, 1969), 1.

4. See, for example, Steven Sverdlik, "Motive and Rightness," *Ethics* 106 (1996): 327–349, 335 (arguing that "motives belong to the conative, desiring side of the causal story").

5. Anscombe, *Intention*, 18.

6. Oliver Wendell Holmes, Jr., *The Common Law* (Boston: Little, Brown, and Company, 1963), 7. According to Frederick Schauer, Holmes overestimates dogs. See Frederick Schauer, "Intentions, Conventions and the First Amendment: The Case of Cross-Burning," *Supreme Court Review* (2003): 197–230, 197

(asserting that "[i]n claiming that 'even a dog distinguishes between being stumbled over and being kicked' Justice Holmes demonstrated his limited knowledge of the canine world").

7. See, for example, Richard H. Fallon, Jr., *Implementing the Constitution* (Cambridge, Mass.: Harvard University Press, 2001), 93 (describing the "point" of Holmes's aphorism as the fact that "we often cannot even characterize an act without understanding what motivated it"). But see Schauer, "Intentions," 197 (understanding Holmes's claim more modestly as pointing to the fact that the "distinction between what someone intends and what in fact occurs is an important feature of law generally").

8. Linda Hamilton Kreiger provides a summary of some of that literature for a legal audience—and explains its significance for antidiscrimination law in Linda Hamilton Kreiger, "The Content of Our Categories: A Cognitive Bias Approach to Discrimination and Equal Employment Opportunity," *Stanford Law Review* 47 (1995): 1161–1248.

9. *Id.* at 1239–1240.

10. Gregory Mitchell and Philip E. Tetlock, "Antidiscrimination Law and the Perils of Mindreading," *Ohio State Law Journal* 67 (2006): 1023–1121. Mitchell and Tetlock argue that studies purporting to show unconscious bias are less meaningful than their authors suppose and especially that the reliance on them by legal scholars is not warranted. In particular they argue that the fact that people more easily and quickly connect whites with positive traits and blacks with negative traits under experimental conditions does not show that people are biased or have negative attitudes toward blacks. Rather, these results are at least partially accounted for by a number of other explanations including anxiety in test conditions and knowledge about statistically valid differences between blacks and whites as groups. Moreover, Mitchell and Tetlock argue that scholars are not justified in drawing conclusions based on these studies about whether people are likely to treat blacks and whites differently in real situations that differ in important ways from the laboratory environment. Mitchell and Tetlock's critique has, in turn, engendered replies. See, for example, Samuel R. Bagenstos, "Implicit Bias, 'Science,' and Antidiscrimination Law," Washington U. School of Law Working Paper No. 07-04-01, available at http://papers.sssrn .com/sol13/papers.cfm?abstract_id=970526. Bagenstos rightly points out that many of the so-called flaws that Mitchell and Tetlock identify are not failures at the level of science (as they suggest) but rather reflect normative disagreement about what wrongful discrimination consists in. For example, Mitchell and Tetlock say that one of the causes for the observed differences may not be bias but rather unfamiliarity with persons of other races. Bagenstos does not disagree. Rather, he argues that whatever the cause, this difference in treatment is cause for concern.

11. *Webster's Third New International Dictionary* (Springfield, Mass.: G. and C. Merriam Company, 1981), 1240.

12. Larry Alexander, "Rules, Rights, Options, and Time," *Legal Theory* 6 (2000): 391–404.

13. Alexander ("Rules") adopts Matthew Adler's conception of constitutional rights as "rights against rules" in his argument here. See Matthew D. Adler, "Rights Against Rules: The Moral Structure of American Constitutional Law," *Michigan Law Review* 97 (1998): 1–173.

14. I do not intend to adopt a view about whether Adler's conception of constitutional rights as rights against rules is correct, nor does Alexander. Nonetheless Alexander's point that many constitutionally permissible rules exclude people is surely correct—however one conceives of constitutional rights. This fact—which one might call the *discrimination conundrum*—was first articulated by Joseph Tussman and Jacobus tenBroek in their classic article, "The Equal Protection of the Laws," *California Law Review* 37 (1949): 341–381. To accomplish a myriad of important and mundane tasks, laws and policies must draw distinctions among people (must *discriminate*—to use that term without its normal pejorative connotations).

15. Alexander, "Rules," 400.

16. *Id.*

17. *Id.* (arguing that "[g]iven constitutional optionality and the permissibility of switching, the courts must treat legislative motivation as material") and *Id.* at 400–401 (claiming that "it is material whether they [laws] were enacted for reasons that were also constitutionally optional as opposed to constitutionally forbidden").

18. *Id.* at 400.

19. See, for example, the distinction between constitutional "operative propositions" and "decision rules" proposed by Mitchell Berman. Mitchell N. Berman, "Constitutional Decision Rules," *Virginia Law Review* 90 (2004): 1–168 (distinguishing "operative propositions," which elucidate constitutional meaning, from "decision rules," which allow courts to apply that meaning).

20. To be clear, let me explain the relationship between Alexander's term *real rule* and the phrases I have been using: classifying on the basis of X trait and wrongfully discriminating. When Alexander asks what the real rule is, he is asking about X. In other words, he is interested in the descriptive sense of discrimination, about classifying on the basis of X trait, but he is raising a question about what is the X on the basis of which the classification is made. To identify the real rule is to find the X on the basis of which the rule classifies.

21. The term *disparate impact* refers to a possible test for when a violation of the constitutional guarantee of equal protection has occurred. The Supreme Court has rejected the claim that a disparate impact on a constitutionally protected group (like a racial minority) is enough to establish that the policy in question violates the Constitution. See Washington v. Davis, 426 U.S. 229 (1976) (rejecting a challenge to the use of a written test in hiring decisions for the D.C. Police Department on the grounds that the fact that the test had a disparate impact on

African American job seekers was not sufficient to shift the burden to the police force to show that the test was a good predictor of job performance).

22. The Supreme Court's disparate impact cases suggest that impact alone cannot be sufficient to establish intent—though it is unclear, at least theoretically, why not. In my view, disparate impact alone could establish the objective meaning of the law, but in the kinds of cases that have come before the Court—like *Washington v. Davis*—there is additional important objective evidence that cuts in the other direction. For example, the fact that there are good reasons to test police officers for the skills the test in question evaluated is relevant to the objective meaning of the law. Note that I am not suggesting one ask whether these reasons actually motivated the police in adopting the test.

23. Larry Alexander and Kevin Cole, "Discrimination by Proxy," *Constitutional Commentary* 14 (1997): 453–463.

24. This is the School C that Alexander and Cole describe; see Alexander and Cole, "Discrimination," 454.

25. Alexander's focus is on disparate impact cases largely as he sees these as the sites of the sorts of conceptual puzzles he finds both troubling and illuminating.

26. Alexander, "Rules," 401, note 33.

27. This is the first reason offered by Harvard President Lawrence Summers to explain the under-representation of women as tenured professors in the sciences, as well as in other demanding jobs, in his remarks at the National Bureau of Economic Research (NBER) Conference on Diversifying the Science and Engineering Workforce that created so much controversy. The controversy was due to the second reason he offered (innate differences in abilities between men and women). See Lawrence H. Summers, Remarks at NBER Conference on Diversifying the Science and Engineering Workforce, Jan. 14, 2005, available at www.president.harvard.edu/speeches/2005/nber.html.

28. See, for example, Warren Quinn, *Morality and Action* (New York: Cambridge University Press, 1993), 177.

29. Judith Jarvis Thomson, "Physician-Assisted Suicide: Two Moral Arguments," *Ethics* 109 (1999): 497–518, 510.

30. 521 U.S. 793, 802–809 (1997).

31. *Id.* at 802 (asserting that "[t]he law has long used actors' intent or purpose to distinguish between two acts that may have the same result").

32. *Id.* and *Id.* at 802–803 (citing Personnel Administrator v. Feeney, 442 U.S. 256, 279 (1979) (upholding a Massachusetts law which accorded veterans an "absolute lifetime" preference in civil service jobs). The law was challenged on the ground that because the class of veterans was overwhelmingly male, the law constituted unlawful sex discrimination. Justice Stewart, writing for the majority, held that " 'Discriminatory purpose,' however, implies more than intent as volition or intent as awareness of consequences. It implies that the decision-maker, in this case a state legislature, selected or reaffirmed a particular course of action at least in part 'because of,' not merely 'in spite of,' its adverse effects upon an identifiable group." *Id.*

33. 521 U.S. at 807, note 11.

34. This objection has been raised by James Rachels, Jonathan Bennett, and most powerfully by Judith Jarvis Thomson. See James Rachels, "More Impertinent Distinctions and a Defense of Active Euthanasia," reprinted in *Killing and Letting Die*, 2nd ed., eds. B. Steinbock and A. Norcross (New York: Fordham University Press, 1994), 139–154 (original copyright 1978); Jonathan Bennett, "Morality and Consequences," *The Tanner Lectures on Human Values II* (Salt Lake City: University of Utah Press, 1981), 46–116; Judith Jarvis Thomson, "Self-Defense," *Philosophy and Public Affairs* 20 (1991): 283–310. For a thoughtful discussion of this view, see Alec Walen, "Intention and Permissibility: Learning from the Failure of the DDE," Draft on file with author.

35. T. M. Scanlon, "Intention and Permissibility," *Aristotelian Society Supplementary Volume* 74 (2000): 311 (emphasis added).

36. *Id.*

37. It might be tempting to draw the analogy even more closely to Scanlon's and argue that what makes the hiring decision wrong is that a particular job applicant ought to be hired. This is a mistake however. In the context of jobs or places at schools, it is not the case that particular candidates are entitled to those spots. The employer or school can choose whichever applicants it wishes. Rather, morally as well as legally, the employer or school is merely proscribed from basing its decision on certain characteristics in certain contexts or in certain ways.

38. Sverdlik, "Motives," 341–349.

39. I explain the terminology *proxy, target,* and *motive* in more depth in an article in which I describe two forms of discriminatory laws—ones that work by proxy and ones that do not. See Deborah Hellman, "Two Types of Discrimination: The Familiar and the Forgotten," *California Law Review* 86 (1998): 315–361.

40. The purpose or goal may be aimed at as a means toward another end as well. See Mitchell N. Berman, "Coercion without Baselines: Unconstitutional Conditions in Three Dimensions," *Georgetown Law Journal* 90 (2001): 1–112, 24 (describing this relationship as "nested purposes" and endorsing the view that a bad purpose matters: "wherever a putatively bad purpose may lie within a chain of nested purposes, the purposes animating state action, like its effects, constitute familiar respects in which the Constitution can be violated").

41. When we focus on the target, this inquiry seems very close to the inquiry discussed earlier in the chapter. Here we are analyzing whether it matters that an actor uses a benign trait to target a suspect classification—like race or sex. That is, we are assuming that is what the actor is aiming to do and asking whether that intention ought to have legal significance. This inquiry is not the same as the inquiry into whether one must consult intention in order to *detect* the case in which that actor uses a benign trait to target a suspect class.

42. Alexander and Cole, "Discrimination," 453 (defining the antidiscrimination principle in the following way: "Government cannot use racial classifications,

even as the most cost-effective proxies for other traits, unless using them as the most cost-effective proxies is necessary to further a compelling interest").

43. *Id.* at 455.

44. Judith Thomson believes that in many DDE cases, we often confuse a judgment of the actor with a judgment of the action. This distinction may be relevant here. We may judge a person who attempts to evade a legal prohibition (by circumvention) to be a bad person regardless of whether the action he or she adopts is morally permissible or not. As Thomson puts it, "a failure to take seriously enough the fact—I think it is plainly a fact—that the question whether it is morally permissible for a person to do a thing just is not the same as the question whether the person who does it is thereby shown to be a bad person." Thomson, "Physician-Assisted Suicide," 517. Tim Scanlon endorses a similar view. See Scanlon, "Intention," 301–317, 306 (agreeing "with Thomson that this confusion involves a failure to distinguish clearly between features that make an action wrong and description of the flaw that an agent exhibits in performing it").

45. See, for example, Owen M. Fiss, "Groups and the Equal Protection Clause," *Philosophy and Public Affairs* 5 (1976): 107–177; Cass R. Sunstein, "The Anti-Caste Principle," *Michigan Law Review* 92 (1994): 2410–2455.

46. Justice Thomas makes an argument along these lines in his opinion, concurring in part and dissenting in part in *Grutter:*

> The Constitution abhors classifications based on race . . . because every time the government places citizens on racial registers and makes race relevant to the provision of burdens or benefits, it demeans us all. "Purchased at the price of immeasurable human suffering, the equal protection principle reflects our Nation's understanding that such classifications ultimately have a destructive impact on the individual and our society."

539 U.S. at 353–354 (quoting Adarand Constructors, Inc. v. Pena, 515 U.S. 200, 240) (Thomas, J., concurring in part and concurring in the judgment).

47. 413 U.S. 528, 534 (1973) (striking down a provision of a federal food stamp program that limited assistance to households of "related persons" on the grounds that the statutory limitation was unrelated to the goals of the program [to raise nutritional levels of poor households and to support agriculture] and because there was evidence in the legislative history suggesting that the classification had been inserted to keep hippies and hippie communes from applying for food stamps).

48. 517 U.S. 620 (1996).

49. *Id.* at 634.

50. Richard J. Arneson, "What Is Wrongful Discrimination?" *San Diego Law Review* 43 (2006): 775–808, 779.

51. This example raises the question of what we should say about attempts to wrongfully discriminate. At this point, I am not quite sure. However, I believe that the fact that civil law puts much less emphasis on attempts than criminal law reveals a well-founded intuition that attempts, though morally blame-

worthy, are not impermissible acts unless they are impermissible without reference to what they are attempts to do.

52. Arneson adopts a similar view. In response to challenges—like that of Judith Thomson—to the view that intentions matter to the moral permissibility of actions, Arneson suggests that sometimes it may be the case that an act, described without reference to the intention (*thinly* in his terms) is permissible but that when described with reference to the intention is not. In considering the example of refusing to share his ice cream with his brother out of spite or malice: "it might be the case that this act thinly described is morally permissible, doing it from spiteful malice is bad, and the combination of the act thinly described and doing it from spiteful malice is impermissible." *Id.* at 782. Arneson thinks this explains what makes wrongful discrimination wrong in cases where the actor has discretion about whom to select. He thinks such cases pose a problem because no candidate has the right to the job in question (in the employment setting, for example). And so, he thinks he needs this alternative explanation. But the candidate denied a job because of his race (in most instances) has had a right violated notwithstanding the fact that no candidate has a right to the job. The candidate has a right not to be rejected on the basis of a trait when doing so demeans him or her—which race-based hiring does in most instances as explained in Part I of this book.

53. Alec Walen, "The Doctrine of Illicit Intentions," *Philosophy and Public Affairs* 34 (2006): 39–67, 60. Walen himself thinks that when an *unconstrained* terror bomber bombs a legitimate target (but would have bombed an illegitimate one if the opportunity to bomb one had arisen), he acts impermissibly because Walen believes it is impermissible to form and act on illegitimate intentions.

54. The Civil Rights Act of 1991 makes relevant the issue of whether a less discriminatory alternative is available that also meets the employer's legitimate needs. See 42 U.S.C. §2000e-2(k) (2000). Machael Selmi argues in a recent article that an expanded conception of intent could also handle such a case. Michael Selmi, "Was the Disparate Impact Theory a Mistake?" *UCLA Law Review* 53 (2006): 701–82 at 762. Perhaps it could, but it would be misguided in my view.

55. Arneson, "Wrongful Discrimination," 782.

56. Holmes, *Common Law*, 33.

Conclusion

1. This is not the same thing as saying that people are entitled to have an equal amount of something.

2. Even here a distinction is drawn between brute luck and option luck. Brute luck is luck plain and simple—the good luck of being born into a well-to-do family, of having many talents and good looks, the bad luck of poor health, being born to a poor or dysfunctional family, or having few talents or talents not valued by the market, etc. Option luck, by contrast, is the luck of having one's choices turn out well or poorly. If one chooses not to buy insurance, for

example, and then does not get sick, this is good option luck. If one does get sick, that is bad option luck. It is brute luck that the egalitarian wishes to equalize, not option luck, as option luck is the freely chosen gamble that one undertakes.

3. Jonathan Wolff, "Fairness, Respect, and the Egalitarian Ethos," *Philosophy and Public Affairs* 27 (1998): 97–122. But see Timothy Hinton, "Must Egalitarians Choose between Fairness and Respect?" *Philosophy and Public Affairs* 30 (2001): 72–87 (arguing that it need not be demeaning).

4. Elizabeth S. Anderson, "What Is the Point of Equality?" *Ethics* 109 (1999): 287–337.

5. *Id.* at 305–307 (arguing that such an egalitarian view "disparages the internally disadvantaged and raises private disdain to the status of officially recognized truth").

6. Samuel Scheffler, "What Is Egalitarianism?" *Philosophy and Public Affairs* 31 (2003): 5–39, 21.

Acknowledgments

This book is the result. I am grateful to have been supported in this endeavor by fellowships from the Edmund J. Safra Foundation Center for Ethics at Harvard University, where I was a Fellow during the 2004–05 academic year, and the Woodrow Wilson International Center for Scholars at the Smithsonian Institution, where I was a Fellow during the 2005–06 academic year. I owe a tremendous debt to both institutions for their support. In addition, I would like to thank my home institution, the University of Maryland School of Law, for allowing me to be away during those two years and for supporting and encouraging my work throughout.

Many people helped me with this project along the way. Frederick Schauer was the first to suggest that my ideas warranted a book. In addition, he read drafts of several chapters and provided incredibly useful critiques. David Luban also read portions of the work and has been an intellectual mentor of mine since college. Others who have read portions of the work and provided tremendously useful critiques and commentaries include Arthur Applbaum, Sarah Babb, Samuel Bagenstos, Mitchell Berman, Richard Boldt, David Enoch, Richard Fallon, Jim Flemming, Heather Gerkin, Doug MacLean, Jim Rasenberger, Connie Rosati, Mike Seidman, Seana Shiffrin, Jana Singer, Robert Wachbroit, David Wasserman, Alan Wertheimer, Susan Wolf, Greg Young, and the other fellows at the Center for Ethics and the Wilson Center.

I have had wonderfully able research assistance in this project. Susan Mc-Carty at the law library at the University of Maryland and Ron Day of the law library at the University of Pennsylvania have been extremely helpful in preparing the manuscript for publication. In addition, Megan Moran-Gates, Jason Patil, and Richard Elkind also provided very helpful research assistance.

Finally, I have presented chapters of this manuscript at workshops and conferences, including The Analytic Legal Philosophy Conference; and legal theory workshops at UCLA, the University of Oregon, American University, and

Dartmouth College, as well as at the School of Law and the Institute for Philosophy and Public Policy at my home institution, the University of Maryland. The discussions at each of these sessions were highly useful.

Friends and colleagues have disagreed with parts of my book. I have attempted to answer their concerns. Any errors or inadequacies in doing so are mine.

Index

CPSIA information can be obtained
at www.ICGtesting.com
Printed in the USA
JSHW050806261221
21493JS00002B/11